K H Blacker ms
May 1986

Psychoanalysis In a
New Context

PSYCHOANALYSIS IN A NEW CONTEXT

by
Arnold H. Modell, M.D.

International Universities Press, Inc.
New York   New York

Library of Congress Cataloging in Publication Data

Modell,, Arnold H., 1924-
  Psychoanalysis in a new context.

  Bibliography: p.
  Includes index.
  1. Psychoanalysis. 2. Affect (Psychology) 3. Interpersonal relations. 4. Psychotherapy. I. Title.
[DNLM: 1. Psychoanalytic Theory. WM 460 M689p]
RC504.M58   1984   616.89'14   84-12965
ISBN 0-8236-5212-2

Manufactured in the United States of America.

For Penelope

TABLE OF CONTENTS

ACKNOWLEDGMENTS

I am extremely grateful to the following: Mrs. Margrethe Bohr and John Wiley & Sons, Inc., for permission to quote Niels Bohr from *Atomic Physics and Human Knowledge*; to George Braziller, Inc., for permission to quote Meyer Schapiro from *Modern Art*; to E. P. Dutton, Inc., for permission to quote Gregory Bateson from *Mind and Nature*.

I am grateful to the editors and publishers of the following journals for allowing me to reprint portions of my previously published papers:

Chapter 2 contains sections published under the title, "A Narcissistic Defense Against Affects and the Illusion of Self Sufficiency," in the *International Journal of Psycho-Analysis*, Vol. 56 (1975), pp. 275-282, and "Affects and Their Non-Communication," in the *International Journal of Psycho-Analysis*, Vol. 61 (1980), pp. 259-267.

Chapter 3 appeared in an earlier version under the same title, "Denial and the Sense of Separateness," in *The Journal of the American Psychoanalytic Association*, Vol. 9 (1961), pp. 533-547.

Chapter 4 appeared in an earlier version under the title "On Having the Right to a Life: An Aspect of the Superego's Development," in the *International Journal of Psycho-Analysis*, Vol. 46 (1965), pp. 323-331.

Chapter 5 appeared in an earlier version as "The Origin of Certain Forms of Pre-Oedipal Guilt and the Implications for a Psychoanalytic Theory of Affects," in the *International Journal of Psycho-Analysis*, Vol. 52 (1971), pp. 337-346.

Chapter 6 appeared in an earlier version under the same title in the *Journal of the American Psychoanalytic Association*, Vol. 24 (1976), pp. 285-307.

Chapter 8 appeared in an earlier version in *Psychoanalysis: The Vital Issues*, Vol. II, edited by J. Gedo and G. Pollock. New York: International Universities Press, 1984.

Chapter 9 was published under the same title as an extended book essay considering the works of Habermas, Polanyi, and Ricoeur in the *Journal of the American Psychoanalytic Association*, Vol. 26 (1978), pp. 641-658.

Chapter 10 was published under the same title in *The Annual of Psychoanalysis*, Vol. I (1973), New York: Quadrangle/New York Times Book Company, pp. 117-124.

Chapter 11 was published under the same title in *The Annual of Psychoanalysis*, Vol. VI (1978), New York: International Universities Press, pp. 167-180.

Chapter 12 was published under the same title in *The Psychoanalytic Quarterly*, Vol. 39, pp. 240-250.

Chapter 13 was published under the same title in *The International Journal of Psycho-Analysis*, Vol. 56 (1975), pp. 57-67.

Chapter 14 was published under the same title in the *International Journal of Psycho-Analysis*, Vol. 62 (1981), pp. 391-402.

Chapter 16 appeared in separate versions in the *Smith College Journal of the School for Social Work*, Vol. 8 (1981), pp. 28-30, and in *The Future of Psychoanalysis*, edited by A. Goldberg. New York: International Universities Press, 1983.

I wish also to express my gratitude for the stimulation I have received from my students both at the Beth Israel Hospital (Boston) and at the Boston Psychoanalytic Institute. They are in many instances the first to have heard the ideas that I have developed in this volume.

Finally, I wish to express my appreciation to my wife Penelope, to whom this work is dedicated. She has patiently supported my labors and assisted in the editing. I am especially grateful for her pursuit of my wayward commas.

The whole region of Psychology may be divided into areas of research according to the number of persons concerned. Thus we may speak of One-Body Psychology, Two-Body, Three-Body, Four-Body and Multi-Body Psychology.

JOHN RICKMAN, M.D.
(from *Selected Contributions to Psychoanalysis*)

INTRODUCTION

The new context to which the title of this book refers is that of a two-person psychology. It would be cumbersome but more accurate to speak of a "new" context, for what is new is only relatively new. Balint (1950) explicitly recognized this problem when he observed that our theory and technique refer to events occurring between two people and not simply within one person. This assumption of a two-person psychology is also intrinsic to the work of Winnicott (1960), who said that "there is no such thing as an infant." It has long been recognized that the language of theory is narrower than the language in which technique (a two-person process) is described (Habermas, 1968).

Harry Stack Sullivan (1953) introduced the two-person context into psychiatry. His contribution remains idiosyncratic; it consists mainly of technical advice and as such has proved resistant to attempts at systematizing (Havens, 1976). Although it has relevance for psychoanalysis, essentially it remains outside of psychoanalysis.

This book presents a series of interconnected chapters written during a span of approximately 22 years. Some chapters have been published; most have been extensively revised; and some appear here for the first time (for details, see the "Acknowledgments"). As is so often the case, I had been working on this problem long before I was fully aware that this was the real focus of my interest. This investigation started with the paper on "Denial and the

Sense of Separateness" (Modell, 1961, Chapter 3), where
I observe that denial cannot simply be thought of as an
intrapsychic defense (a splitting of the ego): It requires as
well the presence of a protective Other, a belief in an omnipotent object or an omnipotence contained within the
self.

The limitation of the traditional intrapsychic context of
the process of defense became most apparent to me as a
result of my increasing experience with the psychoanalysis
of the so-called narcissistic personality. In working with
such a patient, one may spend years with someone who
does not relate, that is to say, someone who does not communicate genuine affects, or communicates affects that are
false or dramatic exaggerations intended primarily not as
a communication but as a manipulation. This state of nonrelatedness is a defense, but it is not an intrapsychic defense: It is rather a defense that is protective of the fragility
of the self with its illusion of self-sufficiency. For affects
are object-seeking, and the communication of genuine affects is an exposure of need. As I shall describe in Chapter
2, affects are the medium through which defenses against
objects occur. This description may cover some of the same
ground as Winnicott's "false self," but unlike Winnicott I
place a special emphasis on the mediating role of affects.
I am suggesting, not that this two-person context replace
the traditional intrapsychic context, but that traditional
psychoanalysis has narrowed its theory to include only the
latter. Affects may still be considered within an intrapsychic context, as for example when Freud (1900) described the affects of dreams as "discharged" into the
interior of the mental apparatus. But affects are also contagious; they are communicated; and they are the medium
through which the affirmation or negation of the sense of
self by the other occurs.

In Chapters 4 and 5 I describe two forms of guilt: The

first I consider in the context of individuation and the second in relation to the self and the nuclear family. The first is the guilt that results when one obtains something for oneself, and the second when one separates from the nuclear family. Both forms of guilt can be traced to a primal fantasy: that to have something for oneself means that the other has been deprived; the guilt of becoming individuated and separated from the nuclear family carries with it a sense that those who are left behind are damaged. In this regard the *current* fates of other family members are of paramount importance. The locus of guilt appears here in a different context from that usually associated with ego/superego conflict. This form of guilt may clinically appear to be intertwined with a more familiar oedipal guilt, but it has a separate origin and a separate function.

Transference and countertransference phenomena have never been considered anything but events occurring within a two-person context. Although there is now, as there always has been, a diversity of opinions regarding matters of technique, it can be argued that there is increased awareness and acknowledgment of the immediate, interactive, and experiential aspects of psychoanalytic technique. I am referring to the increased use of the analyst's countertransference as a perceptual instrument and the emphasis upon the use of transference as a "here and now" experience as opposed to its use in reconstruction (Gill, 1982).

In Chapters 6 and 7 I attempt to make explicit a theory of technique and a theory of the therapeutic action of psychoanalysis that has remained hidden in the work of Winnicott so that its full implications for psychoanalysis and psychotherapy have not been realized. He put it simply (Winnicott, 1954): "The setting of analysis reproduces the early and earliest mothering techniques." He meant that the psychoanalytic setting, that is, the set-up in itself, func-

tions as a "holding environment." Although his initial observations were derived from the more severely disturbed
patients, the principles learned there were later understood to have relevance for the healthier patients as well.
The sicker patient confronts us with certain aspects of
mental functioning that are present in us all and thus
teaches us about these issues with great clarity.

I have understood the idea of the "holding environment" to contain the principle that conflicts, especially
those of separation/individuation, are carried forward *symbolically* into the analytic setting and the analytic process.
I emphasize the term "symbolic," as the recreation of what
Winnicott described as the early and earliest mothering
techniques does not imply an undoing of psychic structure
or a regression in the transference to the beginning of life.
This capacity to symbolize earlier developmental periods
forces us to question our thinking about regression (see
also Loewald, 1981). The symbolic action of the holding
environment is most evident in the psychoanalysis of the
narcissistic patient, where the setting itself, the area of
relatedness between the patient and the analyst, at least in
the initial stages, becomes the principal locus of the therapeutic action of the psychoanalysis. This symbolic "holding" may lead if successful to a middle phase where
conflicts concerning separation and individuation become
central. I have discussed the function of interpretation in
these cases, believing that its ostensive or truth-giving function is mutative only when self/object differentiation has
been accepted. Prior to that the analyst's interpretative
activity, although necessary, is experienced as a piece of
symbolic action (Chapter 7).

Throughout this work I shall re-examine our concepts
concerning the "regression" that occurs in the psychoanalytic process with the neurotic patient. The belief of ego
psychologists such as Hartmann and Rapaport that evo-

lution leads to an increased independence of the organism from the environment has resulted in a corollary in the psychological sphere, namely, that maturation is equated with growing autonomy from the environment achieved through the process of internalization. For example, Rapaport (1960):

> While the instincts of animals on lower evolutionary levels appear to be directly and more or less rigidly coordinated to specific external stimuli, the instincts of animals on higher evolutionary levels appear to be less rigidly coordinated to such specific stimuli. This difference may be characterized as a progressive internalization of the regulation of behavior. The psychoanalytic theory of drives assumes . . . that the regulation of human behavior is to a large extent internalized [p. 58].

Rapaport did not, of course, believe that the individual is totally autonomous from the environment, but he described a *relative* autonomy.

We are indeed more open to the environment than had been previously thought. This openness is reflected in the communication of affects. We know that young children and their mothers remain an open system and that the mother, if empathically "good enough," automatically perceives the child's affective states. Conversely, the child is sensitively attuned to the affective state of the mother. This is not a process that ever becomes completely internalized and autonomous. The capacity to perceive the affective state of another is, of course, the fundamental basis of affective knowledge. And the most mature of individuals requires from time to time the affective affirmation of the self by another.

There is therefore a greater "permeability" of the individual's relationship to the environment; the ego's "relative" autonomy is even more relative than ego psychology supposed. We are less separate than we wish to believe. In *Object Love and Reality* (Modell, 1968) I indicated that there are mature forms of dependency, that in a certain sense one never outgrows one's need for forms of transitional relatedness. There is a continuing need to maintain the illusion that denies the separateness between the self and the other. This illusion forms the basis of loving and creativity. The presence of continued forms of transitional relatedness was also described by Horton (1981). Kohut, who made very similar observations using the term "self object" (1977), claimed that the continuing presence of self objects is as vital to us psychologically as breathing is physiologically (1980).

Kohut's self psychology is, I believe, potentially a two-person psychology. But this has not been recognized by those who identify themselves as self-psychologists. By focusing on the self in contrast to the self *and* the object, as had Winnicott, the self psychologists have artificially accentuated their difference from the work of Winnicott and others who have more explicitly embraced the context of a two-person psychology. As I have indicated, there are many similarities between my own observations and those of Kohut. But there are also significant differences. Unlike Kohut, I view disturbances of the self to be exquisitely conflictual, but the conflict occurs between the self and the object; so that the context of conflict and the context of defense is not intrapsychic but interpsychic. Furthermore, unlike Kohut, I believe that unconscious guilt is intrinsic to disturbances of the self. But perhaps my most significant difference with Kohut is that I see the two-person context as extending and potentially enriching classical psychoanalysis; it is not a new psychology or a replacement for the structural concepts, which I believe to be indispensable.

In Chapter 8 I will compare my clinical observations and those of Kohut. I do believe, as does Kohut, that self psychology raises significant epistemological issues for psychoanalysis, and the solution I propose uses the strategy of complementarity: the traditional intrapsychic context of psychoanalysis and the two-person context are complementary. This is a solution that Kohut also considered but then rejected in favor of viewing self psychology as a superordinate psychology essentially replacing classical psychoanalysis. These issues will be examined in Chapter 15.

If one thinks of psychoanalysis as a two-person psychology, this will influence one's approach to problems of metapsychology and the larger issue—the nature of psychoanalytic knowledge itself. These issues will be addressed in the final section of this-book, "The Problem of Psychoanalytic Knowledge." I have alluded to the fact that our knowledge of the psychoanalytic process is far richer and broader than is our metapsychology. This has contributed in no small measure to the burgeoning criticism and disillusionment with metapsychology. In Chapters 9, 13, and 14 I shall present an overview of some of the critics of metapsychology: chapter 9 is a review of the contributions of Ricoeur, Habermas, and Polanyi; Chapter 13 examines the problem of metapsychology and the structural paradigm contained in Freud's "The Ego and the Id"; Chapter 14 considers the current status of metapsychology in the light of its critics.

In this book I have placed special emphasis on the role of affects. It is evident that affects are the medium through which events in a two-person field occur. The "permeability" I have mentioned in the individual's relation to the environment means also that we no longer believe in a sharp distinction between self and object, between knower and known. Psychoanalytic knowledge arises in the context of a two-person intersubjective psychology. Words by themselves do not necessarily constitute the primary data

of psychoanalysis. What endows words and other bits of
behavioral data with significance is the affective perception
of the observing analyst. There is something queer in the
assumption, "I feel, therefore I know"—it is Descartes' *cogito* turned on its head. In this intersubjective psychology
there occurs some blurring of the self and the object which
is not at all in keeping with Descartes' premises. These
issues will be examined in Chapters 10 and 11. In Chapter
11 I examine affects in relation to what is the central epistemological paradox for psychoanalysis—that it is both
a hermeneutic and a scientific discipline.

Finally, the paradox implicit throughout this work—the
fact that one-person and two-person psychologies employ
different metaphors and different assumptions, that the
ego and the self occupy different conceptual spheres, is
addressed in Chapter 15, "Context and Complementarity."

Part I

**Defense in a
New Context**

Chapter 1

Psychoanalysis as a One-Person and as a Two-Person Psychology

W hether in everyday life, in art,[1] or in science, perceptions are assigned to an implicit or an explicit context. This
placement acts as an organizing "frame" for the perceptual
experience. We know that Freud chose for psychoanalysis
the "frame" of the mind, which pertains to an intrapsychic
one-person psychology. The process that occurs between
two people, between the subject and the object in the psychoanalytic situation, is referred to the mind of the subject,
who is the patient. This produces in us a certain intellectual
unease when, for example, we describe dependency, a
process occurring between two people, as an event in the
mind of one person. Traditional psychoanalysis has not
yet acquired the theoretical language that would enable it
to describe a process occurring between two separate personalities in terms encompassing the events in both individuals. We are forced to describe the actual object as a

---

[1]Gombrich (1960) observed that the test of an image, that is, its capacity to
create an illusion, is not its likeness, but its efficiency within what he calls a
"context of action." Gombrich referred to both mythic and everyday action, such
as interpreting speech sounds by means of the context in which they occur.

"representation" in the mind of the subject. That is to say, traditional psychoanalysis is a one-person psychology.

It is not too difficult to understand how psychoanalysis arrived at this state of affairs. For I believe that this focus upon the mind follows inevitably from Freud's early neurological investigations and his commitment to certain scientific ideals. Historians have established that Freud wished to do for human psychology what Brucke and Helmholtz had achieved in biology and physics. The biology of Freud's intellectually formative period did not appreciate the dynamism that exists between the organism and its environment. In laboratory experiments environmental conditions were controlled so that the true focus was understood to be upon events occurring within the organism. Freud's early scientific ideals were consistent with the oath that Brucke had pledged:

> No other forces than the common physical-chemical ones are active within the organism. In these cases which cannot at the time be explained by those forces one has either to find the specific way or form of their action by means of the physical-mathematical method or to assume new forces equal in dignity to the chemical-physical forces inherent in matter, reducible to the force of attraction and repulsion [Jones, 1953, p. 40].

Fechner's constancy principle, the principle according to which the psychic apparatus tends to keep the quantity of excitation at as low a level as possible, to which Freud adhered throughout his life, can be considered as an example of a "force equal in dignity" to those of physics and chemistry. This principle became the cornerstone of Freud's economic theory (Laplanche and Pontalis, 1973).

Freud's patients, of course, were not studied in a relatively controlled environment. We know that Freud first believed that neurosis resulted from an actual seduction—that fantasies were an attempt to deal defensively with memories of "primal scenes": "Fantasies are psychical outworks constructed in order to pave the way to these memories. At the same time, fantasies serve the purpose of refining these memories or sublimating them" (Bonaparte, A. Freud, and Kris, 1954, p. 196-197). When Freud learned that he was mistaken, that the fantasies and not the memories were in fact primary, that all fathers were not perverts, psychoanalysis could be reaffirmed as a primarily one-person psychology. The field of investigation shifted from that of a relationship, that is, the actual interaction between the child and the adult, to events that occurred within the mind of the child, that is, to the fantasy which ultimately could be traced back to the instincts arising from within the interior of the mental apparatus.

In Freud's famous letter to Fliess on September 21, 1897, where he confessed "that I no longer believe in my neurotica"—that the fathers of his hysterical female patients could not all have been perverts—he also stated, "there was the definite realization that there is no 'indication of reality' in the unconscious, so that it is impossible to distinguish between truth and emotionally-charged fiction" (Bonaparte, A. Freud, and Kris, 1954, p. 216).

What Freud had discovered was the pre-eminence of psychic reality, which was to become the ultimate subject matter of psychoanalysis. Given that psychic reality has an existence of its own apart from the presence of another, if it is true that the unconscious does not distinguish between truth and emotionally charged fiction, the contribution of the actual relationship could be minimized and psychoanalysis could remain a one-person psychology.[2]

The concept of psychic reality is not without ambiguities

---

[2]Anthony (1981) from a somewhat different perspective also reviewed the history of Freud's turning from the external to the internal environment.

(Laplanche, 1976). As Freud indicated, it may be impossible to distinguish with certainty between truth and emotionally charged fiction, or to be able to establish whether one is observing a fantasy or the memory of a trauma. The consequences of an actual seduction as compared to a fantasied one are very different indeed. Freud, as Laplanche showed, never quite abandoned his search for the "actual." In his "Three Essays on the Theory of Sexuality," he fully acknowledged the importance of the mother's seductive influence: "A child's intercourse with anyone responsible for his care affords him an unending source of sexual excitation and satisfaction from his erotogenic zones. This is especially so since the person in charge of him, who, after all, is as a rule his mother, herself regards him with feelings that are derived from her own sexual life: she strokes him, kisses him, rocks him and quite clearly treats him as a substitute for a complete sexual object" (Freud, 1905, p. 223).

Freud here is by no means minimizing the importance of the contribution of the environment. This is a clear illustration of what has come to be known as the "counter Oedipus" complex of the parent (Devereux, 1960). So that the Oedipus complex is not something arising only within the interior of the mental apparatus; its intensity and other vicissitudes do depend upon the sexual life of the parent, as Freud illustrated.

Although psychic reality can in fact exist independently of the "Other," can psychoanalytic truth exist independently of the "Other"? I believe that the ultimate validation of psychic reality cannot occur in complete isolation. Even Freud, whose self-analysis may have been a unique example, required the presence (however distant that presence may have been) of an idealized Fliess.

Although a one-person psychology is the traditional context of psychoanalysis, Freud by no means adhered exclusively to it. Furthermore, Freud's interests were not restricted to the psychology of the individual. It was Freud's general view that the psychology of groups preceded the psychology of the individual. In the chronology of his works, it appears that he followed this principle in that his ideas seemed to be given a prior exploration in the context of a group before he brought them into the context of the psychology of the individual. "Totem and Taboo" (Freud, 1913a) and his "Group Psychology and the Analysis of the Ego" (Freud, 1921) necessarily preceded the "Ego and the Id" (Freud, 1923). As a background to the theory of instincts Freud described the Lamarckian transmission of the traumatic experiences of groups; the memory of the collective murder of the father by bands of brothers was, he thought, the ultimate origin of the Oedipus complex.

Today there are few if any Lamarckians among biologists (although in Freud's day Lamarck still had his respectable adherents), and there are few psychoanalysts who would accept Freud's account of the origin of the Oedipus complex as something other than a scientific myth. But if we dismiss these Lamarckian particulars, there is agreement that the origin of the Oedipus complex can be found in our evolutionary history and that the incest taboo, which favors exogamy, served the adaptive needs not only of the individual but also of the nuclear family and the extended tribe. Although it is inaccurate to claim that psychoanalysis was for Freud a one-person psychology, it is true that for Freud individual and group psychology remained separate subjects. As a consequence we have yet to establish a science of relationships that encompasses the intrapsychic and the psychoanalytic group of two.

We know that psychoanalysis along with other learned

traditions has developed its own institutionalized rigidities. Freud's discoveries became codified and as the discipline aged, there developed an "official intrapsychic position." For example, Rapaport (1954), who brilliantly attempted a codification of psychoanalysis, in describing the psychoanalytic theory of affects, chose to ignore Freud's more speculative ideas that affects and instincts evolved within the context of a group. We first met these speculations in "Totem and Taboo" (Freud, 1913a), and he did not later change his mind in *Inhibitions, Symptoms and Anxiety*: "Affective states have become incorporated into the mind as precipitants of primaeval [group] traumatic experiences, and when a similar situation occurs they are revived like mnemic symbols. I do not think I have been wrong in likening them to the more recent and individually acquired hysterical attack and in regarding them as its normal prototypes" (1926a, p. 93). Rapaport instead considered Freud's theory of affects exclusively in the context of the psychic apparatus.

Those psychoanalysts who challenge this official intrapsychic position have done so, for the most part, at the expense of being viewed as outside of the psychoanalytic establishment.[3] For example Balint (1950), who rejected Freud's belief in primary narcissism, quoted Rickman as follows: "The whole region of psychology may be divided into areas of research according to the number of persons concerned. Thus we may speak of One-Body Psychology, Two-Body Psychology, etc." (p. 123). Balint went on to say: "Each of these psychologies has its own field of studies and ought to develop its own 'language' of technical terms, sets of concepts, etc., for the proper description of its findings. Until now this has been done only in the One-Body Psy-

---

[3]Langs (1981) also espoused the need for a two-person psychology. Unfortunately, he unnecessarily polarized the distinction between a one-person and a two-person psychology, assuming along the way an overly polemical stance.

chology. Psycho-analytic theory—as I have tried to show is no exception; almost all our terms and concepts were derived from studying pathological forms hardly going beyond the domain of the One-Body Psychology . . ." (p. 124). As I noted above, Winnicott's contribution is implicitly within the context of a two-body or, as I prefer, two-person psychology.

Balint and Winnicott, although influenced by different traditions, are members of what has come to be known as the British object relations school. Yet within this broad designation their position needs to be contrasted to that of Melanie Klein and Fairbairn, who, although they do not in any sense diminish the importance of the "object," attempt to preserve the classical viewpoint of psychoanalysis by referring not to the actual object but to the representation of the object in the mind. As Winnicott (1965b) observed, the term "object relationship" could mean "relationship to inner" or to "external objects" (p. 174). He contrasted his own position (Winnicott, 1962a) to that of Melanie Klein as follows:

> . . . she paid lip-service to environmental provision, but would never fully acknowledge that along with the dependence of early infancy is truly a period in which it is not possible to describe an infant without describing the mother whom the infant has not yet become able to separate from a self. Klein claimed to have paid full attention to the environmental factor, but it is my opinion that she was temperamentally incapable of this [p. 177].

Fairbairn, despite other differences with Melanie Klein (1948), adhered to the Kleinian stance of describing object relations in terms of the vicissitudes of internalized objects. He proposed a complex theory of endopsychic structures—"a central ego, internal saboteur, libidinal ego, rejecting ego, exciting object, etc." (1952, p. 105).

This tradition has been carried forward today in the work of Kernberg (1975), who described the psychopathology of borderline states in terms of the complex vicissitudes of the internal images of the object inside the mind of the subject. As did Fairbairn, he spoke of "internalized object relationships." Loyalty to a one-person psychology has, in my opinion, become a deforming Procrustean bed. Now it is true that in the psychoses when relationships with actual persons have been abandoned, as Freud observed in "Group Psychology and the Analysis of the Ego" (1921, p. 130), "the ego now enters into the relation of an object to the ego ideal which has developed out of it, and that all the interplay between an external object and the ego as a whole, with which our study of the neuroses has made us acquainted, may possibly be repeated upon this new scene of action within the ego." The erotic relationship with hallucinated voices that develops in some schizophrenic patients illustrates this substitution of an internal object for an actual one (Modell, 1958). But a representational psychology that attempts to portray relations with actual objects by means of internalized analogues makes no distinction between the actual object and one that is completely created by the subject.

There are further problems: Can the image of the object and the image of the subject be thought of as symmetrical and separate structures in the mind? Or is this a reification of certain endopsychic experiences? Under the sway of intense ambivalence external objects and the self are both idealized and intensely denigrated. Does this so-called "splitting" mean necessarily that the images of the object and the images of the self exist as split "structures" in the mind? Or have we, as I suspect is true, invented "structures" in the mind that homologize with the patient's endopsychic experience?

In my earlier book, *Object Love and Reality* (1968), I observed that Freud's concept of the "presentation of the object," accepted uncritically by generations of psychoanalysts, had its origins in an eighteenth-century philosophy. I suggested that Freud may have acquired this notion from John Stuart Mill, whose translator he was. In turn Mill, as a representational psychologist, would have acquired the idea of "object representations" from Locke. This was Locke's answer to *the* epistemological question—the correspondence between objects in the world and objects in the mind. Locke proposed that this correspondence was "simple"; that "object representations" are fundamental entities analogous to the elementary particles in the physical world.

The psychoanalytic concept of "internalized objects" has, I believe, retained some aspects of this Lockeian atomism. Internalized objects exist, to be sure, as fantasies, but are they psychic structures, and can internalized objects stand as a notational system for actual, that is, external object relations? Despite my earlier interest in the concept of internalized objects, with increasing clinical experience in psychoanalyzing the so-called disturbed patient, I have become skeptical of the broad extension of this concept. Patients may have a fantasy that there is something "bad" inside of them. I recall one such patient who was dominated both in her dreams and waking fantasies with the image that her insides were like a deep, dark-blue, bottomless well in which a shark-like object dwelt. This could be considered the introjection of an intensely ambivalent early object; the biting mother was transposed inside the self, an internalized object. This endopsychic experience of the self as damaging contributed to her near conviction that everything she touched withered and died. A central and dominating fantasy to be sure, but can this "internal object" be considered in any sense to be analogous to an external object?

Internalized objects can be thought of as analogous to external objects only under very special and restrictive conditions. Internalized objects may actually substitute for external objects in some schizophrenic illnesses, where the hallucinations that both protect and persecute do in fact substitute for the actual object relations that have been lost (Modell, 1958). Also, in the withdrawal that accompanies severe mourning it could be said that the constantly recurring images and memories of the loved one who has been lost serve as a substitute in the mind for what has been lost in actuality. Freud described this process in "Mourning and Melancholia" (Freud, 1917b) but there he was careful to note that the "shadow which fell upon the ego" was an internal object only insofar as it was a *substitute* for an actual object relationship.

I have focused on the problem of the internal object as it is, I believe, a failed attempt to retain an object-relations theory that is consistent with a one-person psychology. As I plan to demonstrate in the chapters that follow, psychoanalysis is both a one-person and a two-person psychology. I am not proposing that this "new" context replace traditional psychoanalysis, but merely that the limits of a one-person psychology be recognized—that the addition of a two-person context is intended not to replace classical theory but to extend it. There is a persistent and sustaining duality through much if not all of the subject matter that comprises the body of psychoanalytic knowledge. There is an inherent duality in the theory of affects and the concept of defense, as I shall describe more fully in the next chapter. In the context of the mental apparatus affects have been understood as a discharge phenomenon, under the regulation of the pleasure and unpleasure principles and Fechner's constancy principle, as we have noted. A heightened tension results in a process of discharge, maintaining a certain homeostasis at a lower level of excitation.

This one-person context of affect theory can perhaps be illustrated by the state of sleep and dreaming, where the individual is cut off from external relations. As Freud wrote, "Affectivity manifests itself essentially in motor (secretory and vasomotor discharge) resulting in an (internal) alteration of the subject's own body without reference to the external world" (1915b, p. 179).

But in the waking state affects are the medium of exchange between people. They are inherently contagious, and as I shall describe in the next chapter, are the medium through which the sense of self is affirmed or denied. Affects are object seeking; and the noncommunication of affects, or the communication of false or misleading affects, is the core of the defense of nonrelatedness, a defense in a new context, the context of a two-person psychology. The defense against affects actually defends and manipulates the object carrier that is the source of anxiety. Accordingly, we have in effect a dual theory of affects that is context bound.

As I shall further illustrate in the following chapters, our affirmation of the importance of a two-person context is not to be taken as a depreciation of the central significance of internalization and structure formation. Such concepts are indeed indispensable for us. As Loewald (1980a) noted, "internalization is the basic way of functioning of the psyche, . . . [not] one of its functions" (p. 71; see also Meissner, 1981). I am not suggesting that a two-person psychology replace our more traditional views of structure formation and internalization. What I do propose is that there is a complementarity between these two systems of thought. It is clear that both systems are essential to each other. Both contexts have their own interlocking network of assumptions and theories, which are, paradoxically, incompatible with each other. In Chapters 11 and 15 I discuss the epistemological problems that accompany this paradox. This work expresses a plea to accept paradox: to recognize that paradox is an intrinsic quality of the human mind, and that we must not always attempt to resolve paradoxes by straining for a new synthesis. The paradoxes and inconsistencies which pervade the body of Freud's works may not be something simply to be excused as examples of the lapses in logic for which we forgive genius. They may reflect something deeper. In his quest for truth Freud may have perceived that paradox is intrinsic to human psychology; to achieve a unitary logic may be to destroy the essence of understanding.

This is most evident in our thinking about the self. The self is both a psychic structure, colored by the process of internalization, and also an endopsychic perception, exquisitely dependent upon the immediacy of the response of the other. The self is a permanent structure, but also something always in the process of being reshaped. This is testimony to the fact that we remain forever social animals; the sense of ourselves is constantly molded by the responses of loved ones, friends, as well as the anonymous members of a group. The vulnerability of the self is something that can be exaggerated by pathology so that we can justifiably speak of developmental arrests. But it should also be understood that such developmental arrests with the accompanying difficulty in self-object differentiation are no more than an exaggeration of a process that is present in us all.

Chapter 2

Affects and Nonrelatedness

Brierley (1937) anticipated over 40 years ago that affects are the markers of defenses against object ties: "The child is first concerned with objects only in relation to its own feelings and sensations but, as soon as feelings are firmly linked to objects, the process of instinct-defense becomes a process of defense against objects. The infant then tries to master its feelings by manipulating its object carriers" (p. 51).

It is our contention that affects are the medium through which defenses against objects occur. To make this statement fully comprehensible, let me first review certain assumptions concerning affects, the self, and its objects. In the primitive state there is an affective bond between the adult and child allowing for communication of vital information without the requirement that its contents be made explicit. Communication in this sense is part of the earliest object tie and probably precedes the acquisition of articulated language. This is part of the "holding" function of the human environment and has its obvious analogue in other primate species (Hamburg, 1963).

That the child and its mother are exquisitely tuned to

each other's affects is not open to question. What is of interest to us is that the communication of affects may be the primary source of information regarding the mother's inner world as well as a primary source of information regarding the real world and its dangers. This inference is suggested by the well-known observations of A. Freud and Burlingham (1944) that young children remained calm in a bombing raid if their mothers were not unduly anxious. In this sense the child and the mother remain an open system vis-à-vis each other. No one doubts that this primitive preverbal communication persists throughout life and forms the biological substrate of what we later term "empathy."

We know that there are those who wish to reinstate this primitive tie by demanding that they be understood without the necessity of making the effort of communication. This yearning to return to an "open system" may also be accompanied by what can be described as the involuntary communication of affect. Here the nature of the affect and the act of communication itself remain unconscious to the subject but nevertheless the affect is perceived by the object. This phenomenon is characteristic of certain borderline and psychotic patients where the observer may experience intense guilt, depression, anxiety, and so on, which in a certain sense have been "placed" in the object by an unconscious process in the subject (see further discussion in Chapter 11). We may assume that phenomena of this sort are not limited to the very ill patient but represent the persistence of something that we all experience as children: that we perceive our mother's affects as if they were placed within us in some occult and mysterious fashion.

Affects are then the medium through which vital information is transmitted. This information concerns not only the real world and its dangers, but also the mother's af-

fective state. Since affects are also the medium through
which the process of mirroring takes place, we assume that
the child perceives not only its mother's affects, but also
its mother's perception of his or her own affects. We believe that the analytic process symbolically recapitulates this
earlier mirroring, but what we observe initially is that the
sense of self is protected by means of protracted states of
nonrelatedness. This can be inferred, as I shall indicate,
from the psychoanalysis of the narcissistic patient. In the
initial phase of the analysis, a phase which may last for
years, or may be in some instances never-ending, the vulnerability of the self is protected by a defense of nonrelatedness. I shall first describe this state of affairs and the
analyst's reaction to it and will then attempt to understand
the meaning and function of this particular defense.

There are some patients in whom the state of nonrelatedness is quite evident in the earliest stages of analysis,
whereas in others this state of affairs is masked, and it is
only gradually that the analyst perceives that the patient
is not communicating. In the obvious case the analyst observes a massive affect block as the patient fills the hour
with talk—talk from which the affective charge has been
removed so that the analyst may feel at times that he is
drowning in a sea of words. Although the patient may
report that he is experiencing intense anxiety, his tone of
voice does not convey this—we need to be told—we do not
perceive it ourselves. Our patients may cry silently without
communicating sadness—we identify the affect only by
noticing their tears, not by means of their words.

Until one has developed some experience with patients
of this type, the analyst may tell himself that he is observing
the intellectualization and isolation of an obsessive-compulsive where there is also a massive blocking of affects.
Although the noncommunication of affect may superficially resemble the mechanism of isolation, the effect is

more global as it involves the object relationship to the analyst—the fact that the patient is not relating to us. We are the object that is defended against, and in such states of nonrelatedness our own emotional perceptions, our countertransference, if you will, can be used, and needs to be used, as a perceptual instrument. When I am in the continued presence of someone who is not communicating or is not relating, and I use these words interchangeably, I experience a state of boredom and sleepy withdrawal. Although other people may respond in different ways, I believe that it is axiomatic that when one is a partner in a state of nonrelatedness, the other will experience some significant emotional reaction. The use of the term "countertransference" in this instance does not signify a neurotic response. Countertransference has been increasingly recognized as one of the analyst's perceptual instruments, a recognition which differentiates itself from the view that it is likely to be a reflection of the analyst's neurosis and hence an obstacle. I refer especially to the work of Heimann (1950), McDougal (1980), and Racker (1968).

This noncommunication of affect may be accompanied by other linguistic noncommunicating devices (Rosen, 1967). Some patients omit the links which connect one idea to another. Sentences may be broken off in the middle, reminiscent of Bion's description (1959) of attacks on linking. If one inquires about this, the subject matter is switched so that there is not a dialogue but essentially two people speaking to themselves. There are some who use the method of free association as a means of noncommunication. With true free association there is an underlying structure and cohesiveness, a structure reflective of the primary process. What passes for free association in those who cannot free-associate are forced fantasies, or communication in which the connecting links are omitted so that the communication is in fact incomprehensible,

with the result that the analyst may at times begin to wonder whether the patient has a thinking disorder. The patients that I am describing, however, are not in any sense
psychotic, but employ psychotic-like defenses in that the
locus of the defensive process is the tie to the object. This
pseudopsychotic nature of defense in the narcissistic patient was also noted by Green (1975).

FEIGNED AND MANIPULATED AFFECTS

There are some patients in whom noncommunication
is evident, whereas in others it is more subtle. Some patients in the narcissistic personality group in the opening
phase of the analysis appear to be relating to us. It may
take some time to realize that behind this apparent relatedness there is a certain lack of warmth, a certain emptiness, and ultimately we learn that the affects that we
observe and experience are not genuine but are based
upon a need to comply with what is expected of them. This
does not represent a conscious attempt at deception but
corresponds to what was long ago observed by Deutsch
(1942) in the "as if" personality—a passive attitude toward
the environment with a plastic readiness to pick up signals
from the outer world and to mold oneself and one's behavior accordingly. Winnicott's (1965a) false self based on
compliance covers this same description.

In some patients the affects are not based on a need to
comply but serve a different function. They are false affects in that they are not what they appear to be but reflect
instead a need to evoke a complementary affect in the
analyst.[1] For example, an attractive woman patient was

---

[1]Valenstein's (1962) description of what he called "affectualization" as a defense against communication is, I believe, an observation of a similar process.
He described a patient who used excessive affectivity as a smoke screen that
obscured the analytic field.

overtly seductive. This might be considered simply a manifestation of sexual desire expressed as a wish to seduce.
However, as the analysis progressed, we learned that the
patient herself actually experienced little or no sexual desire; she suffered instead from an absence of desire, experiencing that her sense of self was dead. She hoped that
she would arouse *me* and then I would in turn "place" the
affect in her—a form of psychological pump priming. This
could be described not as a communication of affects but
as a manipulation of the analyst's countertransference in
order to reanimate a sense of self that was experienced as
dead and empty. This observation suggests that we are
witnessing the persistence of a primitive interaction reminiscent of the child who relies on the mother to induce
or place affects within her. This also carries with it the
implication of an indefiniteness of boundaries between the
self and others—that is, a wish to merge.

Certain forms of acting out may also serve a similar
function. For example, there are patients who need to
arouse an affective response in us and therefore may pre-
cipitate a series of external life crises. In an obvious sense
this is a need to learn whether or not we care, but a more
fundamental meaning may be the wish to relieve the sense
of emptiness and deadness of the self.

In this descriptive account of the noncommunication of
affects or the manipulation of affects in the narcissistic
personality, I do not wish to imply that these patients *never*
communicate affects directly. What I am describing, is the
usual, that is, predominant, mode, which is the mode of
nonrelatedness.

It is evident that I have entered into the area of Winnicott's false self. Much of what I have observed is simply
a confirmation of what has been implied in Winnicott's
work, especially his profound and at times enigmatic and
altogether remarkable paper (1963a), "Communicating

and Not Communicating Leading to a Study of Certain Opposites." I have added my own views of affects to Winnicott's observations, as Winnicott did not specifically consider communication in relation to affects. Winnicott (1963a) stated:

> I suggest that in health there is a core to the personality that corresponds to the true self of the split personality; I suggest that this core never communicates with the world of perceived objects, and that the individual person knows that it must never be communicated with or be influenced by external reality. This is my main point, the point of thought which is the centre of an intellectual world and of my paper. Although healthy persons communicate and enjoy communicating, the other fact is equally true, that *each individual is an isolate, permanently non-communicating, permanently unknown, in fact unfound* [p. 187].

And further: "There is room for the idea that significant relating and communicating is silent" (p. 184). Here Winnicott contrasted what he calls silent communication or simple noncommunication with active noncommunication. The latter is defensive, the result of intense anxiety whose content we shall now begin to examine.

WHY DOES SOMEONE WISH NOT TO COMMUNICATE?

I have described a specific character organization of the narcissistic personality that is recreated in the analytic process, which I have metaphorically termed a cocoon (Modell, 1975b, 1976, 1981). This corresponds to the patient's own intrapsychic perception that he or she is walled off from others, encased in a cocoon or a plastic shield, or Sylvia Plath's bell jar. In this cocoon the patient maintains the illusion that he can nourish himself and needs nothing from others—that he is in fact omnipotently self-sufficient. I suggested (following Khan [1963]) that this structural organization is based in part on a need for precocious autonomy, that there has been a relative failure of the parental holding environment resulting in this precociousness of false self organization. Below I shall describe in greater detail the character formation and the response to specific environmental deficiencies. Children with this formation observe quite early that they cannot depend upon their parents to "hold" them symbolically and therefore they must do this for themselves. As they cannot in fact do this for themselves, they must fall back upon fantasies of omnipotent self-sufficiency, often supported by specific fantasies of grandiosity. It is in this cocoon-like state that the non-communication of affects is most pronounced. The cocoon is like a fortress which nothing leaves or enters—it is not only that they do not communicate, but also that they do not receive the communication of others; they do not hear what is said to them.

From this we can infer that noncommunication supports the illusion of self-sufficiency. Or to state it in the obverse: the communication of affects is object-seeking. To communicate affects is to betray a desire.[2] I am reminded here of Fairbairn's (1944) formula that "libido is not pleasure seeking but object seeking." I would state, "Affects are not pleasure seeking but object seeking," to answer the question—Why does someone wish not to communicate? The answer in general is in the area of the *vulnerability of the sense of self*.

There is wide agreement that the child's sense of self is created in part through the mirroring function of the parents, and that the need to reaffirm the self through the

---

[2]Paradoxically, the so-called narcissistic sense of entitlement does coexist with a need to deny the desire to have something for one's self. I have described this in greater detail in Chapter 4, "On Having the Right to a Life."

response of others continues throughout one's life. It is also generally observed that in the narcissistic personality this function is heightened and the sense of self is extremely vulnerable. This is to say, the illusion of self-sufficiency is accompanied by a state of affairs that is its precise opposite: extreme dependency and extreme vulnerability. If one communicates that which is so secret and precious, it is akin to casting one's pearls before swine. An unempathic response at best will lead to a sense of depletion; at worst one will feel shattered. One patient described feeling as if she were an egg: to share feeling was to crack herself open; the precious yolk would run out and be lost forever. One's fate is placed in the hands of the other.

The Fear of the Other's Omnipotent Control

Our patients in the narcissistic group wish to control their affects omnipotently, that is to say, the danger that the self might be demolished is so great that they cannot run the risk of being surprised by an unexpected response from the other. The wish to control the other omnipotently is commonly projected and externalized and experienced as a fear that they will become enslaved. Their view of enslavement is one of absolute domination and control, so that to communicate genuine feeling is to provide the other with the means of domination. To expose the secret self runs the risk of being infinitely exploited, that is, the risk of being swallowed up.

Silent Communication and the Illusion of Merging

There is another facet behind the wish not to communicate. Recall Winnicott's distinction between silent communication and active noncommunication. Simple noncommunication is not defensive, it is not primarily a response to anxiety: it is analogous to the wish to be alone in the presence of another person. With some patients we have the impression, usually in the opening phases of analysis, of a child playing happily by himself content to know that his mother is in the next room. It is as if the patient is talking to himself and is not in the least troubled by the analyst's nonresponse and extended silences. During this period one invariably learns that there is an expectation that he can be understood omnipotently, that is, without having to make the effort to communicate. As Winnicott suggested, it is important for the analyst to differentiate the state of affairs in which the patient is comfortable in his noncommunication from the one in which there is active noncommunication based on intense anxiety and helplessness. Here the need to communicate and the inability to do so can lead to a state of absolute desperation. Here the cocoon is not a safe enclosure but a prison from which there is no escape. In the former instance our interventions (at least in the opening phase of analysis) are not required and may in fact be harmful, whereas in the latter instance it is important that we share with our patient our understanding that nonrelatedness is a defense that is mobilized by the anxiety related to a vulnerable sense of self. To do so is a further recognition that noncommunicating is not done out of simple spite, defiance, or willfulness, that it is in fact a defense analogous to the more familiar intrapsychic defenses. To recognize this prevents the patient from feeling that he has been abandoned.

The Sphere Within a Sphere

The state of affairs in which the patient is silently communicating is a state of contiguity without true relatedness. I have responded to this with a visual image of a sphere within a sphere, that is, the sphere of the patient's self-sufficient cocoon being held within the larger sphere of the analytic setting. In this period the patient is comfortable in attributing to the analyst qualities of omnipotence. Kohut (1971) rightly warned us against refusing to accept this projected omniscience, and Winnicott (1965b) warned us about interpreting it too early.

One may say that in states of simple noncommunication one does not communicate, for to do so will mean the loss of the illusion of the omniscience of the other. In active noncommunication one does not communicate because of the fear of losing the sense of omnipotent self-sufficiency. Finally, the communication of feigned or false affects, or the communication of affects intended to manipulate the other, represents a quest for omnipotent control of the other, a control that protects against a dissolution of the self by the other.

The common thread throughout all these defensive maneuvers is the attempt to maintain control of affects absolutely, that is, omnipotently. To relate to others not only involves repudiation of one's own omnipotence but carries with it the projected danger that the other will do to oneself what one wishes to do to them. The fear of closeness thus is the fear that one will be taken over, that one will become an abject, submissive slave. Not only is this fear based on a projected intent: it reflects a deep dependent wish to merge; there is not only a fear but there is also the wish to be swallowed up (Lewin, 1950).

THE INDUCTION OF NEGATIVE AFFECTS IN THE OTHER PERSON—AN ASPECT OF THE REPETITION COMPULSION

During the analysis of the narcissistic personality there are many sources of dysphoric negative affects. The conflict between the wish to be separate and autonomous and the wish to maintain the illusion of being merged is a generator of negative affects inasmuch as the perception of separateness is not infrequently accompanied by anger. It is not only the anger at the fact of separateness; the experience of anger in itself tends to support a sense of the self and may be a necessary accompaniment to the process of individuation. When these negative affects become chronic, they are apt to induce a corresponding negative countertransference.

There is another type of negativity that one encounters in the psychoanalysis of the narcissistic case that has a different source and a different meaning and function. In this instance the recreation of negative affects in the transference and countertransference can be understood as an attempt to recreate actively what has been experienced passively. It is the attempt to bring trauma, that is, the pain experienced in the conflict with the external world, into the internal world and thus create the illusion of mastery and control. It is as if one protects oneself from the trauma of overwhelming massive pain by inoculating oneself with repeated small doses. What I am describing is a belief consistent with Freud's paradigm of the repetition compulsion (Freud, 1920). Freud's essay of 1920 divides itself into two portions: one derived from psychoanalytic observation and the other a global biological speculation with Fechner's constancy principle as its neurological assumption. If we leave the speculative and quasineurological portions of the essay to one side, there is a suggestion of the beginning of an object-related theory of affects. Freud started by asking the question: If human beings are dominated by the pleasure principle, why is it that they are compelled to recreate painful affects? The most frequently encountered illustrations of the recreation of painful affects are the traumatic neuroses, traumatic dreams, and the recreation of painful events through action rather than remembering in the transference neurosis. In the recreation of the painful event Freud observed that the ego attempts to recreate actively what it had endured passively—by transferring an event from the external world into the internal world, the ego achieves an illusion of omnipotent control. If we assume that every transference affect has its counterpart in the analyst's countertransference, the effect of the patient's repetition compulsion will not be limited to the patient's psyche alone but will involve also the recreation of dysphoric affects in the analyst.[3] To put it simply, the repetition compulsion attempts to master actively what was endured passively by displacing the affects from the primary to the secondary, surrogate objects. This is all familiar to us under the heading of transference repetition; what is not so well known is the unconscious attempt to manipulate the secondary object through the affects induced in the countertransference. In Freud's famous illustration of the child's game, the child's action was intended to influence the mother. This is the game that Freud (1920) observed played by his one-and-a-half-year-old grandchild who threw and withdrew a reel tied by a piece of string over the edge of his cot, accompanying its departure by an expressive, "o-o-o-o," (p. 15) and its retrieval with a joyful, "da" Freud interpreted this game as a re-enactment of the painful departure of the child's mother. Through a magical gesture the child created an illusion that he could control his mother's going and coming omnipotently. We

---

[3]Valenstein (1973) also discussed the relation between dysphoric affects and their object carriers. He understood this to be related to an attempt to maintain an object tie. This is an additional explanation that is not at all inconsistent with our observations of the workings of the repetition compulsion. The attachment to negative affects has a source other than the repetition compulsion which we shall consider in Chapters 4 and 5. There attachment to painful and negative affects may signify an aspect of separation guilt and guilt of the survivor. That is, one may remain attached not only to one's own painful affects but also to those affects that belong to one's parents, as if giving up the affects confronts one with the guilt of separation.

know that Freud did not continue with this line of reasoning but sought an explanation for the repetition of painful experiences in his far-reaching biological speculations about the death instinct.

As in the child's game, a motive behind the noncommunication of affects is to control the object omnipotently. Objects can be controlled through their affects so that the repetition of dysphoric affects in the psychoanalytic relationship signifies not only a wish to maintain ties with those with whom the affects are originally associated but also to control the object experiencing the communication of these affects.

Many of our patients attempt to recreate actively in the countertransference what they fear will occur to them passively. If they fear that their sense of themselves may be demolished by an absence of empathy or a challenge to their grandiosity, they may attempt actively to induce this very criticism in the other so that they can create the illusion that this is something that they are controlling omnipotently. For example, one patient who very much feared that he was incapable of truly caring for others, that is, of truly loving (which was not the case), after some years of analytic work behaved (or at least this is what he reported) as if he were a cold, unfeeling, totally unloving person. He also induced in me the sense that the analytic work, which up until then had yielded considerable results, counted for nothing, that he had no feeling for me, that we in fact had no real relationship, and that it had all been a sham. This could be described as the induction of a negative countertransference response, that the image of himself that he was inducing in me was the one he most feared I would bestow upon him. Despite the suffering that this caused, he had the satisfaction that he was producing it actively.

A NOTE ON NONRELATEDNESS AND CHARACTER FORMATION

When one attempts to delineate a particular character type, one is immediately confronted with the limitations of the concept of character itself. The nosological entity implied in the use of such term as "narcissistic personality" does not imply a category absolutely demarcated from "borderline states" or the transference neuroses. We must allow for transitional forms where assignment to one category or the other may not be possible, which also acknowledges the possibility of overlapping or mixed entities. Such a state of affairs is far from satisfactory, but in spite of this imprecision it is possible to describe the difference between the narcissistic case and the so-called "classical case" by differentiating the transference and the analytic process. In this sense it is an operational definition and it allows at least for a first approximation in the establishment of diagnostic categories. I describe the transference in the narcissistic case and contrasted it to that of the "classical case" in Chapter 6 ("The Holding Environment" and "The Therapeutic Action of Psychoanalysis") and Chapter 7 ("Interpretation and Symbolic Actualization of Developmental Arrests").

Character types may be defined not only by differences in the transference but also by their characteristic forms of defense (Modell, 1975b). We are familiar with the observation that the defenses of the ego are variegated, but if one particular defense predominates, it contributes to the structure of a specific character type (thus the predominance of repression is associated with hysteria, and isolation and intellectualization with the obsessive-compulsive personality). The defense of nonrelatedness may be viewed in a similar fashion. As I have indicated above, the defense of nonrelatedness evokes a specific countertransference response which is one of boredom, sleepiness, or indifference to affects that are spurious and hence do not move us. We feel as if there are not two people in the consulting room. The patient is "emotionally turned off." The analyst's countertransference can usually be relied upon to make the subtle distinction between the defense of isolation, which is an intrapsychic affect block, and the defense of nonrelatedness, which is a defense involving two persons. The obsessive-compulsive may communicate without much feeling, but the analyst still perceives that the patient is relating to him. We have said that affects are object-seeking, and nonrelatedness implies an illusion of self-sufficiency (Modell, 1975b). Although the borderline patient may also have illusions of self-sufficiency, more commonly what is observed initially is a state of intense object hunger. Therefore, the countertransference can be used to distinguish the nonrelating narcissistic case from the borderline case, whose affects are communicated with great intensity. This intensity will correspondingly induce intense countertransference affects in the analyst. (I discuss this in greater detail in Chapter 10, "Affects and Psychoanalytic Knowledge.")

It is implicit that the defense of noncommunication of affects can be traced to a defense against objects, that is, to certain traumas experienced in relation to former objects. Ever since Freud learned that he had been misled by believing his patient's stories of their seductions, psychoanalysts have guarded themselves against any naïve belief in the stories that their patients tell them. We have become distrustful of our reconstructions. Of course there are no definitive guidelines that enable us to separate fantasy from historical fact. All we can say with certainty is that reconstructions correspond to the patient's psychic reality. In spite of these disclaimers, I tend to believe in certain reconstructions. For what we accept as the truth is not what the patient first presents to us but is a picture that only gradually emerges after considerable resistance has been overcome. The trauma that we have reconstructed can be placed in the broad category of disturbance in the parental holding environment. More specifically, the trauma involves disturbances in the communication of affects. I have referred above to the observations of Anna Freud and Burlingham which illustrate the extent to which the child is dependent upon the communication of affect for its orientation in the real world. In a recurrent configuration that I have reconstructed from the psychoanalysis of the narcissistic personality, one or both parents are emotionally absent or the conveyer of spurious information. An intellectually precocious patient observed at the age of two or three that his mother was mad, although this fact was not acknowledged by others. In other instances children correctly observed that their parents' social judgment was "off." Their mothers may have been flighty, fatuous, and actually silly. Such parents became an unreliable source of information about the real world and were unable to provide positive mirroring based on the communication of genuine affects. This affective insensitivity contributed to failures of empathy and overintrusiveness, that is, a lack of respect for the child's requirements for secrecy and privacy. Kohut (1977), Winnicott (1965b), and Guntrip (1968) described similar disturbances in the parental holding environment. We believe that this relative failure in the parental holding environment results, as we have noted, in a precocious maturation. It is as if the child is saying to himself, "I cannot rely on my mother's judgment, therefore I have to be a better mother to myself." This self-mothering can only be sustained by "turning off" from the protective environment and sustaining oneself by means of omnipotent fantasies. These fantasies contribute to the psychic cocoon I described above. Khan (1971)

wrote, "The ego of the child has prematurely and preco-
ciously brought the trauma of early childhood under its
own omnipotence and created an intrapsychic structure in
the nature of an infantile neurosis which is a false-self
organization." This sense of the self, based as it is upon
fantasies of omnipotence, is fragile and vulnerable and
easily disrupted. It represents a precocious separation
from the mother, a separation that is not firmly established,
as it is accompanied by the continued yearning to merge
and the fear of engulfment, all of which is recapitulated
within the psychoanalytic experience.

A COMPARISON TO INTRAPSYCHIC DEFENSE

In describing a defense in a new context—as something
occurring between two people and not confined to an individual psyche—I must acknowledge that I am using the
term "defense" in a manner that is not consistent with the
usual psychoanalytic definition. But I must also add that
I am not the first to have redefined "defense" in this fashion. Balint (1950) observed that the classical concept of
defense was applicable only to those disorders in which
internalization is used extensively, such as the obsessive-
compulsive. He stated further that our theory and technique refer to events occurring between two people and
not simply within one person, so that there was an internal
contradiction between our theory of defense and our theory of technique. Laplanche and Pontalis (1973, p. 103)
define defense as: "a group of operations *aimed* at the
reduction and elimination of any change liable to threaten
the integrity and stability of the bio-psychological individual." Thus, the term *defense* in psychoanalysis can be considered an analogy to the defense mechanisms employed
by the body. These include the physiological mechanisms
designed to maintain internal homeostasis as well as the

behavioral mechanisms related to flight and attack. The term "mechanism," as Freud and later Anna Freud used it, implies an automatic and nearly unconscious process akin to those bodily defense mechanisms. There is, therefore, nothing intrinsic in the term itself to prevent us from using it in the context of a defense oriented toward the external world. The defense of nonrelatedness is in essence an attempt at flight, an attempt to remain hidden and unfound. However, in keeping with an intrapsychic context with its quasineurological assumptions, Freud focused upon the need to secure internal homeostasis; he understood defense to be a process within a mental apparatus regulated by the constancy principle. From this point of view the motive for defense is the anxiety that results from a quantitative increase in instinctual excitation. This still remains the classical view. For example, Brenner (1979) stated: "A defense can probably be defined only with reference to its function. Whatever mental activity serves the purpose of avoiding unpleasure aroused by an instinctual derivative is a defense. There is no other valid way of defining defense" (p. 558).

One could say that that is simply a semantic issue, an arbitrary decision as to the terms we use in our definitions. But if we restrict the term "defense" to its previous usage, we would prevent ourselves from applying it to an entire class of narcissistic patients. We would be excluding from our field of vision, and our field of understanding, aspects of the character structure of the so-called narcissistic personalities as well as the personality structure referred to by the designation "false-self organization." This arbitrary limitation of the concept of defense solely to one's internal homeostasis would prevent us from acknowledging the defensive maneuvers that occupy so much of the opening phase of analysis in the narcissistic personality. If we enlarge the concept of defense to apply as well to events between two persons, we would bring our theory of the technique of the psychoanalysis of the narcissistic case into some congruence with our theory of classical technique. For it is also true that in the narcissistic case our therapeutic efforts must first be addressed to matters of defense before considering content. This will be discussed in greater detail in the section, Therapeutic Action and Psychoanalytic Process. Issues concerning the safety and protection of the self vis-à-vis the human environment must be dealt with before the erotic or instinctual conflicts can be considered. If we enlarge our concept of defense in this fashion, we will also be able to enlarge our theory of technique.

As I hope to demonstrate in the following chapter, the assumption that all of the so-called classical mechanisms of defense are intrapsychic is not correct. Denial is an obvious exception to Brenner's definition of a defense directed against an internal source of unpleasure. The motive of defense here is directed outward; that is, it is a defense against the perception of a painful piece of reality. Denial is of interest to us as it can be considered simultaneously as an intrapsychic defense and a defense in a two-person context; it is a hybrid defense that can be described in structural terms, e.g., "split within the ego," but must also be understood in relation to an illusory protective object. The concept of defense cannot be assigned solely to a one-person or a two-person psychology.

Chapter 3

Denial and the Sense of Separateness

Freud became interested in the problem of denial toward the end of his life. If one compares his formulation of repression to that of denial, it is clear that these two defense "mechanisms" belong to different conceptual orders. Freud's most detailed explication of the mechanism of repression occurs in his paper, "The Unconscious" (1915b). There he described repression essentially as a process affecting ideas on the border between the system UCS and PCS (p. 180), in which there is a disruption of the link between the repressed idea in the unconscious and its verbal representation in the preconscious system. Freud suggested that this disruption was maintained by a withdrawal of libido from the preconscious system as well as an anticathexis maintained by the preconscious system. This force was later understood to be contained within the superego. This extremely complicated account remained within the context of a physiological mechanism, that is, within the context of a mental apparatus. Freud turned to the problem of denial in his last papers, "Fetishism," (1927), "Splitting of the Ego in the Defensive Process" (1940b), and "An Outline of Psychoanalysis" (Freud, 1940a, p. 203). In the latter paper, denial was acknowledged to be a process that occurs between the ego and the external world:

> . . . the childish ego, under the domination of the real world, gets rid of undesirable instinctual demands by what are called repressions. We will now supplement this by further asserting that, during the same period of life, the ego often enough finds itself in the position of fending off some demand from the external world which it feels distressing and that this is effected by means of a *disavowal* of the preceptions which bring to knowledge this demand from reality [p. 203].

There is, as I have said, a dual context to denial: It can be described as a split within the ego as well as an altered relation between the self and the external world, or the human caretakers who are symbolic of that external world. This chapter is a revision of a paper I first completed in 1960. The intent of that paper was to show that denial was sustained by an illusory relation between the ego (and here we would have to speak of the ego and the self, and note the distinctions later) and its objects. I was not then aware of the implications of such a shift in theoretical context. The paper also reflects the language of the period, for example, the term "ego regression." I have used this term to denote a significant arrest in self/object differentiation.

Although I would today avoid any mechanistic explanation of denial, I do believe that splitting of the ego (which may coexist with splitting of the object) remains a useful metaphor of knowing and not knowing. But is "the split in the ego" an explanation or a homology for the observation that knowledge is both retained and disavowed?

Splitting of the ego has been clearly defined by Laplanche and Pontalis (1973, p. 427) as follows: "The coexistence at the heart of the ego of two psychical attitudes towards external reality insofar as this stands in the way of an instinctual demand. The first of these attitudes takes reality into consideration, while the second disavows it and replaces it by a product of desire. The two attitudes persist side by side without influencing each other." Although Freud first described this state of affairs in severe pathological conditions such as fetishism and the psychoses, today we can observe evidence of such splitting in a wide range of personalities, including the narcissistic disorders, which are very much within the category of neurosis. We can frequently observe a hatred of certain aspects of reality; what is hated is the evidence of the limitation of one's omniscience. Many of these individuals still maintain an unwavering belief in the efficacy of the pleasure principle in one portion of their mind, while in another portion of their mind, they fully recognize the reality principle. In this sense, infantile wishes are never abandoned but are maintained alive in a separate province of the mind. What we observe here is a certain organization of thought processes that is in a certain sense psychotic in that it is not in accord with the testing of reality; but it is not necessarily functionally psychotic. Psychosis in this sense is referring only to the organization of thought, not necessarily leading to action.

This splitting of the ego is to be contrasted to the Kleinian concept of splitting of the object, which has been much elaborated by Kernberg (1975). This term refers to an organization of introjects under the sway of intense primitive ambivalence, in which the images of the objects are split into good and bad portions. A further complication is Kohut's (1971) term "vertical split," which, as far as I can understand, corresponds to Freud's splitting of the ego.

Anna Freud (1936) described denial as a defense more appropriate to the immature ego of the child, where abrupt transitions normally occur between reality testing and denial through fantasy or symbolic action. Freud, in his unfinished paper, "Splitting of the Ego in the Defensive Process" (1940b), described a state where part of the ego accepted a piece of reality, namely, the differences between the sexes, that is, the existence of individuals without a penis, while another portion of the ego maintained a belief in the maternal phallus; that is to say, denial resulted in a split in the ego with a resultant loss in the ego's synthetic functions. Denial, according to Freud, is a half measure; reality is perceived but the painful perceptions are disowned only to make a counterclaim at some subsequent time. What is at issue is not so much the perception of reality but its rejection by another portion of the ego. In this rejection there is a restriction of the ego's function of testing reality.

The belief in reality[1]—that there is a world external to the self—assumes a degree of separation between self and object, a separation that is based on the acceptance that there is something outside and differentiated from the self, something that is relatively fixed, and requiring action to bring about change. I hope to demonstrate here that the failure to accept the reality principle, that is, its denial, is maintained in the more severely disturbed person by a regression (or arrest in development) of the ego in relation to its objects, a regression that blurs the distinction between the self and the environment, between the self and the world of objects.

---

[1] I am throughout this paper distinguishing the concept of reality in a psychological sense from the problem of reality in a philosophical sense. The philosophical enigmas concerning appearance and reality and the question of the existence of a world beyond our sense organs are not under consideration here.

Weisman (1958) distinguished reality sense from reality testing, the former referring to the experiential belief in reality and the latter referring to cognitive and intellectual processes. In denial, alterations in both the reality sense and the testing of reality may occur; I would assume, therefore, that these distinctions are relative. Impairment of reality testing would reflect a more severe pathological process.

Lewin, in his now-classic studies on mania (1950), noted that denial was the predominant mechanism used to avoid painful inner reality, that is, the emotional impact of reality. In his investigation of the oral instincts in mania, he emphasized the wish to be devoured or incorporated. Although Lewin did not attempt a direct correlation of this oral wish with the mechanism of denial, it could be said that this wish for fusion, to be one with the object, is based on a denial of separateness from the object, a denial that is consonant with the predominant anxiety of the oral period—the fear of separation. If the object is not separate, it cannot be lost.

Jacobson (1957) noted that if inner reality is denied and treated by the ego as if it were a painful aspect of external reality, one must assume a partial regression of the ego with some loss of differentiation of internal from external worlds. She spoke of regression not to the earliest stage but to a "concretistic" infantile stage where the child, though already aware of the difference between internal and external worlds and between the self and objects, still treats them both in the same manner of a neurosis, showing a significant usage of the more primitive mechanisms of introjection and projection. These mechanisms tend to blur the differences between the self and the object, leading to a relative loss of the sense of separateness.

The case I will present is that of a fetishist studied in a lengthy psychoanalytic psychotherapy. Although Freud considered this disorder to be nosologically distinct from psychosis, I am more in agreement with Glover (1932), who noted that symptoms of perversion existed in patients who represented varying degrees of ego regression, that is, in neurosis, transitional states, and psychoses. The patient to be described here showed sufficient regression of the ego to be placed diagnostically in the borderline group. My remarks concerning denial refer therefore to it in the context of significant developmental arrest without loss of object ties and the development of restitutive psychotic symptoms.

The patient was a young man whose major object tie was a symbiotic or, perhaps more accurately, parasitic relation to his mother. He felt that he could not exist without relying on his mother to perform certain ego functions that should have been his own. The only significant ego functions assumed with a degree of autonomy were those involved in learning. He was a good student and did well but his performance was contingent on its reinforcing fantasies of uniqueness. If these fantasies could not be maintained, that is, if he became aware of competition, he would withdraw from this painful aspect of reality through illness, usually gastrointestinal, which he would aggravate through the overingestion of medication. Following his entry into a good college, his collapse was complete. He gave up active pursuits entirely, remained at home with his mother, and thought of himself as a sort of village idiot.

His sexual activities were confined to masturbation while wearing his fetish, which was a pair of dungarees. This particular article of clothing was invested with a multiplicity of meanings. On a conscious level it provided him with an illusion of masculinity which he felt to be really a masquerade. However, mother wore similar clothing, and in his unconscious mind the dungarees consolidated a primal identification with her. Anal fantasies were prominent. The clothing was associated with fecal odors, symbolized in a concrete way by the first letters in the word *dung*arees. The identification with mother was with a part of the object, and here, as in other cases of fetishism, the identification was with an imagined maternal phallus. His fantasies pointed to a conception of an anal phallus: while using the fetish, he would imagine a bulge in the seat of the pants, representing a column of feces.

What is denied in the fetishist, Freud taught us, is knowledge of the female genitalia—denied as a result of heightened castration fears. Castration anxiety in this patient was reinforced by a traumatic circumcision at the age of six. Knowledge of sexual differences was denied, and there was a profound confusion of the body image and of sexual identity similar to that described by Greenacre (1953). Although sight of the female genitalia was denied, there was an unavoidable counterclaim, a return of what was warded off in the form of a severe and persistent phobia. He would be terrified by Negroes or whites who blackened their faces. This proved to be an instance of displacement upward, for the focus of the anxiety was the specific visual element of the black against the pink of the mouth—symbolic of the vagina. These issues I consider specific for fetishism, and I mention them in passing because it is not my intention to discuss the psychopathology of fetishism per se; rather, I want to use this material to illustrate the more general issue of denial in cases of ego regression. The form of his object ties can be more clearly discerned by presenting some aspects of the treatment relationship.

His initial mode of self-presentation was one of helpless apathy. In contrast to his mother, who accepted this, I insisted that he could do more for himself and made it clear that he would be expected to make certain efforts on his own behalf. I present these details only to note that in attempting to increase his sense of autonomy I became idealized as a good object. A symptomatic improvement followed to the point where he could resume his studies. However, these gains were interpreted by the patient not as the result of his own efforts but as something that was bestowed upon him by the therapist. (It is quite likely that this improvement was the result of an introjective process—an incorporation of a fantasied omnipotent therapist.) There was massive denial of certain aspects of his relation to reality. He was convinced that work was not really necessary and could be circumvented by the therapist, who would do it for him. Indeed, he believed in my ability to soften the harsh demands of reality and to protect him from danger. When he experienced frustration, the frustration was not perceived as something inherent in the work of learning but was instead interpreted as the result of something being withheld from him by me. There was then a massive denial of his own separate existence, a denial of a world outside of himself that required action to bring about desired gratification. This was not, however, a complete regression to the level of the pleasure principle, for he could not exist in society if the demands of reality were entirely ignored. The object of the therapist was interposed between himself and the world in a manner analogous to the young child who relies on the mother to perform certain ego functions and who can thus maintain the illusion that he is safe and that no harm can befall him if his mother is near. The content of the denial was not limited to a specific aspect of reality but was global in its extent. Denial was supported by a transitional object relatedness.

Denial, in contrast to certain forms of repression, is an ineffective defense in that the return of what is denied is inevitable. When these painful aspects of reality are reasserted, the ego tends to become overwhelmed, and in its helplessness, resorts to still more massive denial, with a concomitant regressive remodeling of its own structure. This process can be observed in the following episode.

During the second year of treatment the positive climate gradually began to alter. With the increased recognition that the magical demands placed upon the person of the therapist could not be fulfilled, the negative side of the ambivalence, which had been previously warded off by idealization, became more pronounced.[2] A wish for sleep

---

[2]Gillespie (1940) emphasized the process of splitting in the perversions as a result of the fear of destroying the object.

became accentuated at this time, a wish that could be understood in accordance with Lewin's formulation as a wish for fusion with an incorporation by the primal (maternal) object. There were persistent nightmares of a terrifying nature where he could see himself in danger of being incorporated by an amoeboid breastlike object. The splitting of the person of the therapist became further accentuated: I was perceived as a remorselessly demanding and hence a dangerous object; yet there was a preservation of the illusion that I was an object of absolute constancy—he repetitively noted that I never missed an hour. At this time I did develop a mild but acute gastrointestinal illness, the details of which need to be told because of the specific meaning to the patient. I informed him upon his arrival that day that I was ill and could not see him. I found it necessary to excuse myself hurriedly. The following hour I learned that he did not directly leave the office but had heard my retching in the lavatory. This had an overwhelming impact upon him, for he then made a serious, but entirely unconscious, suicide attempt. He overingested sleeping medication, conscious only of a powerful desire to sleep; there was no thought of suicide and it was only upon his subsequent recovery that he recognized with horror the danger of self-destruction which had been denied. The denial of reality went a step further here: what had been a matter of the acceptance of reality now involved the reality-testing functions as well. (I recognize that these terminological distinctions are somewhat arbitrary and are used merely to denote differing degrees of regression of the institution of the ego concerned with the testing of reality.) He still maintained his conviction during this episode that I would preserve him from harm.

The symbolic meaning of my gastrointestinal illness was subsequently better understood. My vomiting had been interpreted by him as an ejection of himself within me. The existence of a primal identification was seen in the belief that as he had incorporated me, I had also incorporated him: there was minimal differentiation between self and

object.[3] My vomiting provided him with a concrete indication that he was poisonous and that I was ridding myself
of him. He had damaged me; but in ridding myself of him,
I was also damaging him. The object tie to the human object,
the therapist, was reflected in his relations to his inanimate
object, the fetish. The dungarees as well as myself became
"alive" only in the presence of instinctual need and the
expectation of gratification. When I became ill and was not,
for the moment, a need-gratifying object, I was in a sense
dead to him. Similarly, the dungarees became "alive" only
when there was compelling sexual tension—after ejacula-
tion the patient perceived that they were, after all, a dead
thing. With my symbolic death through illness, the patient
then ritualistically killed the fetish by depositing it in a gar-
bage can.

The foregoing material was presented to illustrate my
major thesis that denial can be understood also in the context of a two-person psychology. Avery Weisman (1972),
in his work *On Dying and Denying*, observed denial in the
dying patient. His conclusions were very close to mine. He
stated that denial has been used as a fictitious *mechanism*
and as a hypothetical *explanation*. His investigations demonstrated that denial can only be understood in a social,
that is, a two-person context. Weisman said that "no one
can deny by himself in utter solitude." He observed that
denial helps to maintain a simplified yet constant relationship with significant other people, especially at a moment
of crisis. Denial also serves the purpose of preservation of
an object relationship.

As has been described in other cases of so-called ego
distortion, the regression of the ego becomes part of a
characterological formation and, as Gitelson (1958) ob-

---

[3]Nacht (1958) viewed the loss of differentiation between self and object as
characteristic of borderline cases (ego distortion). He attributed this process to
a terror of the object which is avoided by confusing the self with the object.

served, has a certain adaptational significance. If our patient's transference can be taken as illustrative of his object
ties, it can be seen that the object of the therapist both
stands for the primal maternal object and yet is endowed
through the processes of introjection and projection with
qualities of the self. The object is invested, it is recognized
as outside of the self, but not completely so. The object
could be properly termed a transitional object. Winnicott
described the infant's first possession in an analogous fashion. It was seen as an object with a certain permanency
and protective value that symbolized the breast, and yet
it owed its life, so to speak, to processes within the infant
itself—to an illusion. Nevertheless, it was there, as an object
that was part of the environment; it was not a hallucination.
Winnicott indicated the similarity of this infantile object
to the adult fetish.

The suicide attempt, I believe, represented a still further
regression—one that resulted from the wish for oceanic
fusion with the breast, a wish to achieve the illusion of an
objectless stage, a stage where objects are no longer needed
and hence cannot be lost or destroyed. This was achieved
at the expense of a further regression of the ego with a
resultant denial of psychotic proportions.

This regression of the ego in fetishists was noted by
Greenacre and Bak (1953), who emphasized the process
of primal identification. They, along with other contrib-
utors to the problem of fetishism, placed increasing emphasis on pregenital determinants. Bak described the
fetish as an object that undoes the fear of separation from
mother by functioning as a symbolic substitute, a substitute
of the part for the whole. This would be consistent with
Winnicott's transitional object. In our case, separation anxiety appeared to be fused with castration anxiety. For example, the patient's father lost the tips of several fingers
in an industrial accident. Despite his horror and revulsion,

the patient was compelled to look for and recover the severed members, which he preserved in a bottle of formaldehyde. He wished to preserve them forever; that a body part could be permanently lost was unthinkable.

Denial, like any other defense mechanism of the ego, is set into motion as a result of anxiety. It seems to me that here, as in other borderline cases, separation anxiety (to which castration anxiety may be fused) is the leading motive of defense. The denial of separateness from objects creates the illusion that the object is part of the self and cannot be lost. The awareness of the object's individuality cannot be acknowledged, for if the object is separate, it can be lost or destroyed. In contrast to the transference neuroses, where certain maturational strivings can be counted upon, here self/object differentiation is significantly retarded; to mature is to separate from one's primary objects and is unconsciously felt as an irrevocable loss.

Denial can be described using the homology of a split in the ego to reflect a split in what is known and not known. We assume that there is some sort of barrier that prevents one portion of the mind from access to knowledge that exists in another portion of the mind. But is this a metaphorical description or an explanatory description?

I wonder whether denial can exist without a belief in a protective object. One recalls Weisman's (1972) observation, mentioned above, regarding dying patients, namely, that "no one can deny in utter solitude." The idealized protective object that supports denial may be subjectively created, that is, idealized out of intense need, or the protective object may be found within the self as a vestige of a religious belief which, in this secular age, may find a final resting place as a grandiose fantasy of the self.

Chapter 4

On Having the Right to a Life

Although there are few who would question that the superego is part of every human personality, that conscience and an unconscious sense of guilt are fundamental determinants of human behavior, the interest in the superego by psychoanalysts seems to be inordinately subject to the vicissitudes of psychoanalytic theory.

Not unexpectedly, interest in the superego was at its height in the decade following the publication of Freud's "The Ego and the Id." Thereafter, interest waned, to be only slightly revived during the ascendancy of ego psychology. Sandler (1960b), for example, found that the Hampstead Clinic group, in their classification scheme, made little use of the superego concept. We know that for Freud the superego was inexorably linked to the Oedipus complex—this may have led to a rigid adherence to this linkage—to an either/or system of classification. Either the superego was linked to the classical Oedipus complex or the superego concept could not easily be brought into cases in which the Oedipus complex was not at the center of pathology. Melanie Klein (1948) and her co-workers maintained their interest in the superego by proposing that the

Oedipus complex developed in the first year of life. Thus, they appear to be straining to remain faithful to Freud's original linkage, for if the Oedipus complex occurred in the matrix of disturbances of early object relations, then patients with psychosis or narcissistic disorders could also be understood as suffering from the vicissitudes of an Oedipus complex. Few psychoanalysts other than Kleinians would accept this formulation, as the idea that infants are capable of such complex symbolic transformations is, on the face of it, totally implausible. Kohut (1977) also accepted this rigid linkage of the Oedipus complex to the superego. He contrasted classical oedipal neurosis with narcissistic neuroses as he believed that the Oedipus complex is not central to the psychopathology of the latter disorders. He also believed that these individuals do not suffer extensively from disorders of conscience, for he contrasted "Guilty Man" to "Tragic Man"—the former, a broad heading covering the so-called classical neuroses and the latter corresponding to the more current narcissistic disorders. From Kohut's point of view, the superego and the Oedipus complex are part of one package and belong to the older structural psychiatry, which he wished to replace with a psychology of the self.

In this chapter I will make several interconnected observations: that the severity of unconscious guilt is not necessarily linked to the Oedipus complex; that narcissistic patients with early developmental disorders unrelated to the Oedipus complex do in fact suffer from an intense form of unconscious guilt; and further, that this guilt can be understood as an accompaniment of the process of individuation. The right to a separate life is perhaps invariably accompanied by an unconscious fantasy that separation will lead to the death or damage of the other. Affects traditionally understood within the context of the individual must also be brought into the context of a two-person psychology.

I became interested in the problem of diffuse unconscious guilt as the result of the particular composition of my early analytic practice: I had chosen some patients who proved to be extremely refractory. Today I would categorize them within the broad frame of a narcissistic personality disorder. They were not borderline in the sense that their object relations were not predominantly of a transitional sort, as I have described previously (Modell, 1963), nor was there a major disturbance in reality testing. Nonetheless, there was a certain impairment in their capacity to feel for other persons which interfered with the establishment of a therapeutic alliance. After some time it became apparent that their refractoriness to analysis was due not only to their impaired capacity to form object relationships, but also to something which, although related to this impairment, was more fundamental—they were possessed of a basic belief that they had no right to a better life. Such an attitude is, of course, completely incompatible with the aims of psychoanalysis. What I have been attempting to describe was beautifully portrayed by Sharpe (1931, p. 81):

> The people who enjoy the greatest ease and to whom work and the conditions of life bring the greatest internal satisfaction are those who have justified their existence to themselves. They have won through to a right to live, and a right to live means a life in which physical and mental powers can be used to the ego's advantage and well-being of the community. For a "right to life" is only ultimately based on the right of others to live. In a psyche that had attained that feeling of rightness to live there would be no obsession, no compulsion. . . . I believe "justification of existence" is the very core of our problems, whether we are

thinking of the malaise of the so-called normal or the pathological manifestations of the so-called neurotic.

I am attempting then to understand a human problem which influences to varying degrees the course of most people's lives. I have chosen to describe here extreme examples because the extremity of their pathology will illuminate certain processes which, though less conspicuously, the rest of us share.

CASE 1

The life of this patient was dominated by an urge to destroy all accomplishment, and any pleasure could be experienced only under conditions of self-debasement. He was an unmarried man in his late twenties, with a good intelligence and a considerable musical and scientific talent. Yet he was unable to make use of his gifts in a manner that would secure a role in life that would afford him any degree of pride or satisfaction; whenever a professional goal was in his grasp, he would be forced to prevent himself from attaining it. Despite a good academic record in college, he failed in a professional school. He later became a graduate student in an allied scientific field and, despite genuine ability in this field, presented himself in such an inadequate and infantile manner that he was considered unsuitable as a Ph.D. candidate. He did, however, obtain a Master's degree, but only after some work in analysis. Following this relatively minor achievement, he experienced an overwhelming panic reaction and sought treatment at a hospital emergency room, convinced that he was dying of a heart attack.

The search for sensual pleasure dominated this man's conscious thoughts, and yet he was never able to have sexual intercourse. His one attempt in late adolescence with a prostitute was a fiasco—he was completely impotent and felt so humiliated that he never attempted intercourse again. But he was unable to secure even simpler pleasures for himself without experiencing self-debasement. For example, whenever the opportunity presented itself to enjoy food in a good restaurant or listen to music that he loved, the pleasure would be negated by an obsessive fear that he might vomit. This fear of vomiting was later understood in part as a displacement upwards, for it was a fear of losing bowel sphincter control. It was an expression of the sadistic wish to degrade others, literally to splatter them, and simultaneously to humiliate himself. This sado-masochistic formation was truly the core of his existence. He could properly be classified as an autoerotic pervert. His erotic life was dominated by a specific sado-masochistic fantasy, a variation of which would stimulate him to masturbate: A woman is overcome with an urge to urinate. She dashes for a lavatory, does not arrive in time, and urinates in her underpants. The patient could be aroused sexually by this specific fantasy of a woman suffering from urinary urgency. He invariably masturbated while lying on his back in the female position. Self-degradation was further insured in that it was a necessary part of the act that he "dirty" himself with his own sperm.

This bizarre symptom-formation was intelligible in the light of the patient's early developmental history. He was an only child until the age of five, when a sister was born. Until that time, he had experienced an unusual sensual intimacy with his mother which had as its focus the act of urination. In the middle of the night he would call out, "Mommy, cissie." His mother would then take him to the bathroom where he would first urinate and then watch his mother urinating, all the while experiencing great sexual arousal. He believed that his mother herself was preoccupied with her urinary functions and would frequently refer to her need to micturate, and on some occasions be so overcome with urinary urgency that she would run to the bathroom. He was not only aroused by her but felt that his mother humiliated herself, and for this reason he held her in profound contempt. In his adult life, just the sight of a woman running, for whatever reason, would be sexually arousing. Only the woman who humiliated herself aroused him; the sadistic wish toward mother is apparent.

Before the birth of his sister, he experienced a sense of fusion to his mother. He said, "It was as if she and I were one." His primary identification with his mother persisted and was relatively unmodified by an identification with his father. I consider this failure to form an identification with his father as crucial to the understanding of his psychopathology and will enlarge upon this issue in the theoretical discussion.

He believed that his father, who was preoccupied with certain professional difficulties, abandoned him to his mother's ministrations. His only early memories involving his father were of the fear of being hit by him and the feeling that his father avoided him for fear that he, the patient, might soil him. As he grew older, he related to his father in a peculiarly limited way: he would either arouse him to laughter or provoke his contempt. The patient developed a store of jokes with which he would amuse and stimulate his father or, alternately, he would recount an event in which he had humiliated and debased himself, thereby eliciting his father's disgust. His relationship to his father was limited to this peculiar kind of arousal. An ordinary object relationship with periods of emotionally muted give-and-take seemed never to have been developed. This failure to form a good object relationship undoubtedly prevented his identification with father in the infantile-oedipal period. Instead of relating to his father, he attempted to arouse him and to elicit a response of contempt in a manner reminiscent of the way his mother provoked contempt in him.

Intense preoedipal sado-masochistic fantasies remained unmodified throughout his life. The fantasies themselves were so intact that one had the impression that one was examining an archaeological artifact. He was completely preoccupied with the visual fantasy of a strong man being broken and stretched on the rack, that medieval instrument of torture. He would be alternately the tormentor and the victim. In all of his human relationships this motif would be reenacted. The analysis was a torture situation; the couch was a rack and I was the tormentor, forcing him to confess. We later learned that the man on the rack was not a man but a woman, and the stretching corresponded to his fantasy of the woman's role in sexual intercourse. Oedipal fantasies did develop, but what was most striking was the extent to which they remained unrepressed. At puberty he was conscious of a wish to "fuck my mother" and did not understand why other boys would be embarrassed or ashamed to talk about such matters. He was not quite sure what "fucking" meant but had a vague idea that it involved the genitals in some sort of sexual union. Voyeuristic interest in his mother's genitals was extreme and was not subject to repression or inhibition, for he did manage to see them by constructing an ingenious system of mirrors in her bathroom. It appeared as if the failure to achieve an infantile-oedipal identification with his father had impaired the development of the forces of repression and guilt. Although he had suffered from diffuse, unconscious guilt to the extent that he truly felt he had no right to a life, conscious guilt was relatively absent. He could gaze at his mother's genitals through these mirrors without experiencing conscious guilt or anxiety. He could state in analysis, with great intensity, that he wished to "fuck my mother," again without the experience of guilt or anxiety. His life, however, was under the complete domination of unconscious guilt.

CASE 2

Another patient had achieved the external trappings of success. She had married well; her husband, who was a lawyer, was both wealthy and kind. She had an interesting job at which she displayed considerable talent. But she was compelled to negate whatever she possessed. She dispelled the pleasure in her marriage by unceasing provocations. What she had in fact achieved in life—for she had risen above the economic and social status of her parents—she dispelled by means of the conviction that it was all unreal. She was only acting; she was simply acting the part of a young matron culled from the pages of a women's magazine.

Psychoanalysis was something that she was much too guilty to accept. She could enter analysis if she used the rationalization that she was doing it for her husband's sake. She could not bear having a better life for herself; she had too much already. Her deepest conviction was that she had no right to a life better than that of her mother, which was perceived by her as a life of hardship and degradation. At the beginning of the analysis her unconscious mind did all it could to sabotage the work of the analysis. There was a massive effort, completely unconscious, to present herself in such a manner that I would be convinced that she was unsuitable for analysis. In addition, I suspect that she was able to sense that analysts find it most difficult to accept those who have no feelings for others, and she correspondingly presented herself as someone entirely devoid of human feeling. For example, she related the death of a friend's child without revealing the slightest trace of an emotional response. She presented herself as bizarre, with the unconscious wish that I would think her psychotic; she recounted how she threw her cat against the wall of her apartment in a fit of rage, how she masturbated with a fireplace poker, and so on. In short, she tried to present herself to me as a thoroughly repulsive person. It was only when I realized that the underlying issue was her conviction that she had no right to the analysis, that she had no right to a better life, that we were able to establish the beginning of a therapeutic alliance.

I then learned of an unconscious fantasy that was fundamental and dominated the course of her life. She was the oldest of three children spaced many years apart. She was convinced that she had taken for herself the best that there was of her mother's love (i.e., milk), had in fact drained her and robbed her siblings of their birthrights. Her basic conviction was that love was a concrete substance and that its supply was limited; if she possessed anything that was good, it meant that someone else was deprived. I developed a corresponding concrete image in my own mind: it was as if she and her siblings and parents were all sucking on a closed container, and there was just so much to go round. Whatever she consumed meant that there was so much less for the others. Her life was dominated by intense envy and a correspondingly intense fear of the envy of others. Whatever someone else had she felt had been taken away from her and, correspondingly, whatever she had must be kept hidden for fear of the envy of others. Thus, to have a better life, to obtain something good for herself, meant literally that the rest of her family would starve.

Though the psychopathology here differed in many respects from that described in the previous patient, there were also certain striking parallels. Her life, too, was dominated by sadistic fantasies. She, too, had failed to develop a sense of identity separate from that of her mother. What had developed in this patient was a counteridentification: where her mother was slovenly, she was neat; where her mother was fat, she was thin, and so on. But the counteridentification had to be slavishly and compulsively maintained. It was as if there was nothing else to her; as a separate person she did not exist. As was true with the previous patient, she too failed to develop a good object relationship with her father and was entirely entrusted to her mother's care. Her father, because of his work, spent considerable time away from the home. Here again, the relationship with her father was highly eroticized: her father was the source of much erotic stimulation, exposing his penis to her from her earliest years and continuing to do so until she left home for college. In short, she perceived her relationship to him to be unbearably stimulating and devoid of warmth and tenderness. Here again incestuous sexual fantasies of the oedipal period were not repressed but remained conscious.

Freud (1930) observed, "We ought not to speak of a conscience until a super-ego is demonstrably present. As to a sense of guilt, we must admit that it is in existence before the super-ego, and therefore before conscience too" (p. 136). This observation is of great importance, for it permits one to differentiate the guilt associated with early developmental disorders from guilt that is a function of a structural system, that is, the superego itself. As I shall show below, this distinction is not simply of academic interest.

A feedback model is also relevant, for we would also anticipate a high degree of interrelationship (or feedback) between events in the preoedipal phase and the degree to which the oedipal experience can successfully structuralize and differentiate the preoedipal elements of superego development. That is to say, a good object relationship with the father at a later phase of development may mitigate a primary identification with the mother and lead to a more functional and structuralized superego. Personality development may proceed in a manner reminiscent of the way history textbooks are written: later events determine how earlier events are organized. Such general statements as these have the danger of becoming too abstract and lacking in clinical content so that it is now necessary to return to the specific clinical observations.

An early paper by Hendrick (1936) foreshadowed some of these concepts. Although his discussion was limited to ego defects, his remarks have relevance to the consideration of superego development as well. Hendrick considered that ego defects represented a partial development failure. Intense infantile sadism leading to certain critical fantasies, such as that of oral ejection, interfered with the completion of an identification process. A feedback concept was implicit in his thinking, for he stated that this process of identification would normally terminate the special phase of infantile aggression that preceded it.

In the material presented, we also observed sadistic fantasies of a special intensity: The male patient was dominated by a wish to destroy and humiliate others; the female patient was consumed by envy—she wished to take away anything of value that others possessed and, in turn, feared similar retaliation. It seemed that the guilt of these patients was not only associated with the content of their sadistic wishes, for in both patients there was a failure of development in the phase of self/object differentiation. Although the identification with the maternal object in these patients was not quite so complete as in borderline cases, there was a similar failure to develop a sense of self as distinct from those fantasies that form the nexus of a maternal image. The content of the guilt, as I was able to observe it in each patient, was not only based upon the wish to destroy others but was also related to the belief that the patient had no right to a separate existence, so that it is reasonable to suppose that the guilt is in some way associated with failure of development in the phase of self-object differentiation. I suggest that the belief that one does not have the right to a life is a derivative of what I would like to call "separation guilt." For the right to a life really means the right to a separate existence. Separation anxiety is a familiar subject and requires no elaboration here. But we have paid less attention to the experience of separation guilt. In those individuals who are burdened with intense ambivalence, from whatever source, separation is unconsciously perceived as resulting in the death of the object. A schizophrenic patient whose treatment I had been supervising for several years had finally, after a great struggle, achieved some consolidation of her ego and was beginning to deal with problems of separation from her mother. She directly expressed the belief that in order for her to have a separate existence her mother had to be killed. We see again the working of circular processes, for intense infantile ambivalence will interfere with the development of self/object differentiation. Where there is poor self/object differentiation, there is confusion between self and object; in the infantile mind, the fear of dying upon separation from mother can be confused with the fear of destroying mother.

Although I have drawn my illustrations from disturbed patients, I do not wish to leave the impression that guilt over one's separate existence is limited to the most pathological cases. I believe that vestiges of this problem remain to some extent in many, if not most, people and can be observed in a more disguised form. For example, another patient, whose life was also dominated by a profound sense of unconscious guilt, believed that if she were to become more mature through the efforts of psychoanalysis, her mother could not bear it and would kill herself. She too believed, as did the schizophrenic patient, that if she separated from her mother she would cause her mother's death. One can also discern remnants of this fantasy in the terminal phase of analysis, where patients struggle with feelings of guilt at being permitted to express values and a way of life that are different, that is to say, separate, from those of the analyst.

The two cases I have chosen to illustrate the greatest diffusion of unconscious guilt are conspicuous in that in both instances there was a seriously impaired object relationship with the father, which led subsequently to a failure to achieve good identification with the father in the oedipal period. I recognize that the problem is somewhat more complicated in the female patient, and yet we know that a good father identification based on a love relationship can mitigate the intense ambivalence toward the preoedipal mother and can further the process of self-object individuation. In spite of the waning position of the father in our contemporary culture, in the unconscious mind strength is still equated with the male. It is the internalization of this male strength that provides the unconscious source of instinctual control. I believe that in these patients the diffuse separation guilt of the preoedipal period would have been modified had an identification with the father been successful, and the structural formation of the superego would have been furthered. The failure to achieve a good identification with father resulted in a partial developmental failure of the superego. We have noted the failure to experience conscious guilt that would lead to repression of forbidden thoughts. For example, I have told how the male patient in puberty had conscious wishes to "fuck" his mother. The existence of diffuse unconscious guilt, such as I described above, suggests a failure of function, that is, a failure to form structure. Yet the developmental failure is only partial, for these patients are not amoral sociopaths. What is conspicuous, however, is the extent to which unconscious guilt pervades the entire personality structure. It is not contained and bound up in symptoms, nor do we see guilt leading to restrictive inhibition of a segment or a sector of the personality as, for example, would occur where oedipal guilt in a male might lead to a work inhibition but would permit him to function in other areas. For the patients I have described all pleasure that can be experienced with dignity and self-respect is undone and negated. Pervasiveness of diffuse unconscious guilt is unquestioned, but this should not lead one to describe the superego as strong. Intensity of guilt, as I have tried to show, is a result of a partial developmental arrest of the superego.

The concept of unconscious guilt has been criticized as semantically inconsistent, for strictly speaking, as Freud (1923) indicated, feelings cannot properly be considered

unconscious. Unconscious guilt is an inference of an affect
and not, of course, an actual feeling. Whether the affect
of guilt is experienced is not the crucial issue, for the effects
of guilt will influence behavior regardless of how conscious
the guilt is. The life history of the patients whom we have
described, who feel they have no right to a life, illustrates
the manner in which this guilt can pervade all of their
actions. The situation is really not so different with regard
to unconscious anxiety. Although we do not often use the
term "unconscious anxiety," its presence is a basic clinical
inference in the acting-out patient or the counterphobic
patient, who appears unanxious; when the acting out of
such patients is controlled by analysis, intense anxiety
emerges. Further, we know that signal or secondary anxiety, when used as a motive for defense, need not be, and
frequently is not, conscious. Whether guilt is experienced
by the ego or warded off through projected rage or by
means of a variety of character defenses is an extremely
complex issue which attests to the extent to which the ego
and superego functions are interrelated (see Brenman,
1952).

   To summarize: Certain forms of the negative therapeutic reaction can be understood as a manifestation of a more
basic feeling of not having the right to a life, that is, not
having a right to a separate existence. Separateness refers
not merely to the earliest developmental stages; it can refer
also to events in adult life; this form of unconscious guilt
may be especially severe in those who enter into a different
cultural stratum from that of their nuclear family. There
is not only a sense of disloyalty in abandoning those they
have left behind, but in addition there is a feeling, at times
close to consciousness, that their differentiation from those
who remain in the nuclear family will cause the death of
the latter individuals. Differentiation from one's primary
objects may also involve a giving-up of an attachment to

painful affects. One may find that a patient has become identified with the affects associated with a parent, a certain chronic depression or a grinding lugubriousness; to become joyous would be experienced as a disloyal abandonment.

I have traced the origin of this feeling to the phase of self/object differentiation. Separation from the maternal object is unconsciously perceived as causing the death of the mother; to obtain something for one's self, to lead a separate existence, is perceived as depriving the mother of her basic substance. It will be understood that if such individuals are in addition experiencing a heightened degree of sadism, for whatever reason, this will augment the intensity of separation guilt.

I believe that separation guilt parallels the more familiar guilt of the Oedipus complex. Although these two forms of guilt may become condensed one upon the other clinically, their separate origin may also be noted; for example, the guilt of individuation, unlike oedipal guilt, is not sex linked in that a son may feel guilty for leaving his mother as well as surpassing his father.

The locus of guilt appears here in a different context from that usually associated with ego/superego conflict. We cannot think of this affect simply as a signal arising from internalized structures alone but as an affect that is evoked by events occurring between the individual and his nuclear family. We are reminded here that Freud first described the origin of oedipal guilt in "Totem and Taboo" (Freud, 1913a) in the context of a group—the primal horde, which shared remorse among its members after the murder of their father. We need to be reminded of this as Freud's later structural psychology may have led us to overemphasize the internalization of guilt. In Chapter 5 I will develop further the idea that certain forms of guilt may serve the adaptive needs of the group.

Chapter 5

On Having More

In addition to guilt over becoming separate from the nuclear family, there is also a type of guilt that accompanies the recogntion that one may have more than others. What we shall describe here is perhaps a universal, that is, primal fantasy that the available "good" is a concrete substance in limited supply. To the unconscious mind, the possession of "good" means that the others in the nuclear family have been deprived. Having more of anything, whether it be good fortune, good health, or good intelligence, suggests to its possessor that it has been obtained at the expense of the other. This belief is referable ultimately to the guilt of the survivor, whose appropriate contexts include the psychology of groups and not simply the context of the psychology of the individual. It is relevant to recall that Freud's observations of the affects accompanying hysterical symptoms provided the "objective" data for the origin of psychoanalysis itself (the "subjective" data were, of course, Freud's own deepening self-analysis). Freud understood the hysterical symptoms as a transformation of affect, an affect that had been separated from its ideational content by means of repression. Freud hoped that his observations of hysteria would lead to the demonstration of general laws of the psychic apparatus analogous to the laws of physical science. Freud had before him the example of Helmholtz, who had discovered that the law of conservation of energy applied to living organisms. Fechner's constancy principle, discussed above, was accepted by Freud as analogous to Helmholtz's application of physical laws to biology. Accordingly, Freud interpreted the intensity of affects in hysterical patients as evidence of the pathology that ensues where there is a departure from the constancy principle.

In this stage of his thinking Freud viewed affects as part of this regulatory mechanism—affects were the vehicle for the discharge of instinctual tension. It is important to note, however, that the clinical reference is to dreaming, a state in which the individual is effectively cut off from the external world. In "The Interpretation of Dreams" (1900, pp. 467-468) Freud declared: "I am compelled—for other reasons—to picture the release of affects as centrifugal, as a centrifugal process directed towards the interior of the body analogous to the process of motor and secretory innervations."

Freud's view of affects here would seem to divorce them from all communicative functions. Of course, this theory has not escaped criticism. Rycroft (1956) stated: "None of the various theories of affects reviewed by Rapaport attaches central importance to what is to my mind the most obvious and important factor about an affect—the fact that it is perceptible by others and that it has an intrinsic tendency to evoke either identical or complementary affective responses in the perceiving object." Other prominent critics of what has come to be called the discharge theory of affects include Schactel (1959) and Novey (1959, 1968).

But as I observed in Chapter 1, Freud was not entirely committed to a one-person psychology of affects. There was a more speculative side to Freud which does not seem to be at all related to his physicalistic model of the psychic apparatus. I am referring to Freud's highly imaginative ideas that trace the origin of both instincts and affects to the inheritance of group traumatic experiences.

In "Group Psychology and the Analysis of the Ego" Freud (1921) also recognized that the communication of affects—affective contagion, as he described it—characterized the psychology of the group. Affective experience in groups tends to become intensified and in a certain sense more archaic. Groups display impairment of intellectual judgment, a lack of restraint, and a relative incapacity for moderation and delay.

Ethological research also suggests that affects are more usefully viewed as a group than as an individual phenomenon. Those biologists who are the most concerned with the evolution of behavior have come to realize that the survival value of inherited behavior may consist of those behavioral elements that ensure the adaptation of a group rather than that of an individual. For example, field observations of primates (DeVore, 1965) show that affects function primarily as signals serving the needs of the group. The needs of the individual tend to be subordinate to those of the group; the group is more effective than individuals in obtaining food and protection against predators. Accordingly, the evolution of behavior in primates may be such as to ensure the survival of the individual by means of group behavioral mechanisms. For example, under natural conditions individual animals cannot safely respond to their own motivational pressures without endangering the group; i.e., a thirsty baboon cannot safely leave the group and go away seeking water: such behavior could endanger not only the individual but other members of the group. There are presumably inherent behavioral prohibitions that would prevent the individual baboon from satisfying his own thirst—something perhaps analogous to the response to guilt in human psychology (see also Hamburg, 1963).

Ethologists have noted that for a primate group affects are the medium through which intragroup communication is achieved. Whether through vocalization or facial or postural expressions, vital motivational information is conveyed.[1] Through vocalization, facial and postural expressions, rapidly changing moods are easily communicated; it is knowledge of these moods that will ensure the survival of the group as a whole.

We do not have an adequate psychoanalytic theory of affects because psychoanalysts have not sufficiently acknowledged that the theory of affects cannot be confined to individual psychology; it needs also to be placed in the context of a process that serves the adaptational needs of the group. I include, of course, the psychoanalytic group of two.

THE ORIGIN OF A CERTAIN FORM OF GUILT

There are certain people who behave in a quite peculiar fashion during the work of analysis. When one speaks hopefully to them or expresses satisfaction with the progress of the treatment, they show signs of discontent and their condition invariably becomes worse. One begins by regarding this as defiance and as an attempt to prove their superiority to the physician, but later one comes to take a deeper and juster view. One becomes convinced, not only that such people cannot endure any praise or appreciation, but that they react inversely to the progress of the treatment . . . [Freud, 1923, p. 49].

Freud assumed the content of the guilt of the negative

[1]For an experimental investigation, see Mirsky, Miller, and Murphy (1958).

therapeutic reaction to therapy to be that accompanying incestuous and rivalrous impulses. However, I have come to believe, as I indicated in Chapter 4, that the content of the guilt frequently relates to the conviction that one does not have a right to the better life that would be the consequence of a successful psychoanalysis. Patients in this group, I believe, share a common fantasy: *to have something good means that somebody else would be deprived*—having a better life through a successful psychoanalysis is a "good" which therefore is unacceptable to them. Some of these individuals suffer from a particularly intense form of envy and greed, i.e., they wish to take away everything that others possess. In an additional sense, therefore, the negative therapeutic reaction can be understood as a wish to deprive the analyst of the "good" that he possesses by virtue of his therapeutic skill. This particular reaction to envy has been described by Melanie Klein (1957) as a fantasy accompanying the envy of the breast, the source of what is "good." I agree that such fantasies may contribute to the negative therapeutic reaction. However, as I shall recount, I differ from Klein in that I do not believe that oral sadism is the sole determinant; rather, I think that attention must be paid not only to that which is most deeply unconscious in one's inner reality, but also to external reality; that is, the actual fate of other family members may in some persons be of equal importance.

Since I reported my observations in 1965 I have become increasingly convinced that this issue is not confined to a particular diagnostic group, but that it represents a fundamental human conflict. The intensity of the guilt may be understood as the consequence of two complementary factors. One is a quantitative instinctual element, i.e., the intensity of oral sadism, but there are others in whom the instinctual element does not seem to play a prominent part. Guilt of this sort is a consequence, as it were, of environmental accident; it is a question of the evaluation of the actual fate of other individuals in the nuclear family. There is, I believe, in mental life something that might be termed an unconscious bookkeeping system, a system that takes account of the distribution of the available "good" within a given nuclear family so that the current fate of other family members will determine how much "good" one possesses. If fate has dealt harshly with other members of the family, the survivor may experience guilt, as he has obtained more than his share of the "good." One may feel guilty because of the instinctual wish to take away more than one's share, because of greed, or one may feel guilty because fate has given one more than one's share. This internal accounting system may, of course, in some individuals extend beyond the nuclear family—there is the "conscience of the rich."

Those who have survived the Nazi concentration camps or the atomic bombings of Japan demonstrate this type of guilt in its most blatant form. Although this form of guilt has been well recognized and well documented (Krystal, 1968; Lifton, 1967), it has not been generally recognized that guilt for having survived may exist in a much subtler form. For example, a woman who has had an extremely envious, rivalrous relationship with an older sister is not able to make full use of psychoanalysis because she perceives that she is the only woman left in her family capable of having a loving relationship with a man. Her older sister was trapped in an unhappy marriage and her mother, who divorced her father, was never able to love a man. She is the lone survivor of this family in the sense of being the only one who still has the opportunity to love.

Another example is that of a man who achieved great professional success but needed to deaden his feeling for people and to destroy part of himself through excessive drinking. In his analysis it was learned that he was inflicting talionic punishment upon himself because of the fate of an older sister who was in fact psychically dead from an incurable schizophrenic illness.

The familiar obsessive mechanism of doing and undoing may also in part be determined by this particular form of guilt, for doing may mean obtaining something good and undoing may mean not having something good. This can lead to an eternal alternation of success and failure. In severe forms of obsessive-compulsive neurosis, the doing and undoing of the analytic work may lead to a tedious stalemate where every step forward is balanced by a step backward.

To reiterate: I have learned that in the understanding of unconscious guilt, in addition to our usual consideration of sadistic impulses and the need for talionic punishment, we must also consider current reality, i.e., the fate of other family members.

A familiar source of guilt in those who actually survived social holocausts is the belief that their survival has been obtained at the expense of someone else's death. What I shall now report comes from a lengthy psychotherapy with a patient who was in fact a survivor of a Nazi concentration camp. Although I knew him for a period of over eight years, he was not able to tell me what actually happened to him until he became desperately depressed following a five-year interruption of the treatment, and then it took nearly a year of sitting with him until he was able to tell his story. At the time of his return to treatment he was suffering from severe depression and an almost unbearable state of hypochondriasis. He was nearly consumed with the belief that he was about to die from a heart attack. As is true of such intense states of hypochondriasis, no amount of realistic assurance had any effect.

He was 13 when the Nazis overran the East European

country in which he lived. His parents, an older sister, and he were collected by the Nazis and sent to a concentration camp for eventual extermination. As was customary, when they arrived at the camp, the men were separated from the women, and he never saw his sister and mother again. He and his father remained together for a brief period, but his father was later transferred to another camp. The patient bitterly accused himself for not joining his father (he claims he did have a choice in this matter). He chose instead to remain with an uncle and believed that had he chosen to remain with his father he could have supported his father's will to live and perhaps have ensured his survival. It was his guilt for causing his father's death that later became the center of his hypochondriacal quasi-delusions. As I shall relate, this patient did experience in reality what remains for most survivors merely a fantasy—he survived at the expense of someone else's life. It was the custom in these camps to have a daily inspection of the prisoners, who were forced to place their arms over their heads in order for the examining official to determine how much flesh remained on their ribs. Those who were becoming emaciated were separated for extermination, while others possessing suf- ficient muscle were allowed to continue to work. There was a daily quota to be filled. During such an examination my patient ran away from the line and hid himself. He did in fact successfully escape death, and presumably someone else was chosen for his place in the line. A few months after this, the camp was freed by the invading Russian armies.

The patient's hypochondriacal anxiety appeared nearly 25 years later at a time of his life when he was finally able to enjoy the fruits of his industriousness. He had entered a scientific field and obtained a fair measure of success; in addition, he had made a good marriage and was beginning to enjoy his growing family. Although the focus of his guilt may be interpreted as oedipal in that he castigated himself for his father's death, there was a more fundamental sense of guilt—he felt guilty for being alive. Our patient recreated in his symptoms the actual suffering of the concentration

camp where unexpected death was the nature of things
(every day he would see others dropping dead in the lines
or in the marches). He became his own victim, suffering
the agonizing torment that he was always in immediate and
imminent danger of death from a heart attack. As long as
his life continued to be painful, i.e., as long as he was struggling to achieve a measure of success in this country, he was
not overwhelmed by guilt. But as soon as he began to obtain
this success and a greater sense of ease of living, his guilt
overwhelmed him.

An analysis of the origin of this guilt led to a nearly
complete resolution of this nearly overwhelming hypochondriacal anxiety. I recognize, however, that the effectiveness of the therapeutic intervention does not necessarily
prove the correctness of my interpretation. What I shall
now suggest is a biological speculation.

In many primitive societies there are unavoidable times
of hardship during which the band is threatened by ex-
tinction through starvation. The prevalence of infanticide
as a means of population control in primitive societies attests to the need to adapt to a limited food supply. The
altruistic impulse to share food promotes the survival of
the group.[2] The alternative would be survival of a few of
the stronger individuals who would greedily hoard the
available food supply, but, as has been observed, there is
a survival value in maintaining the group rather than the
isolated individual. It is reasonable to suppose that evolution might favor the survival of those individuals who
experience guilt when they behave greedily and that the
guilt leads to the prohibition of the wish to have everything

[2]This was written prior to the advent of the movement currently known as
"sociobiology" (Wilson, 1975). I do believe, with the sociobiologists, that altruism
does in fact have its origin in our evolutionary history, but I wish to disassociate
myself from the sociobiologists' simplistic belief in the genetic origins of complex
characterological and cultural phenomena.

for oneself. This form of guilt, which in man's earlier history contributed to the survival of the group, continues to be inherited and to exert its influence upon modern man, although its original function may no longer be relevant. However, as a result of man's capacity for metaphorical thinking, the experience of guilt did not remain limited to its original object, the obtaining of food, because food can be symbolically elaborated as the acquisition of that which is "good." This would suggest that the idea that one should feel guilty for greedy and envious thoughts—an injunction of many religions—does not arise from religious doctrine; rather, religious doctrine has made use of a pre-existing biological given.

The guilt of having something for oneself may lead to the inhibition of acceptable egoistic strivings, that is, an inhibition of realistic demands. As I have noted, the description of narcissistic personalities as "entitled" has become a cliché. Although one cannot doubt the existence of wishes to be treated as an exception, what may be more characteristic is an inhibition of what might be termed reasonable demands for oneself. In severe cases this may take the form of what can be called a malignant passivity, a failure to do what is necessary to obtain what one needs for oneself. In a larger sense such people may fail to embrace life out of a deep sense that to do so will deprive others.

The belief that having something for oneself means that it was stolen from others is an example of a "primal fantasy."[3] In the case I presented, my patient's life had been "stolen" from another. Freud first used this term in 1917 in his "Introductory Lectures":

I am prepared with an answer which I know will seem

---

[3]See Laplanche and Pontalis (1973) for a discussion of the relation between primal fantasy and instinct.

daring to you. I believe these *primal phantasies*, as I should like to call them, and no doubt a few others as well, are a phylogenetic endowment. In them the individual reaches beyond his own experience into primaeval experience at points where his own experience has been too rudimentary [1917c, pp. 370-371].

As I mentioned above, Freud's neo-Lamarckian belief in the inheritance of acquired characteristics may have discredited his theory of the origin of these primal fantasies, but this should not cause us to underestimate their importance. His most complete discussion of primal fantasies occurs in "Moses and Monotheism" and his paper on the Wolf Man. I quote first from "An Infantile Neurosis" (1918, p. 119):

... phylogenetically inherited schemata, ... like the categories of philosophy, are concerned with the business of "placing" the impressions derived from actual experience. I am inclined to take the view that they are precipitates from the history of human civilization. The Oedipus complex, which comprises a child's relation to his parents, is one of them—is, in fact, the best known member of the class. Wherever experiences fail to fit in with the hereditary schema, they become remodelled in the imagination—a process which might very probably be followed out in detail. It is precisely such cases that are calculated to convince us of the independent existence of the schema. We are often able to see schema triumphing over the experience of the individual; as when in our present case the boy's father became the castrator and the menace to his infantile sexuality in spite of what was in other respects an inverted Oedipus complex.

And in "Moses and Monotheism" (1939, p. 100)

If we assume the survival of these memory-traces in the archaic heritage, we have bridged the gulf between individual and group psychology [emphasis added]: we can deal with peoples as we do with an individual neurotic. . . . And by this assumption we are effecting something else. We are diminishing the gulf which earlier periods of human arrogance had torn too wide apart between mankind and the animals. If any explanation is to be found of what are called the instincts of animals, which allow them to behave from the first in a new situation in life as though it were an old and familiar one—if any explanation at all is to be found of this instinctive life of animals, it can only be that they bring the experiences of their species with them into their own new existence—that is, that they have preserved memories of what was experienced by their ancestors. The position in the human animal would not at bottom be different. His own archaic heritage corresponds to the instincts of animals even though it is different in its compass and contents.

Separation guilt and the guilt that ensues when one has more are further examples of primal fantasies. Primal fantasies are in a certain sense beyond individual psychology and according to Freud "bridge the gulf between individual and group psychology."

Part II

**Therapeutic Action
and
Psychoanalytic Process**

Chapter 6

The "Holding Environment" and the Therapeutic Action of Psychoanalysis

At the Congress in Marienbad in 1936, Glover (1937) observed that "it is essential that our theory of therapeutic results should keep pace with the complexity of ego development and with the complexity of our etiological formulae" (p. 127). As I have shown in previous chapters, our increasing experience with the psychoanalysis of the so-called narcissistic case has led to a comparison of our concept of defense with that of the "classical case." It is not surprising then that we have also been led to a reexamination of the psychoanalytic process and the nature of the therapeutic action of psychoanalysis.

The understanding of the factors which underlie therapeutic change in psychoanalysis is not a secure area of knowledge; it is easier to identify the forces that interfere with the progress of an analysis than to understand what contributes to its therapeutic success. Our theory of therapeutic change is, I believe, itself constantly changing as a result of the changing nature of the neuroses (see Chapter 16). This theory is obviously linked to the subject of transference, where a final understanding also seems continually to elude us.[1]

I believe that most analysts would accept James Strachey's statement (1934) that structural growth is effected by means of sparingly employed mutative interpretations. Interpretations are only effective when certain conditions are met: in Strachey's words, "every mutative interpretation must be emotionally 'immediate'; the patient must experience it as something actual" (p. 286). He stated, further, that the interpretation must be directed to the "point of urgency." This means that very precise conditions must be present regarding the state of the patient's affects. The patient must be in a state of affective relatedness so that the psychoanalyst can, by means of empathy, perceive the "point of urgency"—that is to say, there must be an affective bond. The patient's affective experience, furthermore, must be of a certain intensity—that is, sufficient to experience the immediacy of feeling but not so great as to overwhelm him. Strachey believed that the transference interpretations are likely to have the greatest "urgency" and that mutative changes are most likely to occur through the interpretation of a transference. There are differences of opinion about this: some would place transference interpretation at the very center of the therapeutic process, whereas others, like Anna Freud (1969), would give equal weight to interpretive reconstruction utilizing memory, free association, and dreams. Further controversy exists over the effectiveness of interpretation in the presence or absence of a therapeutic alliance: most believe that transference interpretations are mutative, that is, that they produce structural change only when self/object differentiation has been achieved so that the patient can accept the analyst

---

[1]Since a thorough examination of the theory of the therapeutic action of psychoanalysis is beyond the scope of this chapter, the following account is necessarily simplified.

as a separate person and can collaborate actively (Zetzel, 1956b). Kleinian analysts take a minority view, believing that transference interpretations can be effective even in the absence of a therapeutic alliance. (For a discussion of this controversy see Greenson [1974] and Rosenfeld [1974].) But if we leave these controversies aside, all analysts are united in the view that interpretations can be effective only when there is, in Strachey's terms, a "point of urgency," that is to say, affect that is genuine and communicated. It is further agreed that mutative interpretations lead to structural change by means of a series of innumerable small steps. This results in a growing identification of the patient with the analyst's "analytic attitude" (Bibring, 1937). Strachey emphasized the modification of the patient's superego, but we would now include the modification of the ego and the sense of self.

The theory that the therapeutic action of psychoanalysis requires a certain state of affective relatedness would have to be modified as it applies to the psychoanalysis of the narcissistic personality. For as I have indicated above, in the opening phase of the treatment (which may last for months or years) there is a persistent state of affective nonrelatedness. Strachey's criterion for interpretation—the state of affective relatedness, "the point of urgency"—is lacking and, further, there is an absence of a therapeutic alliance. In the absence of both a transference neurosis and a therapeutic alliance, and without a point of affective urgency that permits mutative interpretations, what then provides the motive force for the therapeutic action of psychoanalysis?

Kohut (1971) attributed the structural growth that occurs in such cases to a process that he called "transmuting internalization." He described it as follows: "Preceding the withdrawal of cathexis from the object there is a breaking up of those aspects of the object imago that are being internalized" (p. 49). And further, "there takes place a depersonalizing of the introjected aspects of the image of the object" (p. 50). Later, after he had given up the psychology of drives, Kohut (1977) reformulated "transmuting internalization" as the "neutralization of microstructures" (p. 31). I find his concept of "transmuting internalization" an unsatisfactory explanation of the therapeutic action of psychoanalysis in narcissistic patients. It is not that I question that the process occurs, for this has long been recognized. My principal objection is his theoretical frame of reference—one that focuses nearly exclusively on changes in the self, describing them in terms of a distribution of narcissistic object libido. Kohut did not make use of the psychoanalytic theory of object relations; to describe qualitative differences in libido is reminiscent of Freud's 1914 paper, "On Narcissism," a paper that preceded structural theory. Although Kohut employed structural concepts, he separated narcissism from the development of object relations, a view antithetical to object-relations theory. (For a similar criticism see Loewald, 1980a, and Kernberg 1974.)

Theory has a selective influence upon what we choose to observe. Kohut's theoretical position that narcissism and object relations proceed along separate developmental lines would minimize the interplay of the human environment upon the vicissitudes of development and the sense of self. This is not a minor theoretical disagreement but a radically different model of the mind (see my discussion in Panel, 1971). Object-relations theory describes intrapsychic processes in the context of a human environment. Such a view is consistent with contemporary biological theory in that it views the world around the organism with the organism in it. This is what, in psychoanalytic jargon, has come to be called a "two-body" theory.

It is our contention, therefore, that the syndrome of the

narcissistic character disorder that Kohut has so accurately described requires a theory of object relations for its fuller understanding. There is a theory of the therapeutic action of psychoanalysis that derives from the object-relations point of view. We are referring to those analysts who view the analytic setting itself as containing some elements of the mother-child relation. This point of view includes the contributions of Winnicott (1965b), Balint (1968), Spitz (1956), Loewald (1960), and Gitelson (1962), among others. It is a view that would see the analytic setting as an open system, a view in which the ego must be considered in relation to its human environment.

We have adopted Winnicott's term, "the holding environment," as an evocative description of this human environment, but it should be understood that in applying this term we are emphasizing a theory that is not exclusively Winnicott's. Winnicott introduced the term as a metaphor for certain aspects of the analytic situation and the analytic process. The term derives from the maternal function of holding the infant, but taken as a metaphor, it has a much broader application and extends beyond the infantile period—where the holding is literal and not metaphorical—to the more general caretaking functions of the parent in relation to the older child (Khan, 1963). We suggest that the mother, or more accurately, the caretaking adults, stand between the child and the actual environment and that the child and its caretakers are an open system joined by the communication of genuine affects. As Winnicott put it, ". . . the analyst is *holding* the patient, and this often takes the form of conveying in words at the appropriate moment something that shows that the analyst knows and understands the deepest anxiety that is being experienced, or that is waiting to be experienced" (1963b, p. 240). The holding environment provides an illusion of safety and protection, an illusion that depends upon the bond of affective communication between the caretaker and the child. The holding environment suggests protection not only from the dangers without, but also from the dangers within. For the holding implies a restraint, a capacity to hold the child having a temper tantrum so that his aggressive impulses do not prove destructive to either himself or the caretaker. In this regard it is not uncommon to observe at the beginning of an analysis that patients will test the analyst's capacity to survive aggressive onslaughts. The holding environment provides, in Sandler's terms (1960a), a background of safety. When there is a loss of this holding environment, which may occur for a variety of reasons such as the illness of the parents or their emotional unavailability, the child is forced into a premature maturation and, in a sense, ceases to be a child, at least for a period, for to have a childhood requires the presence of a holding environment. A child who is forced into a premature self-sufficiency does so by means of an illusion (Modell, 1975b), an illusion for which the ego pays a price.

THE HOLDING ENVIRONMENT AND THE ANALYTIC SETTING AS AN OBJECT RELATIONSHIP

Others, however, have questioned whether the analytic situation does in fact recapitulate an early mother-child relation. Anna Freud (1969, p. 40) stated:

> There is, further, the question whether the transference really has the power to transport the patient back as far as the beginning of life. Many are convinced that this is the case. Others, myself among them, raise the point that it is one thing for the preformed object-related fantasies to return from repression and be redirected from the inner to the outer world (i.e. to the person of the analyst); but that it is an entirely different, almost magical expectation, to

have the patient in analysis change back into the prepsy-chological, undifferentiated, unstructured state, in which no division exists between body and mind or self and object.

Leo Stone (1961) was also skeptical about whether the an-alytic setting can reproduce aspects of an early object re-lationship. As Anna Freud indicated, it would be foolish to insist that regression in analysis goes back to structurally undif-ferentiated states of the first or second year of life. Never-theless, there are actual elements in the analyst's technique that are reminiscent of an idealized maternal holding en-vironment, and these can be enumerated: The analyst is constant and reliable; he responds to the patient's affects; he accepts the patient, and his judgment is less critical and more benign; he is there primarily for the patient's needs and not for his own; he does not retaliate; and he does at times have a better grasp of the patient's inner psychic reality than does the patient himself and therefore may clarify what is bewildering and confusing.

Strachey (1934, p. 285) underlined an important para-dox that is implicit in psychoanalytic technique. He stated: "It is a paradoxical fact that the best way of ensuring that his [the patient's ego] shall be able to distinguish between phantasy and reality is to withhold reality from him as much as possible." This paradox is also relevant to our consideration of the "holding environment." For although there are "real" caretaking elements in the analyst's cus-tomary activity, if he does in fact assume an actual pro-tective role (such as might be necessary in certain emergencies), this will interfere with the analytic process. We wish to reiterate, therefore, that the caretaking ele-ments we have described are implicit in the classical analytic technique itself (in Eissler's terms, without parameters). If active measures are introduced into the analytic situation, there is the paradoxical effect of weakening the analytic holding environment. (The same point was made by Rosenfeld [1972] and Gitelson [1962].)

It should also be made clear that when we speak of "real" elements in the object relation between patient and analyst as part of the care-taking function, we are not referring to the very different issue of the patient's perception of the analyst as a "real" person (Greenson and Wexler, 1969). The word "real" is used here in a different context. Again, to refer back to Strachey's paradox, the introduction of special measures to reveal to the patient the "reality" of the analyst's personality may, in the treatment of the neuroses at least, have the opposite effect. The use of this technique in borderline and other psychotic illnesses is a separate issue.

We have discussed the so-called "actual" elements in the object tie between the patient and the analyst. The situation is further complicated by the fact that this actual object tie is penetrated by the products of fantasy. That these fantasies may be primitive and may occur in young children does not mean that the patient has in fact regressed in a structural sense to the age of one or two, as Anna Freud has questioned. The fantastic elements include the magical wish to be protected from the dangers of the world and the illusion that the person of the analyst in some way stands between these dangers and shields the patient. It is the illusion that the patient is not "really in the world." There is the wish that the analyst can make the world better for the patient, without the patient's being required to do any work—that mere contiguity to the powerful analyst will transfer the analyst's magical powers to himself.

A patient in the termination phase dreamed that she was lying on the floor holding a life-sized doll while I was seated watching her. The patient identified the doll as the analytic process that she was in danger of losing. What is of interest

here is that the analytic process itself was invested with the
qualities of a transitional object, apart from the person of
the analyst. Although the qualities of the holding environment are generated by the analyst's technique, they may
become separated from the analyst and take on a life of
their own. The analytic process is not infrequently observed in dreams as a more or less protective container,
such as a house or an automobile.

The gratifications that result from the analyst's functioning as a "holding environment," we must again emphasize, are not the consequence of the analyst's special
activity, that is, actively giving reassurance, love, or support, but are an intrinsic part of "classical" technique. Here,
gratification appears to contradict the rule of abstinence,
but the nature of the gratification is quite different from
that associated with libidinal or aggressive discharge. It
moves silently; it is not orgastic. I have suggested elsewhere
(Chapter 13) that the instincts subserving object relations
are of a different order than what Freud described as the
instincts of the id. Although this assertion remains controversial, it is not controversial to assume that the healing
forces of the "holding environment" have biological roots.

THE PSYCHOANALYTIC PROCESS IN
NARCISSISTIC PERSONALITIES

The First Phase—The Cocoon: Defensive Structure and the
"Holding Environment"

The description of the psychoanalytic process in the narcissistic personality as consisting of an initial, a middle, and
a termination phase is likely to be judged as overly schematic. The sequence of each phase may vary enormously.
In some patients, the initial phase may extend for years,
and some do not ever enter a middle phase and achieve

a certain sense of individuation. For these patients, it could be said that they may have obtained therapeutic benefit from the psychoanalytic process but in a certain sense remain unanalyzed. Despite these reservations, I believe that this schema remains a useful system of classification.

The initial period, the first phase, usually extends for a year, it is a period of great frustration for the psychoanalyst: The patient behaves in the main as if there are not two people in the consulting room, remaining essentially in a state of nonrelatedness. The patient feels encased in a cocoon. I have chosen the cocoon metaphor because it implies a potential for life. A cocoon, unlike a mummy or a plastic bubble, contains something alive and must be attached to something else that is essential for its nourishment. As I have described above (Chapter 2), the illusion of self-sufficiency and disdainful aloofness defends against yearnings that are insatiable. Some patients believe themselves to be inside a plastic bubble which reflects an endopsychic perception of deadness and a belief that they are not "really in the world." The illusion of self-sufficiency defends against a feared total dependence upon the human environment. (See also Volkan, 1973.)

During this phase, although the analyst may experience boredom and indifference, the patient may be enjoying the analytic experience.[2] At times we have the impression of a child playing happily by himself content to know that the protective person is in the next room. The patient may be talking to himself but nevertheless experiences a sense that he is safe in the analytic setting.

Although the analyst in the initial period may have a feeling that nothing is happening, we believe that the analytic process is set in motion by the holding environment.

[2]Some patients, if they are able to, will come very early to their appointments to obtain the feeling of safety and pleasure of remaining alone in the waiting room with the knowledge that the therapist is next door.

During this period there cannot be said to be a therapeutic alliance, for this requires a sense of separateness that has not yet been established. Instead of a therapeutic alliance (Zetzel, 1958), we see a magical belief reminiscent of what has been described in borderline patients as a transitional-object relationship—the object stands between them and the dangers of the real world. It is as if the patient really believes that he is not "in the world" and that there is no need for him to obtain anything for himself—there is a denial of the need to work.

What I am describing corresponds, of course, to some aspects of Kohut's idealizing transference. This positively toned transference gradually gives way, for reasons to be described, to negative transference. For a cocoon is also similar to a fortress, where nothing leaves and nothing enters. The analyst begins to observe that his comments tend to be forgotten or not even heard—nothing seems to get through. The analyst's emotional position is one of acceptance, patience, and empathy—he must be able to wait. As Winnicott observed (1969, p. 86): ". . . it is only in recent years that I have been able to sit and wait for the natural evolution of the transference arising out of the patient's growing trust in the psychoanalytic technique and setting, and to avoid breaking up the natural process by making interpretations." Interpretations at this stage tend to be either dismissed, not heard, or resented as an intrusion. (We will return in a following section to discuss the function of interpretation.)

The Middle Period: Individuation and the Development of the Therapeutic Alliance

In this portion of the analysis the positively toned transference gradually changes into its opposite. We begin to enter the period that can be described as one of narcissistic rage. The time of onset of this phase may be due in part to the emotional capacities of the analyst, that is, how long he can tolerate the patient's prolonged state of nonrelatedness. But we suspect that even with the most tolerant and accepting analyst the process would shift of its own accord, for, as the regression deepens, the insatiable demands that have been warded off by denial will become more manifest. The analyst becomes more aware of the patient's insatiable needs for admiration and total attention and, in turn, becomes more confronting. This is not simply the empathic acceptance of the patient's grandiose self that Kohut has described.

Here I share the observation of Loewald (1980a, p. 348) who stated: "To my mind a not inconsiderable share of the analytic work consists of more or less actively and consistently confronting these freed narcissistic needs of the narcissistic transferences" (see also Kernberg [1974] on confrontation). The confrontation of the patient's grandiosity gradually gives way to a systematic interpretation of the cocoon fantasy itself.

With this activity on the part of the analyst, the affect block and state of nonrelatedness is gradually and imperceptibly altered and gives way to genuine affect, albeit that of intense rage. We have arrived at the "point of urgency" that Strachey described as the necessary precondition for giving mutative interpretations. This rage in some patients takes on murderous proportions or may lead to a defensive indifference, a regressive movement back to the earlier cocoon fantasy. I believe, with Winnicott (1969), that the rage itself supports the process of individuation. In contrast to the rage that accompanies the Oedipus complex, the wish to destroy the parent of the opposite sex, this rage is not aimed at the analyst as a parental imago. It is less definite and more diffuse. For example, as the analyst is equated with the environment itself, he becomes the target of rage directed against external reality. A developmental sequence is symbolically recapitulated in the interaction between the analyst and the patient. The analyst becomes, in the patient's mind, the representation of reality and the wishes of the earlier period of the analysis are in intense conflict with this reality. These wishes are: the wish to be understood without communicating, the wish for the analysis to proceed by mere contiguity to the analyst without the need for activity, that is, work on the patient's part, and in some cases, the wish for the analyst to be conjoined to the patient so that the analyst will be able to eradicate the patient's painful affects. Dealing with these wishes and the accompanying rage requires persistent confrontation and interpretation. The need for this does not represent a failure of the analyst's empathy; it is simply a piece of reality.

The patient's rage may also be fueled by envy—the envy itself is again diffuse and nonspecific: the patient may envy the analyst for what he is and for what he has, that is, his knowledge. As one moves through this stormy period in the analysis, a period that may occupy months or perhaps a year or longer, one observes that the cocoon transference has been gradually dissolving—the patient no longer believes in his self-sufficiency, he is able to acknowledge his demands more directly, and his extreme dependency is no longer denied. With this comes the beginning of individuation, a sense of separateness, and the development of the therapeutic alliance. Although this may be a difficult and painful period, there is a sense that two people are present. The patient gradually, although reluctantly, begins to accept the fact that he has a responsibility for the work in the analysis.

We believe that the holding environment of the first phase has led to sufficient ego consolidation to permit a shift in the focus of therapeutic action of psychoanalysis in the second phase. And we believe that the motive force for the therapeutic action of psychoanalysis in the second phase is interpretation. Interpretation effects the dissolution of the cocoon transference in a manner analogous to the use of interpretation to effect the dissolution of a transference neurosis. It should be understood that, in contrast to the classical case, the dissolution of the cocoon transference permits the establishment of a therapeutic alliance. We can say that at the end of this middle phase the patient is emerging from the cocoon—he is beginning to hatch. With this there is a greater sense of aliveness. As patients report it—they feel as if they are beginning to live their own lives.

The Third Phase: The End Phase

In this phase the analysis approximates that of a classical case, without being identical to it, in that the potentiality for regressive movement is ever-present. During weekend separations, for example, there may be a renewal of the cocoon transference. Elements, however, of the historically idiosyncratic transference neurosis begin to emerge—that is, there is a repetition of imagos of whole persons and not the externalization of parts of the self.

We have now entered the realm of the Oedipus complex. In the male, indications of castration anxiety appear in the transference, which has shifted from the conflict with the environment to recapitulate historically determined facets of the transference neurosis. Correspondingly, there is a shift of focus, both within the transference and outside of it, from dyadic to triangular relationships. While the vicissitudes of the Oedipus complex may not emerge as completely as in a "classical" case, they are unmistakably present.

Affects are now experienced with great intensity—now it is only rarely that the analyst experiences the sense of boredom and sleepiness that so characterized the opening phase. In short, during this period the analysis is not unlike that of a classical neurosis, with the exception that there is the readiness to reestablish the narcissistic affect block that characterizes the cocoon transference.

Because of the patient's extreme dependency, the phase of termination may be prolonged. It should be clear that a true termination can be achieved only if the cocoon transference has been resolved through interpretation. In some patients with narcissistic character disorders, the stormy middle phase in which the cocoon transference is resolved is never traversed. Consequently, the patient remains unanalyzed and persists in a state where the analytic situation itself is used as a transitional object. It can be said with some truth that such patients become addicted to the analytic process.

Empathy and Mutative Interpretation

We have suggested that interpretations only become mutative during the second phase of the treatment of narcissistic character disorders, that is, when there is a state of affective relatedness. Interpretations are, of course, not confined to the second phase of analysis, and we suspect that their therapeutic action in the first phase may be of a different order. Interpretations may function principally as a sign of the analyst's empathy and understanding—that is, they may function as part of the analytic holding environment. I believe Rycroft (1956, p. 472) had something of the same idea in mind when he stated:

> In addition therefore to their symbolic function of communicating ideas, interpretations also have the sign-func-

tion of conveying to the patient the analyst's emotional attitude towards him. They combine with the material setting provided by the analyst to form the analyst's affective contribution to the formation of a trial relationship, within which the patient can recapture the ability to make contact and communication with external objects.

It is unlikely therefore that interpretations can be mutative until there is sufficient maturation of the ego for the acceptance of self/object differentiation. In the opening phase, the analyst's interpretations, although accurate, may not be distinguished by the patient from the analyst's general empathic response (see also Gedo and Goldberg [1973] for a discussion of the hierarchy of treatment modalities).

The Narcissistic Transference and the Transference Neurosis

It is the underlying assumption in this paper that as our psychoanalytic nosology is broadened to include syndromes of varying disturbances of ego structure, we will correspondingly have broadened our understanding of the analytic process and the process of transference. This is the point of view developed by Gedo and Goldberg (1973). We believe it is important to resist a tendency to blur the nosological distinction between the transference neuroses and the narcissistic character disorders. We suspect that the increased attention to the narcissistic disorders may reflect an actual increase in their frequency—a shift in the ecology of neuroses—and that a shifting nosology of neurosis may be the manifestation of yet unidentified psychosocial processes.

Fenichel (1938) observed that "neurotics who demand analytic treatment today differ from those that went to Freud thirty or forty years ago." And today we say that the neurotics who seek treatment differ from those who consulted Fenichel in 1938. For we have now come to view the capacity to form a transference neurosis as a sign of health. Elements of the transference neurosis appear only after a certain degree of ego growth and consolidation has been achieved. The development of the transference neurosis requires a capacity for illusion (Khan, 1973). (For a more general discussion of the transference neurosis, see Blum [1971].) As Greenson noted (see Workshop [1974]), it is fluid, changeable, and different in every patient. This is in marked contrast to the narcissistic transferences, which are uniform to the extent that they can be said to form an operational basis for defining the syndrome. This is not to say that the delineation of the narcissistic transferences occurs regardless of the analyst's technique or skill. Nevertheless, their uniformity suggests that they are based upon the externalization of psychic structures, that is, various portions of the self, or self-object, and that they do not require a condition of basic trust for their emergence. This suggests that the more familiar externalization of the superego is also a noncreative structural transference element, to be distinguished from what takes place in the transference neurosis.

Ego Distortion and the Ego's Conflict with the Environment

In his paper, "Neurosis and Psychosis," Freud (1924b) suggested that the ego's conflict with the environment was characteristic of psychosis: ". . . neurosis is the result of a conflict between the ego and its id, whereas psychosis is the analogous outcome of a similar disturbance in the relations between the ego and the external world" (p. 149). Our psychoanalytic experience with narcissistic character disorders has shown us that Freud's formula no longer applies, for this syndrome, where the ego is in conflict with the environment, must be categorized as a neurosis. Yet in the same paper Freud suggested a solution to this apparent contradiction, for he stated that it is possible for the ego to avoid a psychotic rupture by ". . . deforming itself, by submitting to encroachments on its own unity and even perhaps by effecting a cleavage or division of itself" (pp. 152-153). Freud had a specific form of ego distortion in mind, which he elaborated in later papers (1927, 1940b). This is the ego's capacity, as in cases of fetishism, to maintain two opposite views simultaneously, with a resultant loss in its synthetic functions. An example given was that of the fetishist's accurate perceptions of the female genitals held in the mind side by side with the belief in the existence of a female penis. Splitting of this sort, with a loss of synthetic functions, exists in narcissistic character disorders; Kohut described it as a "vertical" split.

In our description of the cocoon defensive organization we suggested that the underlying fantasy of self-sufficiency is the consequence of the ego's conflict with the environment. The belief in a state of omnipotent self-sufficiency exists side by side with an intense and overwhelming dependency expressed as a craving hunger for admiration and approval. This deformation of the ego is also a split, as Freud described, whose content follows directly from the ego's conflict with the environment. As we have indicated above, the specific deformation provides the basis for a specific transference response in which the ego's conflict with the environment is relived in the analytic setting.

We are led to a closer consideration of the nature of the trauma and the resultant ego disturbance or distortion. It would be naïve to suggest that there is a simple or direct relationship between developmental trauma and a specific characterological syndrome. We know of many instances in which similar developmental traumas result in quite variable characterological responses. Furthermore, we know that the reconstruction of childhood trauma from the analytic material of an adult patient is on a less firm footing than our direct observations of the psychoanalytic process itself. Nevertheless, we are not able to minimize the importance of trauma in the etiology of the narcissistic character disorder, which in a very general way may be described as a developmental failure of the "holding environment."

In our patients we can infer through historical reconstruction that there has been a relative failure in the parental holding environment which can take several forms, as discussed in preceding chapters. Kohut showed that the mothers of such patients are lacking in empathy and are overly intrusive, an observation we were able to confirm. This failure of empathy can also take the form of a relative failure of the parents' protective function, that is, of guarding the child against excessive stimulation. This may mean the failure to protect the child from sadistic or bullying attacks from other members of the household, as well as a failure to protect the child from excessive sexual stimulation. For there to be a failure of the holding environment, we believe that it is necessary that both parents in some way be involved. We have the impression that in the older child the father's role is significant either in opposing or in augmenting the maternal element.

Although the specific form of the failure of the parental shield may vary, we believe there is a common denominator in that it induces the formation of a precocious and premature sense of self, a sense of self that retains its fragility and must be supported by omnipotent, grandiose fantasies (Modell, 1975b). It is this defensive structure that we see re-emerging in the psychoanalytic process—the cocoon. The conflict with the environment that emerges in the middle period of the analytic process reaches a climax when there is a breaking up of the cocoon, so that the hatred transferred to the analyst is the patient's hatred of reality.

To return to our question—that of the failure of the holding environment in the "classical" case: trauma and conflict with the environment are of course not absent in the histories of our so-called classical cases, but do not lead to a structural deformation of the ego. We have the impression that such traumas may be reflected in periods of "acting in" during the early phase of psychoanalysis and in the relative abandonment of the therapeutic alliance, as if the patient needs to experience regressively the illusion of the magical protection of the analytic setting. In contrast to the patients with narcissistic character disorders, such episodes do not require any lengthy period of ego consolidation before yielding to interpretation.

We approached the problem of the "holding environment" from several points of view. We believe that there are elements of caretaking functions implicit in the object tie of the patient to the analyst, functions that are part of ordinary psychoanalytic technique. Loewald (1960) said that the analytic setting represents a *new* object tie. In addition to these "real" elements, there is the fantasy that the analytic setting functions in some magical way to protect the patient from the dangers of the environment, a fantasy similar to that of perceiving the analyst as a transitional object (Modell, 1968). These fantasies commonly reappear in the termination phase and then are no different from other transference fantasies that can be dealt with by interpretation. In the so-called classical case, the analytic setting functions as a "holding environment" silently; it is something that is taken for granted and can be described, as it was in the earlier literature, as part of the "confident" transference. However, where there has been a significant developmental arrest, the analytic setting as a holding environment is central to the therapeutic action.

There is implicit here a theory of the therapeutic action of psychoanalysis that places a special emphasis on the interactional elements between the analyst and the patient. This has been implicit in Winnicott's work, but as was characteristic for him he did not advance these ideas in any systematic fashion. In 1954 in the paper "Metapsychological and Clinical Aspects of Regression," he proposed that "The setting of analysis reproduces the early and earliest mothering techniques." He first understood this principle in his work with more seriously ill patients. Later, however, he gradually came to understand that it was not necessarily limited to them, but that it was seen in this group with greater clarity. As I shall attempt to illustrate in the next chapter, I do not view the reproduction of early mother-child interaction in analysis as a regression. To do so misses the most significant point: that the analytic setting, as experienced through the object tie to the analyst, recreates a human environment in which early developmental conflicts can be brought forward *symbolically*.

Chapter 7

Interpretation and Symbolic Actualizations of Developmental Arrests

In our description of the analytic process as a "holding environment," there is an apparent paradox. We have described the re-emergence of a very early developmental period, that of merging and fusion with the maternal object, and yet our patients for the most part are mature, responsible people who in many instances have achieved a certain success in their chosen careers. How can we reconcile this relative maturity with the appearance in psychoanalysis of phenomena reminiscent of the first years of life? Does the analytic process, in fact, induce a deep regression, or are there other ways of understanding this? As we have noted above, Anna Freud (1969) remained extremely skeptical of the power of transference to induce a deep regression: "The transference rarely has the power to transport the patient back as far as the beginnings of life." She wrote, further: "It would be an almost magical expectation to have the patient in analysis change back into the pre-psychological, undifferentiated, and unstructured state in which no divisions exist between mind and body

or self and object." Thus, it is nonsensical to believe that
patients in analysis undergo a structural regression back
to the first years of life. In resolving this paradox, we must
consider alternative ways of understanding the therapeutic
action of psychoanalysis; our customary way of thinking
about regression and developmental arrests in psychoanalysis may simply be muddled and wrongheaded.

In the previous chapter, we observed that the technique
of analysis—what the analyst does as an analyst in the con-
duct of analysis—without "parameters" is symbolic of certain caretaking functions. We understand this analytic
activity to recreate, symbolically, the "holding" that occurs
between the mother and the child. Many aspects of ordinary "good" analytic technique can be seen as symbolic
equivalents of aspects of the parent-child relationship—the
considerations that the analyst is constant, reliable, and
primarily there for the patient's needs, has a more benign
and less critical judgment than the patient, is empathically
capable of enabling the patient to feel understood, and can
help the patient clarify what is bewildering and frightening
because of his better grasp of the patient's psychic reality[1]
(Modell, 1978a). The holding environment also means setting limits, analogous to holding a child having a temper
tantrum, or accepting what is obnoxious, as the mother
accepts the child's soiling.

I have emphasized the observation that the elements of
a holding environment are symbolically actualized here by
ordinary classical psychoanalytic technique. There is no
introduction of special active measures, no playing of roles,

[1]Of course, one can also enumerate those aspects of the analytic relationship
that are completely unlike a parent-child relationship. One does not give advice
or offer oneself as someone to emulate; one does not exert moral persuasion
or interfere directly in the patient's life, and so on. This is only to remind us
that the psychoanalytic situation is indeed unique as it carries with it *some* symbolic
attributes of the parent-child relationship but is shorn of other qualities. It is
not, as some would claim, a type of reparenting.

nor is there any conscious intent on the part of the analyst to introduce this form of symbolic gratification. The gratification is intrinsic to analytic technique. I have also suggested that the symbolic actualization of the holding environment occurs in every patient; it is this that permits the patient to entrust himself to the analytic process—to free associate—and to allow the unfolding of the transference neurosis.

But for patients who have suffered a significant degree of developmental arrest, the symbolization of the analyst's activity as a holding environment is not a silent background to the analytic process; it becomes the center of the process itself.

How then can we understand the difference in response in these two groups of patients? The symbolic meaning of the analyst's activity may be perceived as similar in both groups but in one group, that of the so-called narcissistic personality, the privation from previously experienced relative failures in parental holding accumulates and becomes like a coiled spring waiting release. The symbolic action of the analytic function serves as a releasing mechanism. *The patient and analyst acting conjointly recapitulate an early developmental phase.*

From the analyst's point of view, what begins as the "frame" of the analysis, that is, the ordinary psychoanalytic technique, gradually becomes part of transference and countertransference phenomena. To repeat, the transference in the narcissistic case is a developmental recapitulation, thus explaining its uniform character, and is to be contrasted to the transference neurosis, which is idiosyncratic, the recreation of a specific "image." In the psychoanalysis of the narcissistic personality, I have described two broad phases. The first, or opening phase, which may continue for a year or up to several years, depending on the severity of the conflicts, is analogous to the early developmental stage of full or partial merging of the mother and the child, where the child expects the mother to know when to anticipate the child's needs without the child having to make an effort to be understood. The other phase is roughly analogous to a phase of individuation.

The analyst is inevitably drawn into the recapitulation of this conflict and may need to make implicit or explicit the fact that the patient must assume responsibility for communication. The content and intensity of this symbolic recapitulation will, of course, vary enormously, depending on the severity of the developmental arrests and a multitude of other factors. For some patients, the issues around individuation may not focus upon communication, but on other factors, such as the continued belief that the analyst in some way can alter their own internal affective states—can dip into their own psyches, so to speak, to remove painful affects. To tell such patients that they must come to terms with some feeling, be it rage or guilt, will be as if one is speaking to them in a foreign language. It is as if they cannot even imagine that there are some things that the analyst cannot do for them—some processes that are totally private and internal, that is, within the boundaries of the self. In many instances, this process leads, I believe, to a necessary and useful confrontation with the principle of reality, of which the analyst is the prime representative. My point here is that the analyst, as the representative of reality, is drawn into some degree of confrontation with the patient, which symbolically recreates an early phase of individuation.

The principles of treatment of the narcissistic personality still remain controversial, and there are those who would disagree with this therapeutic advice and would claim that such measures are an unwarranted introduction of educational techniques. Leaving this controversy concerning technique to one side, we note that the interaction of the analyst and the patient illustrates the fact that there is a symbolic recapitulation of a developmental phase into which the analyst is drawn as an active partner by means of transference and countertransference phenomena. It is apparent that this kind of symbolic actualization differs in kind from the symbolic meaning of the analytic setting as a holding environment. I recognize that for some students of psychoanalytic technique, the use of the analyst's affective response may appear to be an unwarranted breach of analytic distance and neutrality. However, I believe it is essential to the treatment of the narcissistic personality that at certain measured, controlled points, the patient be aware that he is able to elicit a genuine emotion in the analyst. This introduces a necessary element of authenticity into the analytic dialogue, an element which is frequently lacking in the patient's own family. To this extent, it is important that the analyst, as always, monitor and control his own affective response and at times be prepared to use those responses to authenticate elements of the transference and countertransference interchange. In a larger sense, the patient has enlisted us as stage manager and we are actors, giving them a second chance to re-experience what they had lacked in earlier development.

I have been reiterating here that the development of the ego, in relation to the sense of separateness, is never complete; that conflicts concerning individuation are part of everyday life; and that the experience of merging and fusion is not limited to the sexual act. And further, that everyday life, as well as the analytic situation, offers opportunity for symbolic actualization.

The fact that we have learned most about these phenomena from our sickest patients has cast a certain prejudicial pall over these issues. We have become accustomed to thinking of such phenomena as deeply regressive, or even psychotic or psychotic-like. Yet we know that our patients, many of whom in other aspects are highly functional social beings, have the wish to merge but fear that their sense of self may be totally fractured by an unempathic response, and so on. These people are in no sense psychotic. We have been misled by an ego psychology which equates maturation with internalization. From that point of view, phenomena such as we have described are interpreted as evidence of a dedifferentiation of psychic structure, that is, of an ungluing of the personality itself. If the analyst, because of his theoretical preconceptions, believes this to be the case, it will have an unhappy practical consequence, that of confirming the patient's worst fears about himself. In addition to which, it may simply be untrue.

The concept of regression itself is misleading. As Loewald (1981) observed: It is one of those terms which cannot bear too much weight (p. 23). Loewald observed further that "life is not seen only as a series of developmental steps from the cradle to the grave; we have become transfixed by the idea of development" (p. 28). We have been overly influenced by a misplaced biologic analogy—the observation of development as an orderly system of hierarchical structures. The layering of psychic development in the adult is not a matter of one phase being laid upon another like the layers of a cake. Conflicts and wishes from earlier, indeed the earliest developmental periods, can be carried forward without the implication that a regression has taken place, or that there has been a disruption of psychic structure or psychic functioning. It seems to me probable that unresolved early developmental conflicts are carried forward symbolically without necessarily implying a structural or organizational pathology. To the extent that the sense of self remains fragile (and we are all fragile to some extent), the need for the affirmation of the other continues throughout life. That this phenomenon makes its appearance at an early stage of life and persists through development does not imply that a regression has taken place. In a larger sense, this is simply testimony to the fact that man is a social animal, and dependency on another individual or dependency upon the attitudes of a group is testimony to the preeminence of group over individual psychology, but should not for this reason be labeled childish. The sense of separateness is a hard-won achievement, an achievement which, in a certain sense, is never complete. Freud recognized, in "Civilization and Its Discontents," that the "oceanic feeling" is not necessarily pat'ological but is a "source of religious energy which is seized upon by the various churches and religious systems, directed by them into particular channels, and doubtless also exhausted by them" (1930, p. 64). Stated somewhat differently, this religious experience provides an opportunity for a working-through of conflict which may have had its origin in the earlier stages of development.

We have noted how the use of the analyst's activity in the analytic setting varies if we compare the transference neurosis to the narcissistic personality. In the former, it is a silent background; in the latter, it is the center of the analytic process. From this, we may conclude that a symbolic use of the analyst's activity, that is, a symbolic actualization, takes place in each type of patient according to his need. I do not wish to imply any overly schematic division between the narcissistic case and the classical transference neurosis. For we know that the transference neurosis is usually "latently" present in the narcissistic case; it is only that problems of self/object differentiation have a certain priority; for some patients it is not that oedipal conflict is absent but that it is never reached therapeutically.

Transference interpretation may be effective not only for its truth-bearing or ostensive function, since the analyst who makes a correct interpretation in the face of an intense affective involvement is also demonstrating to the patient that he is able to continue to function as an analyst, that he has not been drawn into the game. That is, the interpretation has, in addition to its ostensive meaning, the function of a symbolic act which communicates to the patient that the analyst continues to function as an analyst despite intensive erotic or aggressive provocations. This is analogous to the well-functioning parent who is involved but remains above the battle, does not lose control, and does whatever is necessary in the best interests of the child. We should also not overlook the effect of the act of interpretation upon the analyst. For example, Klauber (1972) suggested that interpretation is a regulator of psychic tension between the analyst and the patient.[2]

Developmental arrests are in the nature of potentials for symbolic action. In such fashion, those people who have not accepted their own separateness, who have not mourned the loss of their own and their parent's omnipotence, will invest the analyst's activity with the power of an omniscient protector. I have described the analyst's endopsychic experience of this process as a visual image of a "sphere within a sphere": that is, the sphere of the patient's self-sufficient, self-contained, self-created, omnipotent environment held within the larger sphere of the analytic holding environment. Within the holding environment, many early developmental conflicts will be acted out or, more precisely, "acted in." Although this "acting in" is analogous

---

[2]What I have described as "symbolic actualization" has some relation to what has been called a "working through" of developmental conflict (Shane, 1979) as well as the developmental approach to the understanding of the therapeutic action of psychoanalysis (Settlage, 1979). This symbolic actualization can also be thought of as a manifestation of the repetition compulsion if we follow Loewald's (1980b) view of the repetition compulsion in its creative potential: "repetition means reactivation on a higher level of organizing potential, which makes possible novel configurations and novel resolutions of the conflict" (p. 89).

to the transference neurosis, it is quite different from it in that the content is remarkably uniform. What is symbolically recapitulated is a struggle to maintain a sense of autonomy and self-sufficiency with the fear that to communicate (that is, to share and to express feeling) leads to the control, humiliation, and, ultimately, the destruction of the sense of self. Alongside of this fear of the loss of autonomy, there is paradoxically a lack of acceptance of the sense of separateness of the self; the belief that the self is, in fact, unconsciously merged, that communication is not necessary; that the mere contiguity with the analyst will affect a magical cure. Even if the analyst uses a pristine classical technique, his response provides a new object relationship which is different from that which the patient experienced in the past. The analyst now understands the patient's anxiety; he respects the patient's autonomy and his right to make choices; he does not intrude, he does not retaliate; and he provides an effective, steady holding environment.

With this symbolic recapitulation of developmental arrests, the analyst does not function only as a screen to receive the patient's projections but as an actor whose actions promote a symbolic working-through.

To describe a symbolic actualization is reminiscent of an earlier concept, Sechehaye's (1951) concept of symbolic realization used in the treatment of schizophrenia. What Sechehaye described was the deliberate introduction of specific symbols, such as a balloon, to symbolize the maternal breast, and so on. In contrast, what I am describing is not the introduction of specific artificial symbols, but the fact that the analytic process itself, that is, the analyst's actions, will be invested with symbolic meaning. As Winnicott has previously indicated, it is the patient who gives the signals:

An infant is merged with the mother, and while this remains true the nearer the mother can come to an exact
understanding of the infant's needs the better. A change,
however, comes with the end of merging, and this end is
not necessarily gradual. As soon as mother and infant are
separate, from the infant's point of view, then it will be
noted that the mother tends to change in her attitude. It
is as if she now realizes that the infant no longer expects
the condition in which there is an almost magical understanding of need. The mother seems to know that the infant
has a new capacity, that of giving a signal so that she can
be guided toward meeting the infant's needs [p. 50].

It is very important, except when the patient is regressed
to earliest infancy and to a state of merging, that the analyst
shall *not* know the answers except insofar as the patient
gives the clues. The analyst gathers the clues and makes the
interpretations, and it often happens that patients fail to
give the clues, making certain thereby that the analyst can
do nothing. This limitation of the analyst's power is important to the patient [1960, pp. 50-51].

It is the patient who permits the analyst to be empathic,
and the patient may become virtually incomprehensible,
that is unknowable, so that the analyst is forced to respond
to this fact, which in turn confronts the patient with the
fact of his separateness.

THE FUNCTION OF INTERPRETATION

Psychoanalysis has long considered interpretation to be
its most effective tool. Indeed, for many, it is the act of
interpreting that distinguishes psychoanalysis and psychoanalytic psychotherapy from other forms of treatment
which are viewed as purely supportive. The function of
interpretation, its part in psychoanalytic technique, and
technical advice were well summarized by Fenichel (1941).

He began with advice: "One should always start interpretation at the surface; interpretation of resistance precedes interpretation of content; one should avoid too deep or too superficial interpretations." As to the results of interpretation, Fenichel continued that what is to be interpreted is isolated and draws the patient's attention to his own activity within himself; that he himself has been bringing about that which he has up to now thought he was experiencing passively. Finally, interpretation enables the patient to comprehend meaning and motives for this activity.

One might ask, why does a patient accept interpretations? Fenichel would answer that: one, because he recognizes as true within himself that which has been interpreted to him; two, the positive emotional attitude toward the analyst induces the patient to take a less skeptical view concerning anything expressed by the analyst; three, the interpretations are accepted as a result of identification with the interpreting analyst.

Fenichel's description of interpretation is still accurate, but perhaps restricted in its application. It applies to the so-called classical case where there is a good differentiation between self and object. In this instance, an interpretation may be considered as ostensive, because the patient will respond primarily to the manifest content, that is, to its truth-bearing function. At the other end of an imaginary continuum, the manifest, or ostensive content of the interpretation is relatively ignored and what is responded to is the act of interpretation itself. By making an interpretation, the analyst performs something that is experienced as a symbolic act. The content may be acknowledged, ignored, or perceived to be of secondary importance. For this reason, we learn, to our discomfort, that our well-meaning interpretations may have released consequences that we did not anticipate or did not intend if the patient wishes to remain unfound. (This is irrespective of the accuracy or inaccuracy of the interpretation.) Therefore, Balint (1968) and Winnicott (1963a) have cautioned the analyst against too active interpretations in the opening phase of the treatment of narcissistic disorders. Balint had advised the analyst to be "non-intrusive" and Winnicott taught us the importance of being able to wait. If a patient needs to maintain the illusion of omnipotent self-sufficiency, the fact that the analyst will confront him through an interpretation with something that he had not thought of himself threatens this narcissistic defensive structure. Or if the patient wishes to be known, interpretations can be enormously reassuring. If, on the other hand, the analyst merely confirms or understands something that is already in the patient's awareness, this may reinforce a sense of oneness with the analyst.

It is for this reason, I believe, that Kohut's recommendation of the extended use of empathy is effective in the opening phase of the treatment of the narcissistic patient. It is important, however, to note that empathy and interpretation differ in that interpretation includes making conscious something that has been unconscious, whereas an empathic response need only reaffirm what is already known. However, even an empathic response may be invested with a variety of unwelcome symbolic meanings: it may be experienced as a violation of the patient's need to be hidden and unfound; it may reinforce a fear of being merged and swallowed up, that is, the analyst's knowledge of the self may be a threat to one's autonomy.

We know that interpretations that go beyond the patient's conscious awareness or interpretations that are confronting or in any sense painful may be dismissed as if they have not been heard. At certain periods in the analysis, they may be totally ineffective or worse, experienced as cruel intrusions. It is as if the patient does not wish to hear anything that he has not thought of himself. Some patients

need to preserve a belief that their system of thinking can
be omnipotently controlled by themselves and thus resent
our activity, in that they experience it as the intrusion of
alien thoughts. Other patients appear to be functioning at
a level of taking in what is pleasurable and ejecting what
is painful. If, however, the patient feels cut off, abandoned,
in desperate need to be understood, that is, he wishes to
be found, an interpretation will, as I have indicated, be a
source of immediate gratification and result in the reduction of anxiety. The same action of the analyst will be
invested with opposite symbolic implications, depending
on the patient's developmental position. This, of course,
is confusing for the analyst and accounts, I believe, for our
uncertainty concerning the use of interpretation.

I believe that this is further evidence for the view that
where there is a significant developmental arrest, interpretation will be experienced not in terms of its ostensive
content, but as a symbolic act. We are not suggesting that
the truth-bearing content of the interpretation or empathic
response is inconsequential. The analyst cannot speak non-
sense to the patient, and interpretations that are clearly
off the mark will tend to be ignored. But in these instances
the locus of therapeutic action is not the truth-bearing
function itself, that is, making the unconscious conscious,
but the therapeutic effect, whether positive or negative,
may follow from the symbolic meaning accorded to the act
of interpretation.

From this, it also can be inferred that the establishment
of "psychoanalytic truth" can occur only when there has
been an establishment of a certain sense of separateness.
For analyst and patient, there needs to be a mutually val-
idating response; although the analyst may be convinced
of the truthfulness of his reconstruction, it still requires
the patient's validation and vice versa (Loch, 1977). Although we still believe (despite the skepticism of others;

see Gedo [1979], Schafer [1982], and Spence [1982]) that there is an analytic truth that can be discovered, it is difficult to conceive of a successful analysis in which there has not been at some points the establishment of this "psychoanalytic truth." As has also been noted, this "psychoanalytic truth" is not a construction but a reconstruction. That is to say, we cannot believe with any certainty that it corresponds to a historical reality, but it does correspond with, and it is an affirmation of, the patient's psychic reality. This does not mean that "psychoanalytic truth" is a historical truth in that one can establish with certainty the distinction between memory and fantasy, but it is, in fact, an act of collaborative reconstruction. Perhaps history itself is no more than this.

We have said no more than Freud (1937b) had previously noted in "Constructions in Analysis":

> What we are in search of is a picture of the patient's forgotten years that shall be alike trustworthy and in all essential respects complete. But at this point we are reminded that the work of analysis consists of two quite different portions, that it is carried on in two separate localities, that it involves two people, to each of whom a distinct task is assigned. . . . We all know that the person who is being analyzed has to be induced to remember something that has been experienced by him and repressed; and the dynamic determinants of this process are so interesting that the other portion of the work, the task performed by the analyst, had been pushed into the background. The analyst has neither experienced nor repressed any of the material under consideration; his task cannot be to remember anything. What then *is* his task? His task is to make out what has been forgotten from the traces which it has left behind or, more correctly, to *construct* it [pp. 258-259].

I have been attempting to convey that the analyst's activity, whether a construction, a reconstruction, or a transference interpretation, has a symbolic penumbra. Although I have emphasized developmental arrests in this chapter, I would not wish to leave the impression that I consider this to be the only condition under which the analytic setting and the analyst's activity are used to "work through" conflict concerning individuation. Throughout this work I have suggested that we may have been caught in a dialectical response to structural ego psychology. Although the concept of internalization is indispensable, the very success of this theory may have carried us too far in one direction. Self/object differentiation and the associated need for affirmation of the self through mirroring are not limited to the preoedipal period as if it were an archeological stratum with a point of closure. We are less completely internalized vis-à-vis our human environment than structural theory would lead us to believe. The need for transitional object relatedness, that is, to maintain an illusion of connectedness with a protective object, is never ending.

We also know that religion as well as art provides for the illusion of connectedness. If one grants this to be true, it is to be expected that similar illusions will be created in the analytic relationship regardless of whether there has been in fact a significant developmental arrest or a pre-existing state of deficiency; it is only that in the presence of developmental arrests we observe this process with greater intensity and clarity.

A NOTE ON REGRESSION

As I shall show in Chapter 14, there are some mistaken biological notions that have become incorporated into Freud's metapsychology, the foremost of which is the assumption that instincts are forces arising in the interior of the organism without the participation of the facilitating environment. Therefore, what is taken in from the environment is not necessarily to be equated with what is learned and adventitious. Modern biology teaches us something that is quite different: what is provided for genetically requires, at every stage of development, a fitting-in of something from the environment. For example, Freedman (1982), in reviewing the account of the puberty of Victor, the wild boy of Aveyron, noted that although sexual arousal was present in him, it did not seem to be connected to any interest in women or their genitals. A human environment was needed to provide an aim and an object for the sexual instincts. This principle is also true at the level of cellular development, for both dendritic arborization and the structure of the neuron are significantly affected by the environmental conditions under which it is maturing (Hubel, quoted by Freedman [1982]).

If the environment at all levels, from that of cellular interaction to object relations, is crucial, it is reasonable to suppose that individuals, in a certain sense, remain an open system vis-à-vis the psychological, that is, the human environment. This consideration is at variance with a premise of ego psychology that maturation can be equated with internalization (Hartmann, 1939). According to this view, self-object differentiation, a process beginning in early childhood, is completed with adult maturation. Although it is true that in certain borderline and narcissistic character disorders there has been an arrest in development leading to a certain failure in self/object differentiation, it is also true that self/object differentiation is a process that is never completed. It may be a cultural bias of the West to insist that a sharp differentiation of the self from others is a sign of maturity. Transitional object relatedness (Modell, 1968) and self-objects (Kohut, 1980) persist throughout life. This would account for the fact that the analytic process can symbolically actualize these early stages without implying that the individual had undergone a differentiation of psychic structure.[3]

---

[3]In my previous work *Object Love and Reality* (Modell, 1968) I devoted considerable attention to what I then described as forms of topographic and structural regression. Although I still believe that the concept of structural regression is useful in its application in certain psychoses, I no longer consider the notion of topographic regression as applied to transference phenomena in the neurosis to be a valid concept.

Chapter 8

Self-Psychology as a Psychology of Conflict

Throughout this work there has been an implicit if not explicit comparison to Kohut's self-psychology. If self-psychology is, as I believe, an unacknowledged two-person psychology, this comparison is inevitable. This chapter will make this comparison more explicit. As I have noted, the failure to acknowledge self-psychology as a two-person psychology can be traced in part to Kohut's emphasis on a "new" psychology of the self which was seen as discontinuous with earlier contributions. Although the role of the object is implicit in Kohut's emphasis on the process of mirroring, he has chosen to focus attention upon the self rather than the self *and* its affirming object. This placing of the contribution of the object to one side was, I believe, further accentuated by his insistence that narcissism and object love occupy separate developmental lines. In contrast, I cannot conceive of the preservation and safety of the self apart from its protective object.

In breaking with Freudian tradition, Kohut's focus upon the self exclusively is analogous to the exclusive reference to the intrapsychic which is the assumed position of classical psychoanalysis. In the history of psychoanalysis there are other instances of those who have radically modified Freudian psychoanalysis and yet maintained an exaggerated "classical position." Melanie Klein, in her unswerving belief in the death instinct, remained more "classical" than most Freudians. In the *Restoration of the Self* (Kohut, 1977) reference to two developmental lines was dropped; the focus was now entirely upon the self. This focus upon the self as opposed to the ego does introduce a new epistemological problem for psychoanalysis, as the self is primarily an endopsychic perception in contrast to the ego conceived as a structural organization, functioning in part automatically and unconsciously. Earlier in the development of self-psychology, Kohut tried to reconcile self-psychology with classical Freudian theory, proposing that they were complementary; but at the end he took the position that classical psychoanalysis could be placed within the supraordinated framework of a psychology of the self (p. 230).

This has not been my position. In this work I have attempted to show that a two-person psychology does not replace Freudian psychoanalysis but is a necessary adjunct. There is no need for a new psychology, but I do agree with Kohut that our deeper understanding of the psychopathology of the self does in fact raise significant epistemological questions. I will consider these broader issues of metapsychology in the final section of this book, "The Problem of Psychoanalytic Knowledge," especially in Chapter 15 ("Contexts and Complementarity"). In this chapter I will restrict my attention to the more purely clinical issues. In this more restricted clinical sense Kohut differentiated the psychology of the self from classical psychoanalysis, claiming that self-psychology encompasses not states of conflict but states of deficiency. From what I have presented in previous chapters, the reader will recognize that

I too have described states of deficiency in terms of relative failures of the human holding environment, but I have also described the result of these relative deficiencies or failures as intensely conflictual. My own psychoanalytic experience has led me to the view that Kohut may have been mistaken in suggesting that conflict is less an issue in the narcissistic personality than in the so-called transference neurosis (for similar criticisms see Loewald [1973], Treurniet [1980] and Wallerstein [1983]). In his assumption of a radical stance with regard to classical psychoanalysis, Kohut retained a classical definition of conflict, that is, restricted it exclusively to terms of intrapsychic conflict, as I indicated in Chapter 2. He did not consider that the locus of conflict can be between two people and not only between id and ego or ego and superego. As a corollary the concept of defense plays little or no role in self-psychology. If one adheres to this view, it must have some influence upon psychoanalytic technique.

In similar fashion Kohut contrasted the psychology of guilt with the psychology of the self. In contrasting and comparing the narcissistic disorders of the self with the transference neuroses, Kohut described the former as Tragic Man and the latter as Guilty Man. He explained that he referred to Guilty Man if one's aims are in conflict with one's drives and Tragic Man if the aims are toward the fulfillment of the self. Self-psychology is therefore proclaimed as a new psychology that departs from the old structural psychology in which the Oedipus complex is at the center and in which the superego and the aims of the instincts are in conflict. Kohut proposed that self-psychology is to be contrasted with classical psychoanalysis which he viewed as a psychology of guilt.

It may be that Kohut was again influenced by a classical conception which he retained despite his radical reformulations. This is the assumption that the Oedipus com-

plex and the superego are inextricably linked. I have
shown in Chapters 4 and 5 how separation guilt and survivor guilt can arise in the context of individuation, something quite separate from the Oedipus complex. It would
appear to me that Kohut has understood only two alternatives—the classical Freudian concept of the superego as
the heir to the Oedipus complex, or a new psychology of
the self in which the Oedipus complex and the superego
have little place. (Kohut's break with classical theory is indicated in the contrast between "The Analysis of the Self"
[1971] and the "Restoration of the Self" [1977]).

No one will doubt that the Oedipus complex is a quin-
tessential source of conflict. The love for the parent of the
opposite sex automatically induces guilt and in the male
leads to castration anxiety. As a result of the double nature
of the Oedipus complex—that is, positive and negative
Oedipus—death wishes toward the parent of the same sex
are inevitably poignantly and exquisitely ambivalent.

Although I have described two categories of guilt that
are not derived from the Oedipus complex, I do not question the existence of oedipal guilt and the fact that the
superego is heir to the Oedipus complex. The desire, fear,
and guilt which the child experiences toward his parents
are resolved by means of a set of complex identifications
which permit a modification of the intensity of instinctual
demands and result in the structure known as the superego. That this process may not be as fully internalized as
would be suggested by classical theory, that guilt may arise
in relation to current events within the nuclear family, as
I have described in preceding chapters, does not necessarily challenge this account of the origin of the superego.
But we also know that the superego has a history that
antedates the Oedipus complex (Beres, 1958). Those patients whose psychopathology can be placed within the
broad category of the disorders of the self frequently suffer

from a disorder of the superego as well. As a general statement it can be said that the relatively well-defined structural differentiation that occurs in the transference neurosis, where the Oedipus complex is at the center, supports a relatively healthy development of the superego, as compared to those people in whom structural differentiation is not so well defined. We know also that the quality of object relations contributes to the effectiveness of the superego (see also Chapter 13, "The Ego and the Id: 50 Years Later"). In the absence of an adequate parental holding environment, the child does not internalize parental controls—and so must fall back upon his own superego for control, which tends to be excessively primitive and harsh. Where there are impaired object relations there is often a corresponding disturbance of superego development, leading to a diffuse, unbound, archaic sense of unconscious guilt.

Disturbances of the self may be thought of as states of deficiency, but they are not conflict-free. The intensity of unconscious guilt in narcissistic disorders not only reflects a structural disorder but may be the consequence of the fact that the process of individuation itself, that is, becoming autonomous and having a separate life and a separate fate from that of other family members, is guilt inducing. Let me briefly review what I have presented in prior chapters. What is good is a concrete substance in limited supply. To obtain some good for oneself means that someone else has been deprived.

Paradoxically, the well-known sense of narcissistic entitlement exists side by side with the profound belief that one is not entitled to anything at all, that one does not even have the right to one's own life. This fantasy becomes attached to the process of individuation: To become oneself, to be fully separate, means that the other has been deprived and damaged. To have a separate life will damage the other; ultimately, it is the belief that in order to be born someone else must die. Though such ideas are nearly universal, they become intensified and are central to the psychopathology of those patients who are struggling with problems of autonomy, separateness, and individuation. I have described this as separation guilt.

We know that the presence of unconscious guilt by definition may be unknown to those who experience it, but unfortunately it may also be unknown to the analyst. And if the recognition of this powerful deterrent to recovery is further impaired by a theoretical preconception that such guilt is found only in transference neuroses, this will have a significant influence on the analyst's therapeutic effectiveness. In order to be analyzed, one must believe that one has the right to something and also that taking something from the other will not be damaging. The intensity of unconscious guilt of this type—the number of quanta of it in a given personality, so to speak—depends on complex and variable factors, among them the degree of sadism present and the fate of other family members. If the individual is literally or symbolically the only survivor, it can be understood that his unconscious guilt may be expressed as a profound passivity, a passivity which appears at times to be a form of psychic entropy. It is not so much a matter of active self-destruction as of a failure to embrace life. This failure to act to obtain something for oneself as a result of passivity may be unrecognized, and therefore the analyst and the patient may remain unaware of its truly malignant aspects.

I have set forth in Chapter 2 the defense of nonrelatedness. Implicit in any defense is a danger that must be defended against. Here, the danger concerns the vulnerability of the self. Although the anxiety is multifaceted, states of nonrelatedness and states of inauthenticity can be understood as a defense against the possibility that an unempathic response from the other will shatter the sense of self. Noncommunication is a means of preserving the integrity of the self. At a fundamental and deep level there is a conflict that may be described as the wish to remain autonomous, self-sufficient and hidden, versus the wish to be known, to be found, and to surrender the self to the other.

The psychology of the self is embedded in this fundamental dilemma, namely, that the sense of self needs to be affirmed by the other, and yet a response from the other that is nonconfirming or unempathic can lead at best to a sense of depletion or at worst to the shattering of the self. This results in a defensive quest for an illusory self-sufficiency which is in conflict with the opposite wish to surrender the self to the other, to merge, to become enslaved.

Fairbairn (1940) described the tragedy of the schizoid personality—the fear that one's love will prove to be destructive to the other. I have observed in addition a fear that love will prove to be destructive to the self. The exposure of positive feelings can be viewed as a dangerous humiliation—for love leads to the wish for enslavement, a total surrender, a giving over of the self to the other. Obnoxious behavior and negative affects may have many meanings and functions, as we have seen above, but an additional function may be a defense against the fear that the sense of self can be submerged and swallowed up by the other. A fighting negativistic stance serves to maintain the outlines of the self against the intolerable risk of the loss of the sense of self. The exposure of what is genuine and valued carries the risk of an unempathic rejection. However, not to communicate leads to self-imprisonment. For some it feels as if one is screaming at the bottom of a deep well and no one hears. There is an intense, profound conflict between the fear of psychic abandonment and the fear or wish for merger. This conflict may lead to a near-insoluble dilemma: we must use all of our intuitive skills to judge whether at a given moment the patient needs to be found or whether he fears our intrusion. In the first instance active interpretative work may be required, but in the second instance interpretations may be experienced as cruel intrusions which will only compound the patient's anxiety.

IMPLICATIONS FOR PSYCHOANALYTIC TECHNIQUE

Kohut could maintain his position that self-psychology is a psychology of deficiency states and not of conflict by asserting that oedipal conflict is not inevitable. In his last paper (1982) Kohut suggested that the myth of kindly, protective Odysseus replace the myth of Oedipus the father slayer—that parricide is the consequence of abnormal intergenerational relationships, and that normally there is a joyous interrelationship. My own clinical experiences support a very different view, namely, that the Oedipus complex is autonomous, that parricidal wishes are inevitable whatever the quality of the parental relationship. Although I believe that disturbance in the sense of the self and disturbances in the holding environment may in some cases completely overshadow the influence of the Oedipus complex, the reverse is also true—there may be intense parricidal and incestuous conflict in the relative absence of any disturbance in the sense of self.

I have offered the tentative hypothesis that the sense of self in its relation to protective objects may occupy a separate developmental line from that of the Oedipus complex (Sacks, in press). The preservation of the self becomes manifest in the opening phase of psychoanalysis in relation to the use of the analyst and the analytic setting as a holding environment. I have come to believe that there are implications for psychoanalytic technique that extend beyond the narcissistic patient; although oedipal issues and issues pertaining to the safety of the self may present clinically as if they are intertwined, issues pertaining to the safety of the self should be dealt with *before* considering oedipal derivatives.

The clearest source of evidence for the derivatives of the Oedipus complex in psychoanalysis can be found in the transference neurosis. In Chapter 6, "The 'Holding Environment' and the Therapeutic Action of Psychoanalysis," there is a symbolic developmental recapitulation where the analyst becomes, in the patient's mind, the representation of reality and the wishes of the earlier period of the analysis are in intense conflict with this reality. These wishes are: the wish to be understood without communicating, the wish for the analysis to proceed by mere contiguity to the analyst without the need for activity, that is, without the symbolic acknowledgement of separateness. If one denies that self-psychology is a psychology of conflict and claims rather that it is instead a psychology of states of deficiency, one will assume responsibility, as Kohut suggested, for failures of empathy. But if one believes that the psychology of the self is a psychology of conflict, one will accept that the analyst is symbolically invested with the qualities of reality and the reality principle. It is neither necessary nor advisable to accept responsibility for all empathic failures; although Kohut recognized the growth-promoting effect of empathic failures, he advised us to avoid conflict by extending empathy to the limits of one's capacity. I, in contrast, would view conflict as inevitable, necessary, and something that promotes individuation. Even the anger engendered by conflict is to be welcomed as it sharpens the sense of what is outside and what is inside.

134   THERAPEUTIC ACTION

The wish to be understood without the necessity to communicate denies a separateness of the self and may be linked with the belief that the analyst in some fashion will be able to remove painful affects without the patient needing to make efforts on his own behalf. This confrontation with the fact of reality—this promotes individuation. It is a symbolic act recapitulating a developmental conflict, as described in the preceding chapter. The denial of separateness may enable the patient to believe that the analyst could dip, in some occult fashion, into the patient's psyche and modify the patient's affects.

At times it may be empathic to make no empathic response. Winnicott (1960) warned us of the dangers of excessive empathy. Viewed in the context of a developing child, an excess of maternal understanding inhibits and restricts the child's confidence in his own creative powers of perception. Sometimes patients suffer from therapists who are too quick and too clever with their interpretations, denying to the patient their own area of creative observation.

In some patients, gentle confrontation concerning the limitations of reality may be necessary. In other instances such confrontation is not necessary as the patients will discover for themselves that the illusion that the analyst affords them protection against the pain and dangers of reality cannot be maintained.

Part III

The Problem of
Psychoanalytic
Knowledge

Introduction

With the limitation of the psychology of the individual there is also implicitly a limitation of the concept of the mental apparatus, which is far narrower in its application than Freud had assumed. We are not suggesting, as did Kohut, that the concept of the mental apparatus be abandoned altogether, for it continues to have relevance under certain conditions. Psychoanalysis still has a need for certain concepts that are in part quasiphysiological. A partial list of such phenomena would include: dreaming as a process; the primary-secondary process; and the so-called regulatory principles—the pleasure and reality principles—and to a more limited extent the repetition compulsion. (In Chapter 2 I have shown that the repetition compulsion as applied to transference-countertransference phenomena needs also to be understood within the context of a two-person psychology.) Other concepts such as that of the superego have their origin, according to Freud, within the evolution of a social group and only later become partially internalized. The superego belongs in both contexts. It is never completely internalized, betraying its link to group psychology through the phenomena of guilt of the survivor and separation guilt. In this section, we examine another duality, that of psychoanalytic knowledge itself. We believe that the "facts" of psychoanalysis consist not simply of words, but of words embedded in an affective valence, and that the perceptual organ of the psychoanalyst is that which permits him to perceive the affects of others. As this perceptual organ evolved out of the earliest mother-child affective bond, it is in this sense a biological given. Affects, we believe, are the carriers of semantic content, and conversely, words shorn of their affective covering are not the data of psychoanalysis. We no longer believe in the centuries-old dictum that there is a separation of the faculties of cognition and feeling; nor do we believe in the Cartesian view that separates the knower from the known, mind from matter, the personal from the impersonal.

But there is another dualism implicit in psychoanalytic knowledge, first described in the eighteenth century by the Italian philosopher Vico as the sense in which we can know more about other men's experience in which we act as participants than we can ever know about inanimate nature (Berlin, 1969). This divergence later came to be known as the distinction between *Naturwissenschaft* and *Geisteswissenschaft*, outer and inner knowledge, nature and culture. Although the "facts" of psychoanalysis are perceived through an affective communication, these "facts" are also subject to the schemata that are the products of psychoanalytic assumptions and theories. Psychoanalytic knowledge arises in the context of a two-person intersubjective psychology; these data are processed by a shift from the I-Thou stance to that of the I-It. There is a separation of the observing mind from what is observed. The analyst classifies and forms categories. For example, he separates defense from content; he classifies the forms of defense; he decides whether a transference manifestation represents aspects of a transference neurosis or a narcissistic transference, and so forth. In this, the analyst's position is not unlike that of a naturalist observer. This duality, this shift from the empathic to the naturalist stance, pervades all of what we do as analysts and presents us with a paradox. In Chapters 11 and 15 I suggest that there is an analogy here to the device of complementarity, introduced into physics by Niels Bohr—that we accept two opposed and contradictory views of the epistemology of psychoanalysis, both of which are correct.

In Chapter 9, we observe that philosophers of science are beginning to revise their views of the methods of science. They no longer believe science to be a totally impersonal enterprise in which the truth or falsity of a scientific idea can be determined by impersonal, that is, nonpsychological, procedures. I refer here in particular to the work of Polanyi, who described a "personal knowledge" which is neither subjective nor objective. In this he came close to a similar view of Winnicott's, who spoke of the origin of cultural knowledge as the potential space between the subject and the object. I apply the latter idea to a description of the creative act in Chapter 12.

Chapter 9

The Nature of Psychoanalytic Knowledge

Nearly two decades ago the relationship of psychoanalysis to the philosophy of science was the subject of a published symposium (Hook, 1969). At that time, psychoanalysts were placed on the defensive and were asked to prove that psychoanalysis was, as Freud had asserted, a science. Philosophers such as Ernst Nagel held to their presumably unassailable positivistic doctrine that in order to qualify as science, a theory must be able to be not only confirmed but also negated. Sidney Hook asked what kind of evidence psychoanalysts were prepared to accept that would lead them to declare that a given child did not have an Oedipus complex. In the absence of what the philosophers considered to be a definitive reply from the psychoanalysts, their general opinion of psychoanalysis could be summed up in Nagel's statement: "[I] can only echo the Scottish verdict: not proven (p. 55).

In the ensuing years, the relationship of psychoanalysis to at least some branches of philosophy has undergone a radical transformation. Psychoanalysis is no longer in the dock, required to defend itself against the assertion that it is not a science; it is instead viewed as a new method for obtaining knowledge, which in turn requires a further advance in philosophy for its comprehension. The French philosopher Ricoeur (1970) and the German philosopher and sociologist Habermas (1968) approached psychoanalysis in this fashion. They both considered psychoanalysis a hermeneutic discipline—a claim I shall examine in some detail.

There has been another transformation in modern philosophy which is of interest to the psychoanalyst: the doctrine of logical positivism, which dominated philosophical thinking about science from Freud's day to our own, is being supplanted by a more humanistic, one might say a more psychological, view of scientific method. The judges of psychoanalysis are themselves being judged. In a series of extraordinary works, Michael Polanyi mounted a devastating critique against the belief that science consists of the discovery of eternal, impersonal laws of nature that lie outside of human commitment and human passion.

Although the books reviewed here were not published recently, they may help to illustrate a current and central controversy: is psychoanalysis a science, or do psychoanalysts observe meanings and not causes so that its methods are closer to those of the humanities? When controversy involves the fundamental assumptions of a discipline's "paradigm" (to use Kuhn's [1962] term), the identity of the group is split so that the opposing parties no longer share a conceptual framework. "The same range of experience takes the shape of different facts and different evidence" (Polanyi, 1974a, p. 167). When this occurs, there is no longer a common language and no longer a possibility for communication. It is quite possible that this kind of splintering polarization is now occurring in psychoanalysis.

PSYCHOANALYSIS AS A HERMENEUTIC DISCIPLINE

The term "hermeneutic" is derived from Hermes, the deity of speech and writing. It refers to the discipline of interpretation, originally interpretation of the Scriptures, but it can equally apply to the restoration of meaning of a forgotten language or a secret code. Waelder, in his review of the Hook symposium (1962), understood that such interpretations are essentially historical reconstructions, "because what is reconstructed is the meaning of a sign for those who put it there. There is no complete evidence that this was so; we cannot conjure it up and listen. It might all be a delusion, a vast edifice of interlocking errors—except for the fact that the *reconstructions fit an enormous mass of data from many sources* [emphasis added] and that the probability of all this being a matter of coincidence is so infinitesimal as to be negligible" (Waelder, 1962, pp. 624-625).

Ricoeur believed, as did Waelder, that psychoanalysis is such an interpretative or hermeneutic discipline. He stated, "Psychoanalysis is not a science of observation but an interpretation more comparable to history" (1970, p. 362). Ricoeur supported this argument by what must be described as perhaps the most brilliant exegesis of Freud's text that has yet to appear. It exceeds in subtlety and profundity comparable attempts by Jones and Strachey. I do not intend to review here his "reading" of Freud, except to note in passing certain trenchant observations. He described Freud's "first topography," the metapsychological papers prior to "The Ego and the Id," as basically solipsistic because they lack an intersubjective dimension.[1] If we examine Freud's theory of affects as described in Chapter VII of "The Interpretation of Dreams" (1900) and the

---

[1]Ricoeur's observation of Freud's early apparent solipsism was itself subject to a detailed critique by Sawyier (1973).

paper "The Unconscious" (1915b), where Freud stated that "Affectivity manifests itself essentially in motor (secretory and vasomotor) discharge, resulting in (internal) alteration of the subject's own body without reference to the external world" (p. 179n.), it does appear that Freud is describing essentially a solipsistic process.

The argument that psychoanalysis is a hermeneutic discipline receives its firmest support from the method of dream interpretation, where the manifest dream is analogous to a text that requires deciphering. For this reason, both Ricoeur and Habermas placed interpretations of dreams at the center of their examination of the psychoanalytic method. This, of course, served a tendentious purpose, for without minimizing the importance of dream interpretation, it is only one element in the field of psychoanalytic observation, and we know that it is possible to carry out a successful psychoanalysis in which the interpretation of dreams is not central. At a certain point the analogy to hermeneutics becomes forced and can no longer be maintained. For to preserve the textual analogy, Ricoeur was forced to assert that psychoanalysis does not use the methods of observation, that there are no "facts" (1970, p. 365) in psychoanalysis,[2] that it is not a science and proceeds only by means of interpretation. To further buttress the hermeneutic analogy, Ricoeur minimized the method of free association in favor of the fixed symbols in the dream elements. For if the manifest dream is analogous to a forgotten language or a secret code, as Ricoeur asserted, equal attention must be paid to all of the elements, with the assumption that there are some fixed equivalents between what appears and what is hidden, that is, between the dream symbol and what is repressed. Ricoeur main-

---

[2]Ricoeur subsequently modified this statement: There are facts in psychoanalysis but they do not have the epistemological status of facts in science—"They are 'reports' " (1977, p. 837).

tained that Freud did not pay sufficient attention to the
process of symbolization, that he minimized the existence
of fixed interpretation of symbols in favor of the method
of free association. I believe that this assertion goes to the
heart of the matter—the difference between seeing the
dream as a text requiring translation, or viewing the interpretation of dreams as a source of new and unexpected
observations.

Unlike the deciphering of a secret code, the psychoanalyst is guided by his perception, both conscious and unconscious, of a certain quota of affect, and he directs his
attention to individual elements of the dream. We know
that dreams that are communicated without affect do not
further the work of psychoanalysis. I suggested above that
the analyst's unconscious perception of the patient's affects
is the fundamental instrument of observation in psychoanalysis. In this context it is useful to review Freud's description of the method of free association. He
recommended "an evenly-suspended attention" (1912, p.
111) so that the analyst's free associations complement
those of the patient and, in fact, are in a certain sense
induced by the patient's associations. This suggests an oscillatory process between the patient's communication and
the analyst's perception, leading to the formation of new
knowledge. The translation of a dream's visual metaphors
is in most instances a new discovery and not the translation
of a fixed symbolism, although such fixed symbolisms do
of course exist. However, to maintain the hermeneutic
analogy, Ricoeur must insist: "It is not the dream work
that constructs the symbolic relation but the work of culture" (1970, p. 500).

Although the hermeneutic analogy receives its greatest
support from the interpretation of dreams, Freud himself
noted this analogy when he stated that "the interpretation
of dreams is completely analogous to the decipherment of

an ancient pictographic script such as Egyptian hiero-
glyphs" (1913b, p. 177). But the analogy cannot be pushed
too far, for the dream, unlike the ancient language, provides the observer with a source of new, unexpected responses. I am therefore in fundamental disagreement with
Ricoeur regarding his assertion that there are no facts in
psychoanalysis and that psychoanalysis is not a science of
observation.

Ricoeur's work is not only an exegesis; it also introduces
his own views concerning the nature of symbolization. His
conjecture is immensely attractive but unfortunately may
be untrue. It is understood in psychoanalysis that the motive for symbolization has some relation to the unconscious
and the process of repression. For example, a church steeple in a dream may symbolize a penis, but the penis is not
employed to symbolize a church steeple, because the image
of the church steeple does not need to be maintained in
repression (Jones, 1916). Ricoeur suggested a fundamental
modification of this principle. Substituting for repression
the concept of object loss, he used Freud's example of the
child's game described in "Beyond the Pleasure Principle"
(1920, p. 15), where the little boy magically controls his
mother's absence by throwing and retrieving a reel over
the side of his crib, exclaiming "*fort* (gone)," and hailing
its reappearance with a joyful "*da* (there)." Ricoeur took
this illustration as a paradigm for the process of symbolization in general.[3]

Ricoeur described (1970, p. 384) "a dialect of absence
and presence," suggesting that behind every symbol is an
absent "other." This is very close to Lacan's statement
(1977, p. 65): "Through the word—already a presence
made of absence—absence itself gives itself a name in that

---

[3]I have used the same illustration in my own work (Modell, 1968) but have
restricted its application to the symbolization of omnipotent thoughts.

moment of origin whose perceptual recreation Freud's genius detected in the play of the child." It is difficult for an outsider to judge questions of priority, but I suspect that this area was first staked out by Lacan. This view has had great influence on the French school of psychoanalysis, as can be seen in the title of Andre Green's (1975) paper, "The Analyst, Symbolization and Absence in the Analytic Setting." The concept has a poetic attractiveness, and although I do believe with Ricoeur that loss and separation anxiety are motives for the development of certain symbolic processes, it is a very large leap indeed to assert that *every* symbol contains an absent "other."

Ricoeur's work was also concerned with what he called the "placement" of psychoanalysis, that is, how might psychoanalytic knowledge be understood in relation to the more familiar categories of human knowledge? Without attempting to enter into the history of philosophy, I wish merely to note that there has been a reawakening of interest in the work of one particular philosopher whose ideas have special relevance for psychoanalysis, Vico, who died in 1744, and who has been the subject of a new appreciation by Isaiah Berlin (1976). Vico believed, as I have noted, that there is a sense in which we know more about other men's experiences—in which we act as participants—than we can ever know about nonhuman nature, which we can only observe from the outside. Although Vico did not use the term "empathy," what he described is identical to the analyst's use of empathy; he spoke of imaginatively entering into worlds different from our own. He wrote further that "the skill which permits us to do so is not capable of precise analysis and cannot be taught to the competent but insensitive or ungifted" (Berlin, 1976, p. 97), an observation that every psychoanalytic educator can confirm.

In establishing the major divergence between inner and

outer knowledge, Vico made a distinction that is essential to the problem of psychoanalytic knowledge: historical observations are essentially nonrepeatable—we may describe them as "happenings," whereas the observations of impersonal natural phenomena have recurring configurations and therefore are generalizable. This distinction between the cultural and historical sciences, to which hermeneutics belongs, and the natural sciences, where recurring configurations can be observed and generalized, poses the central dilemma for psychoanalytic knowledge. For even those who believe that psychoanalysis is a branch of the humanities and condemn what they call the scientism of metapsychology do not dispute the fact that there are recurrent configurations that permit at least the establishment of a clinical theory (Klein, 1976). Essentially, this paradox was ignored by Ricoeur, who denied that psychoanalysts observe anything, claiming to the contrary that there are no facts in psychoanalysis and hence no recurrent configurations.

Habermas, a member of the Frankfurt Institute for Social Research, the so-called Frankfurt School, did acknowledge this dilemma and proposed his own solution. Like Ricoeur, he was also concerned with "placing" psychoanalysis, and as a background to this effort, he traces the history of philosophy from Hegel to the positivism of Pierce, as well as the cultural philosophy of Dilthey—who inherited much from Vico. Because this is not of direct interest to the psychoanalyst, I have restricted my attention to just two chapters from Habermas' (1968) work, Chapters 10 and 11—"Self reflection as science: Freud's psychoanalytic critique of meaning," and "The scientistic self misunderstanding of metapsychology: On the logic of general interpretation."

As a philosopher who appeared to know Freud only from the printed word, Habermas was less successful than

Ricoeur in his exegesis of the Freudian text. In the hands of Habermas, the hermeneutic analogy became a procrustean bed that deforms psychoanalysis itself in order to preserve the textual analogy. He sees the entire body of psychoanalysis as a form of language and from this position can state "Psychoanalytic interpretation is concerned with those connections of symbols in which the subject deceives itself about itself" (1968, p. 218). Psychoanalysts would have difficulty in recognizing this statement as having much relevance to what they usually do when they make an interpretation, for Habermas, like many philosophers, ignored the function of affects. He especially ignored Strachey's observation (1934) that interpretations must be emotionally immediate and directed at "the point of urgency." In order to maintain the analogy that psychoanalytic interpretation is essentially that of deciphering a text, Habermas sees neurosis as "deviation from the model of the language game of communicative action" (p. 226).

The importance of Habermas' work does not, however, depend on his misunderstanding of psychoanalysis, but on his recognition of the central dilemma in psychoanalytic knowledge and his proposed solution that "Psychoanalysis joins hermeneutics with operations that generally seem to be reserved to the natural sciences" (p. 214). Habermas criticized Freud for borrowing the positivistic epistemology of the physical sciences and applying it to psychoanalysis. This line of criticism is so well known that there is no need for it to be recapitulated here. What is of interest to us, however, is Habermas' observation that "For Freud the language of the theory is narrower than the language in which the technique was described" (p. 245).

To remedy this situation, Habermas wished to supplant psychoanalytic theory with what he calls "general interpretations" restricted to ordinary language, that is, the language in which the psychoanalyst and his patients converse. This proposal ignores the fact that the language employed in the communication between the patient and his analyst serves a different function from that of a scientific language. The proposal is essentially the same recommendation that Schafer (1976) made—he would have us avoid all metaphors borrowed from biology, such as the metaphor of "ego structures." But to reduce all of psychoanalysis to a problem of language is in a fundamental sense "abiologic." It ignores not only the central function of affects, but also the fact that much of what psychoanalysts observe is derived from psychic structures not taken simply as a metaphor. For the unfolding of psychic development is also in a literal sense an epigenesis, one that results from our evolutionary history. (I discuss this matter in greater detail in the next chapter.)

Habermas went on to assert that the truthfulness of general interpretations can be arrived at intersubjectively by examining the context of the patient's associations to the interpretation. This may be true with regard to the interpretation of dreams, where the truthfulness of interpretation rests ultimately with the patient, but psychoanalytic observations are much broader than that of dream interpretations. The unfolding of the psychoanalytic process is something that can be observed by the analyst but not necessarily confirmed by the patient; the relative absence of a transference neurosis in certain character problems is one example. Here, the determination of the truthfulness of a psychoanalytic generalization is made by other analysts observing the same configuration in the psychoanalytic process. This intersubjective validation corresponds to the methods of the naturalist observer, in contrast to the methods of historical or hermeneutic knowledge.[4]

[4]For a critique of Habermas' general interpretations from different perspectives, see Nichols (1972) and Thomä and Kächele (1975).

This is the fundamental difficulty with the solution that Habermas proposes to the dilemma that psychoanalysis partakes of both historical and natural science. These are fundamentally different categories of human knowledge. We must return to Vico's original distinction between historical knowledge, where the observer enters imaginatively into the world of the subject and describes a unique event, and natural science, with its repeated configurations that yield generalizations. Collingwood (1956), following Vico, regarded historical knowledge as "the re-enactment of the past in the historian's mind" (p. 163). This historical or hermeneutic context is essentially disjunctive with that of the natural scientist, who views recurring and repeatable configurations. Habermas attempted to ignore the disjunction by combining the generalizations of natural science with those of the hermeneutic method, the mixture of which he called "general interpretations."

I believe, as did Freud, that psychoanalysis encompasses both forms of knowledge and that this continues to be the central paradox of its epistemology. Freud maintained and accepted the disjunction between what may be described as the historical or archeological aspects of psychoanalytic knowledge and other generalizations which followed the methods of natural science. However, Freud did not make this explicit and in fact denied that psychoanalysis created a new scientific method (1932, p. 159). Habermas criticized Freud, as have many others, for adhering to an understanding of scientific method that can be described as positivistic. He was doing nothing less, however, than accepting the dominant philosophic view of the times. The domination of the positivistic or "objective" view of scientific inquiry has persisted to our own day and has only recently been questioned by such men as Polanyi, whose work we shall now examine.

BEYOND OBJECTIVITY

It is claimed that it is a self-serving observation of psychoanalysts that only those who have some direct experience with psychoanalysis either as patients or as practitioners can fully comprehend it. This may be self-serving, but it also may be true. Ricoeur, who displayed an extraordinary grasp of the Freudian text, misunderstood the use of free association in the interpretation of dreams as Habermas misunderstood the nature of psychoanalytic interpretations in general. As a psychoanalyst who is not trained as a philosopher, I am undoubtedly subject to the same misunderstandings of philosophy; nevertheless, in our respective ignorance, we can meet halfway. The misunderstandings of the philosopher who is not a practitioner of psychoanalysis apply equally to the philosopher of science who is not a practitioner of science. This limitation, however, is not true of Polanyi, who was a distinguished physical chemist who later became a philosopher of science. The most complete presentation of his views is to be found in *Personal Knowledge: Towards a Post-Critical Philosophy* (1974a). It was first published in 1958 and precedes by four years the better known work by Kuhn (1962), *The Structure of Scientific Revolutions*. Polanyi, whose thinking in certain respects parallels Kuhn's, drew more radical conclusions. Kuhn's work remains more accessible and hence more popular. *The Tacit Dimension* (1967) represents the Terry Lectures delivered at Yale in 1962, and "Scientific Thought and Social Reality" (1974b) is a series of loosely connected essays dealing with science and society. They are dedicated to the memory of George Klein, who, as Polanyi noted in his Preface, he loved and admired. Those who knew Klein in the years before his death can also attest that Klein was filled with enthusiasm for Polanyi's work and its implications for the epistemology of psychoanalysis.

Polanyi's account of scientific method sought to under-mine what can be described as positivism. One of the best known and clearest spokesmen for the so-called "objective" view of science was Popper (1959). It was the positivistic view that was used to deny psychoanalysis the status of science by those philosophers of science participating in the 1958 symposium referred to above. They accepted Popper's dictum that the data of psychoanalysis were not falsifiable and hence not scientific. Popper's view was that science is essentially an impersonal enterprise, eliminating completely what he contemptuously described as "psy-chologism." Although he acknowledged that the process of conceiving a new idea is indeed personal, he sharply distinguished the conception of a scientific idea from the methods and results of examining it. The latter alone is the business of science; the truth or falsehood of a scientific idea can be determined by impersonal procedures that are therefore completely removed from the realm of psy-chology and human interests. As a result of these proce-dures, eternal lawlike generalizations can be formulated. Thus Popper could describe an "epistemology without a knowing subject."

Polanyi believed that such a view of complete objectivity is "a delusion and false ideal" (1974a, p. 18). I am unable here to recapitulate the closely reasoned and wide-ranging scope of his arguments and can only underline his conclu-sions. Unlike Popper, Polanyi believed that scientific truth is established and preserved by intellectual passion and commitment (p. 159):

> I have said that intellectual passions have an affirmative content; in science they affirm the scientific interest and value of certain facts, as against any lack of such interest and value in others. This *selective* function—in the absence of which science could not be defined at all—is closely linked

to another function of the same passions in which their cognitive content is supplemented by a cognative component. This is their *heuristic* function. The heuristic impulse links our appreciation of scientific value to a vision of reality, which serves as a guide to inquiry. Heuristic passion is also the mainspring of originality—the force which impels us to abandon an accepted framework of interpretation and commit ourselves, by the crossing of a logical gap, to the use of a new framework. Finally, heuristic passion will often turn (and have to turn) into *persuasive* passion, the mainspring of all fundamental controversy.

He also stated that "Science is not established by the acceptance of a formula, but is part of our mental life, shared out for cultivation among many thousands of specialized scientists throughout the world, and shared receptively, at second hand, by many millions. . . . Science is a system of beliefs to which we are committed" (p. 171).

Polanyi, to me at least, convincingly demonstrated that the central truths of science are protected not by procedures, as Popper would claim, but by human values.

Polanyi's work moved in the same direction as does psychoanalysis in its refutation of "pure objective" knowledge. Psychoanalysts have long been acquainted with the "objectivity" of their "subjective" empathic perceptions. Polanyi declared that "The personal participation of the knower in the knowledge he believes himself to possess takes place within a flow of passion." He added:

I think we may distinguish between the personal in us, which actively enters into our commitments, and our subjective states, in which we merely endure our feelings. This distinction establishes the conception of the *personal*, which is neither subjective nor objective. Insofar as the personal submits to requirements acknowledged by itself, is independent of itself, it is not subjective; but insofar as it is an action, guided by individual passions, it is not objective either. It transcends the distinction between subjective and objective [p. 300].

Above, I mentioned that Polanyi's views in certain respects parallel Kuhn's concepts of scientific change. Kuhn's notion of a scientific revolution taking place by means of an alteration of a centrally organizing paradigm is an idea that is immediately accessible to psychoanalysts. Although Kuhn did not acknowledge it as such, his is essentially a psychological conception. The process of a shared paradigm's becoming the basis of "normal science" is directly analogous to Freud's (1921) description of the group's being established by means of shared identifications. Both Polanyi and Kuhn maintained that experimental evidence that is in conflict with the central paradigm (Polanyi does not use this term) will be at first dismissed through some form of rationalization. The impersonal procedures, then, that Popper described, which establish the truthfulness of a scientific assertion, do not correspond to the way in which scientists in fact arrive at knowledge.

Polanyi, unlike Kuhn, explicitly acknowledged the process of establishing scientific truth to be psychological or sociopsychological. In *The Tacit Dimension* he wrote, "To rely on a theory for understanding nature is to interiorize it" (1974a, p. 17). For Polanyi the term interiorization is equivalent to that of identification. This interiorization "establishes the tacit framework for our moral acts and judgements and we can trace this kind of indwelling to logically similar acts in the practice of science" (p. 17). He described this again in Scientific Thought and Social Reality: "Indwelling involves a tacit reliance on our awareness of particulars not under observation, many of them unspecifiable. We have to interiorize these and, in doing so, must change our mental existence. There is nothing definite to which we can hold fast in such an act. It is a free commitment" (1974b, pp. 148-149).

Throughout his works Polanyi returned to a recurrent theme that is of the greatest significance to psychoanalysis. He did not elevate this theme to the level of a general principle; instead, he described a quality that can be called the quality of disjunction. This is similar, if not identical, to Bohr's more familiar epistemological device of complementarity. That is, the same ensemble of events have different varieties of coherence and different levels of meaning, levels of meaning that are essentially disjunctive. This is a profound argument against reductionism: biology cannot be explained by physics or chemistry, nor can psychological events be reduced to physiology. From "Scientific Thought and Social Reality":

> I contradict the claims of biologists who affirm that they are explaining life in terms of physics and chemistry. But the fact is they do nothing of the kind. The purpose which biology actually pursues, and by which it achieves its triumphs, consists in explaining the functions of living beings in terms of a mechanism *founded* on the laws of physics and chemistry, yet *not explicable* by these laws [1974b, p. 134].

This concept of disjunction would also apply to the attempt to explain psychological events by means of neurophysiology. George Klein (1976) had recognized the central significance of this observation of Polanyi's for psychoanalysis, but drew conclusions with which I cannot agree—that is, he believed that there was a fundamental disjunction between clinical theory and metapsychology. If metapsychology consisted solely of neurophysiological principles, as Klein suggested, this would be true, but metapsychology also consists of concepts such as the superego which are eminently clinical.

Nevertheless, the principle of disjunction—or, as I prefer, complementarity—is of central importance to psychoanalysis as an epistemological device for resolving what we have repeatedly described as the central dilemma of psychoanalytic knowledge: that psychoanalytic observations are unique and unrepeatable, and yet the same events demonstrate repeatable configurations from which we derive our clinical knowledge and clinical theories. The same phenomena can be understood by means of two mutually exclusive systems of meaning (Chapters 11 and 15) if we use the epistemological device of complementarity, a device that accepts basic dualities without straining for mutual dissolution or reduction. To say this, however, is no more than to restate Polanyi's concept of disjunction.

Ricouer viewed psychoanalysis as a hermeneutic, that is, a historical, discipline and denied that there were observable facts. He believed that psychoanalysis was not a science. Habermas acknowledged the historical and scientific duality in psychoanalysis but ignored this basic disjunction by attempting to combine or merge in his "general interpretations" attributes of historical phenomena observed from the inside with the quality of repeated configurations observed from the outside. I believe that Habermas' attempt was not successful.

These contributions from philosophers to the nature cf psychoanalytic knowledge have not solved the enigma of the epistemology of psychoanalysis, but there is some cause for optimism, for they have clarified the problem.

Chapter 10

Affects and Psychoanalytic Knowledge

If one asks, what is it in psychoanalysis that corresponds to the raw data of other sciences, one discovers that there is not a simple or direct answer. Although science no longer accepts the Baconian notion that there are "facts" in nature isolated completely from the influence of the selective process of theory, nevertheless there is the unassailable belief that at bottom science rests upon a perceptual base. Whether that fact is a fossil bone, a species of bird, or the swing of a needle in a scientific instrument, facts are sensory. In archaeology and paleontology, historical sciences analogous to psychoanalysis, the data can be literally tangible; the bits of broken pottery and broken bones can be touched. As is true of psychoanalysis, and in contrast to the more advanced sciences, there are no instruments interposed between the perceiver and that which is perceived. But what does the psychoanalyst perceive? Is there something that corresponds to the tangible artifacts of the archaeologist? Or does the mind, in Sherrington's words, move ghostlier than a ghost? Are the fundamental data of psychoanalysis elusive and ineffable?

Hartmann (1959) wrote that the data gathered in the

psychoanalytic situation are primarily behavioral data—verbal behavior, silence, bodily movements, and so on. These data are then interpreted with reference to internal, that is, mental, and not behavioristic processes. But is this strictly so? Not all such verbal behavior constitutes psychoanalytic data. One has only to think of the attempts to "objectify" psychoanalysis by means of tape recordings. Without intending to depreciate the value of such studies, these procedures soon demonstrate that all of the patient's words are not data and that if all the recorded words were considered to be of equal significance, one would soon become engulfed by a verbal flood. Words by themselves do not necessarily constitute the primary data of psychoanalysis. Consider those people who use words to communicate nothing, who use speech to create distance, to bore, and to distract. For this reason I believe that the attempt of a certain French school of psychoanalysts to view our science as a branch of linguistics (for example, the work of Lacan [1968], who was obviously influenced by Claude Levi-Strauss) is not entirely convincing. What endows words and other bits of behavioral data with significance is the perception by the observing analyst that these bits of behavior are associated with affects.

It can be justly argued that when words are used not to communicate but to create distance, this too is a form of data, one that is usually classified as a defense, presumably against the closeness of an object relationship. This is unquestionably true, but in contrast to the ongoing psychoanalytic process, where affects are communicated, the patient is here in a state of withdrawal; there is a temporary cessation of the analytic process. Once having observed the nature of this defense, the data do not change and there is no further increment of knowledge. *We would say that the patient's affects are the transmitter of data, and the transmission only occurs when there is an affect bond between the patient and the observing analyst.* The analogy of the patient's mind as a transmitter was described by Freud (1912, p. 115) as follows: "[The analyst] must turn his own unconscious like a receptive organ towards the transmitting of the patient. He must adjust himself to the patient as a telephone receiver is adjusted to the transmitting microphone." The perceptual organ of the psychoanalyst is that which permits him to perceive the affects of others. Such an organ is not so clearly identified as are the organs of sight, hearing and smell. This fact has caused considerable confusion to philosophers and has accordingly interfered with the establishment of an epistemology of psychoanalysis. Because psychoanalysis cannot be fitted into any ready-made epistemology, as Ricoeur (1965) so aptly said, "The understanding of Freudianism requires a new advance of thought." There is something very queer in the assumption, "I feel, therefore I know." It is Descartes' "cogito" turned upon its head. It is beyond my competence and the scope of this paper to pursue what is one of the leading problems of modern philosophy. It is clear, however, that the ancient separation into mental faculties of cognition and feeling is false. There are two recent works which dealt extensively with this specific problem of the philosophical implications of psychoanalytic knowledge: the contributions of Ricoeur and of Yankelovich and Barrett (1970).

When we return to Freud's analogy of the patient's unconscious mind as a transmitter and the analyst's unconscious mind as a receiver, the analyst's unconscious may be correctly likened to a perceptual organ, but in this instance it is a perceptual organ that significantly influences what is perceived, for not only will the analyst's unconscious influence that which the patient produces as data, but also the analyst's interpretations will produce fresh material. However, the perturbing effect of the psychoanalytic observer does not constitute an insurmountable ob-

162   PSYCHOANALYTIC KNOWLEDGE

stacle to scientific objectivity. For an analogous situation
exists in physics. Niels Bohr (1958, p. 11) wrote: ". . . the
necessity of considering the interaction between the meas-
uring instruments and the object under investigation in
atomic mechanics exhibits a close analogy to the peculiar
difficulties in psychological analysis arising from the fact
that the mental content is invariably altered when the attention is concentrated on any special feature of it."

If we take the analyst's unconscious perception of the
patient's affects to be the fundamental perceptual instrument, this places the problem somewhere in the broad
category of the analyst's "countertransference." This term
is not ideal, for in its narrower sense it denotes the analyst's
neurotic responses to his patient, but in its broader sense
it connotes the sum total of the analyst's perception of his
own affective responses. It is the analyst's preconscious
perceptions of his affects that permit him to use the communication of affects as a perceptual instrument. It becomes a neurotic problem for the analyst, interfering with
the analytic process, when his perceptions are under
repression and remain unconscious.

That the countertransference is an observing instrument
has long been known to psychoanalysts, for in 1926 (p.
136) Helene Deutsch observed that:

> This internal experience of the analyst . . . establishes
> between him and the analysand a contact which is outside
> the conscious apparatus, even though this process itself is
> stimulated by a motor-verbal discharge on the one hand,
> and by a reception of the latter through the organ of hear-
> ing on the other hand. However, that which takes place
> between the first stimulation of the senses and the subse-
> quent intellectual processing of this stimulus is a process
> which is "occult," and lies outside the conscious. Thus we
> speak of the analyst's "unconscious perception."

In this paper Deutsch first introduced the idea that empathy takes place by means of the analyst's partial identifications with the patient. Deutsch further proposed a tentative differentiation of classification of this mode of unconscious communication. Her description was clinically confirmed by Racker (1968), although these concepts are by no means familiar to most psychoanalysts. Deutsch differentiated empathy and intuition, which proceed from an identification with the patient, from another process which she termed "a complementary attitude." She wrote (1926, p. 137):

> . . . the essence of all intuition in general. Indeed intuitive empathy, is precisely the gift of being able to experience the object by means of identification taking place within oneself, and, specifically, in that part of oneself in which the process of identification has taken place. This intuitive attitude, i.e., the analyst's own process of identification, is made possible by the fact that the psychic structure of the analyst is a product of developmental processes similar to those which the patient himself had also experienced. Indeed, the unconscious of both the analyst and the analysand contains the very same infantile wishes and impulses.

Deutsch went on to observe, however, that this countertransference is not limited to an identification of certain portions of the patient's ego but also entails the presence of certain other unconscious attitudes which she would like to designate with the term "complementary attitude" (1926, p. 137):

> We know that the patient tends to direct his ungratified infantile-libidinous wishes at his analyst, who, thus, becomes identified with the original objects of these wishes. This implies that the analyst is under the obligation of renouncing his real personality even in his own unconscious atti-

tudes, so as to be able to identify himself with these *imagines* in a manner compatible with the transference fantasies of his patient. I call this process "the complementary attitude," in order to distinguish it from mere identification with the infantile ego of the patient.

I would understand Deutsch's distinction as follows: Knowledge through empathy is a kind of refinding of aspects of the self in the patient, whereas in the complementary attitude the analyst is acted upon by forces in the patient and may unconsciously be manipulated to recreate certain imagos in the patient's past that are alien to his own character. It is as if the patient's unconscious is a stage director who assigns roles to the analyst with the entire process remaining outside of consciousness. Until the analyst becomes aware of what is happening, he might find himself tending to act in the direction of the role to which he has been assigned. In contrast to the act of empathy, which is apt to be pleasurable for the analyst, this complementary attitude is apt to be experienced as something unpleasant; instead of the pleasure of recognition there is the unpleasantness of being acted upon. The analyst is in a comparatively passive position until he has a conscious recognition of what is occurring.

This complementary attitude may bear some relationship to the process of projective identification that has been described by Melanie Klein and her students. Racker (1968) described the process as follows: "The complementary identifications are produced by the fact that the patient treats the analyst as an internal (projected) object, and in consequence the analyst feels treated as such; that is, he identifies himself with this object" (p. 135).

Thus an analyst sometimes experiences unaccountable affects, affects that cannot be attributed to the process of simple contagion, although the analyst may tend to react to the patient's hostility with a corresponding affect (Ry-croft, 1956) and may experience contagious anxiety and depression. The complementary attitude involves affects that are linked to imagos belonging to the patient's past. This fact may remain outside the awareness of both the analyst and the patient.

Although these processes are by no means limited to any single diagnostic group, the observation of schizophrenic patients is useful, as the regression throws these issues into sharper focus and with greater intensity. For example, during one phase of my treatment of a schizophrenic girl, I was unable to understand why I experienced intense guilt concerning the apparent lack of progress of the therapy. I knew that I did not have any exaggerated therapeutic expectations and therefore could not account for the guilt solely as a consequence of my having failed therapeutically. This guilt became understandable only when I recognized that I was experiencing something that corresponded to Deutsch's description of the complementary attitude. This patient believed that her father had driven her mother crazy and was responsible for her mother's own mental illness. What the patient believed had occurred between her parents was now reenacted in the transference, and I was assigned the role of the damaging, destructive father who was now driving the patient crazy. As a result of proc-esses which are still unclear, I did in fact experience this unreasonable sense of guilt.

This passively experienced complementary attitude gives way to a more actively perceived understanding when the analyst succeeds in some degree with his ongoing self-anal-ysis. In this way what is experienced passively becomes transformed into something active and is mastered. Even in most well-conducted analyses, the analyst may at times be thrown "off balance" in this way and go on to achieve a reintegration with the deepening of his understanding of the analytic process.

What Deutsch described as empathy is analogous to what Freud (1925) described for perception in general. That is, Freud stated that perception is always a reperception, a refinding of the object that has been lost. As such it carries with it a certain quantum of pleasure. It has been frequently noted that the analyst's empathy may be heightened by states of mild depression as well as states of mourning, states in which there is some longing for a lost object. This is in contrast, as I indicated above, to the experience of the complementary attitude, where there is the unpleasant experience of being intruded upon.

Both the complementary and empathic countertransference which are first experienced unconsciously or preconsciously become worked over by the analyst's secondary intellectual processes. This is what Greenson (1960) called "insight," in contrast to the more regressive affective response of empathy. Here the analyst's experience of insight entails some measure of recognition and categorizing of what he has first experienced unconsciously. In the experience of the complementary attitude some time may elapse before the analyst recognizes the source of his own affects and understands their origin.

To return to our original question, I hope that I have satisfactorily demonstrated that the fundamental data of psychoanalysis consist in the perception of affects and that this perception corresponds to the visual and tactile organs of other scientists. It is questionable whether affects are ever devoid of mental content, although Jones (1948) presented the hypothetical case of the infant who may experience affects prior to the development of ideational content—a state of affairs he described as "aphanisis." This description remains to be empirically demonstrated. The affects associated with transference are always embedded in the context of identifications with formerly loved objects or aspects of the self (Kohut, 1971). Whether the content corresponds to actual experiences with a loved object or the objects have themselves been created by the subject is immaterial. In this sense the objects have a historical dimension. We know that this historical dimension refers also to the self. For example, it is not uncommon in the analysis of a narcissistic character for the analyst to begin to wonder about his own capacity to care for others. This corresponds to the mirror aspect of the transference that Kohut described.

But there is another dimension to the affects that are experienced in the analytic situation, a dimension that corresponds to the present, that is, to the current, object relationship between the patient and the analyst. This distinction also can be related in the broad sense to the difference between transference and therapeutic alliance (see Zetzel, 1970).

The facts of an analysis consist of more than the affects of transference communications. The method of free association produces memories of the past, dreams, reports of current experiences, and the like. Are these not also facts? I believe that whether an analyst can utilize such products of free association as facts depends upon the quality of the current object relationship between the analyst and the patient. If the patient is withdrawn and communicates without affect, it is as if the unconscious transmitter has been turned off, and the same communications may have to be reheard at a later date if they are to be utilized as analytic facts. It is for this reason that with the more disturbed patient, greater reliance is placed upon communication via the transference as compared to the use of memories of the past. Anna Freud (1969) noted that the unique role given to the transference in the psychoanalytic process to the exclusion of all other avenues of com-

munication is a point of controversy. Where affective
withdrawal may assume major proportions, the analyst
cannot make use of the patient's free associations as such,
and transference and countertransference begins to occupy the center of the analytic process. The analyst is
forced to use his countertransference as a perceptual instrument to observe shifts of engagement and withdrawal.
Although some patients remain in the presence of the object, that is, the analyst, without severing object ties, they
are actually in a state of unrelatedness. This is the "cocoon," described in Chapter 6. There is an apparent interruption in analytic activity, an interruption in the flow
of knowledge; the transmitter, as it were, is turned off and
the analytic process itself seems to be in a state of suspen-
sion until affective contact is regained. However, this only
seems to be an interruption of the analytic process as it
may continue to move silently by means of the holding
environment.

The capacity to know the affective state of another human being is a biological given. In Chapter 5 I offered
some speculations concerning the evolutionary significance of the communication of affects, with special reference to their function in ensuring the survival of the
group. If these speculations are true, it would suggest that
the capacity to know the affective states of another probably antedates the acquisition of language. This more primitive communication of affects becomes grafted onto
verbal expression through the medium of the tone of voice
and inflection. The phenomenology of this process is outside the realm of psychoanalysis and belongs to the area
of psycholinguistics. But as I have attempted to show, the
affective component may also be withdrawn from linguistic
expression so that language ceases to be a source of psychoanalytic knowledge. I am suggesting that we are utilizing a form of innate knowledge in the psychoanalytic

process. In this we are very much in accord with the recent contributions of Chomsky (1971), who proposed that our capacity to understand sentences may rest upon certain genetically determined structures of the mind. It is in the same sense that "facts" of psychoanalysis are perceptually and biologically rooted.

Chapter 11

Affects and the Complementarity of Biological and Historical Meaning

The fundamental assumptions of psychoanalysis were recently questioned by a group of scholars and clinicians (Holt, 1975; Klein, 1976; Gill, 1976; Schafer, 1976) who were all formerly students and collaborators of Rapaport. They mounted a broadly based attack on metapsychology. Although their views differ, especially regarding the important issue of the relation of psychoanalysis to biology, they are consistent in their belief that metapsychology has been a pernicious influence on psychoanalysis and, as a corollary, that structural theory and ego psychology in general represent an unfortunate phase in the history of psychoanalysis and had best be forgotten (see Chapter 14).

The fulcrum of this attack on metapsychology is the observation that, unlike natural science, psychoanalysis is concerned with meaning and not causality. This point of view was also championed by Home (1966) and Rycroft (1966), who argued that if psychoanalysts observe meaning and not causes, the methodology of psychoanalysis is that of the humanities and not of science. Those critics who believe that psychoanalysis is a branch of the humanities claim that the logic upon which psychoanalysis is based is the logic of language. And they are supported in this position by a fashionable movement in contemporary English philosophy based in part on the work of Wittgenstein. We agree that the question of meaning is central to psychoanalytic knowledge, but believe that those who have focused on the problem of language have missed the obvious fact that meaning in the psychoanalytic situation depends not so much on words as on affects, as discussed in preceding chapters (see also Basch, 1976). None of these authors seems to have recognized that affects are at the heart of the problem of psychoanalytic knowledge.[1] Words by themselves do not constitute the primary data of psychoanalysis. We know of an entire category of patients, those who have been described as narcissistic characters, who for long periods of time in psychoanalysis use words in a noncommunicative way (see Chapter 3). Observation of these patients' language alone would not constitute basic facts, as the words are shorn of affects, and thus also of meaning. What endows words and other symbolic structures with significance is the communication of affects. It is the analyst's response to communicated affects that forms the basis of what is called empathy. Empathy cannot be present without the communication of affects.

Some would argue that symbolic meaning is essentially a problem of semantics outside the realm of biology, that evolutionary history and the teleological belief in purposeful adaption are irrelevant to psychoanalysis. It is in this spirit that Schafer (1976) proposed a new language for psychoanalysis, one divorced from what he considered to be the contamination due to biological metaphors. Since affects can only be understood in the context of an evo-

---

[1]An exception is the work of Susanne Langer (1967), who fully recognized the central position of affects. Contemporary philosophers, however, tend to view her position as eccentric.

lutionary process, it would follow that biology is in this sense antecedent to language.

If we view the analyst's unconscious mind as a receiver, it is a perceptual organ that significantly influences what is perceived. For the analyst's unconscious affects influence that which the patients produce as data; the analogy of the unconscious mind to a perceptual organ cannot be carried too far, for it may be described as unique in its capacity to alter the communication that is perceived. But nevertheless, the belief that the capacity to perceive affects in others is a biological given and as such is analogous to the function of other perceptual organs such as the eye, ear, and the skin, is somewhat justified. These other perceptual organs retain their acuity until they are modified by advancing age. However, the perception of affects is dimmed much earlier in our development. It is probably most acute in young children and becomes modified during latency. In this respect it is similar to the esthetic appreciation that most children possess, which unfortunately becomes quickly extinguished, except in a few gifted individuals. We attribute the quality of empathy to those individuals who have retained this ability without which a psychoanalyst cannot function. In one sense the training analysis recaptures this lost esthetic capacity.

We note in Chapter 10 two different modes of perception of affects in the analytic process. One can be described by the familiar term "empathy," which from the standpoint of the analyst is a more conscious, pleasurable and active process supported by trial or partial identifications with the patient (Deutsch, 1926; Kohut, 1959). Affects are also perceived through another route that is subjectively less pleasurable to the analyst. In this instance the process itself is not fully conscious; the analyst may feel manipulated, as if he were the actor and the patient the stage director. I refer here to the use of the analyst's countertransference in perceiving the patient's affects—I use the term not in its narrow sense to denote the analyst's neurotic responses to the patient, but in the broader sense to connote the sum total of the analyst's self-awareness of his own affective responses to his patient. An experienced analyst knows this to be one of his most valued tools. The training analysis enables the analyst to distinguish whether the affects that he is perceiving have their source in his own life history or whether he in fact is being acted upon by a process set in motion by the patient. Deutsch described this as "the complementary attitude." This term, however, has not been accepted and may also coincide with what has been called "projective identification," which has eluded precise definition. I prefer the simpler classification: that the analyst may perceive affects in either the active or passive mode. The active mode corresponds to the process of empathy and carries with it a certain pleasurable recognition. In the passive mode the analyst is acted upon; this is a less pleasurable experience, less under conscious control, and may require some measure of self-analysis from the analyst in order to identify the source of the affects.

We have described the communication of affects at some length to buttress our assertion that assuming that psychoanalysis is a study of meaning, meaning itself is determined by the communication of affects.

THE CENTRAL PARADOX AND ITS SOLUTION

Although the analyst is a participating observer in the analytic process, he does attempt to minimize the intrusive influence of his own personality. We do not believe that he presents the patient with the totally blank surface of a reflecting mirror (Freud, 1912, p. 118), and yet the mirror analogy is still accurate in that the analyst's activity is designed to promote the unfolding of a process that emanates from within the patient, a process that is not primarily a response to the analyst's personality. In this sense, the affects that are perceived are communicated primarily from the patient. Freud's recommendation that the analyst behave as a reflecting mirror permits the unfolding of the transference neurosis in its sharpest outlines. It is a device that minimizes the influence of the knower on the known. In this sense, the analyst is in the position of a naturalist observer. By now the body of clinical knowledge that has been obtained by this method is voluminous. Although each analysis is unique and cannot be repeated, it is assumed that the similar recurring configurations that reappear in these unique experiences make generalizations possible. Although our criteria for testing the truthfulness of our general assertions are imprecise, no one who has had any experience with psychoanalysis doubts that it is possible to observe repeated configurations. It is the fact of this repeatability that provides us with our claim to be a science. The perturbing influence of the analyst observer can be minimized to the extent that we can observe the unfolding of an autonomous process.

It can be justly argued, however, that what we have presented here of the naturalist-observer analogy is completely incorrect; that it is virtually impossible to minimize the perturbing effect of the participating analyst; that the reality of the analyst, his age, his sex, the extent to which he is empathically responsive, will all alter the unfolding development of the analytic process; and that, as we have noted above, the analyst's unconscious perceptual organ influences what is perceived. In this sense, the analytic experience is unique and nonrepeatable. The closest analogy is not to the naturalist but to the historian. We are in the position of Heraclitus, who does not step twice into the same river for the river is never the same.

The analogy between the epistemology of historical inquiry and psychoanalysis is very close indeed. Of special relevance to psychoanalysis is the work of the Italian philosopher Vico, whose contributions have already been cited. Isaiah Berlin (1969, 1976) described Vico's belief that we can know more about other men's experience than we could ever know about nonhuman nature. What Vico described comes very close to our own concept of empathy. He spoke of "imaginatively entering" worlds different from our own. Vico's method consisted of a "series of self-analyses, tracing the phases of the development of one's own individual mind from childhood to maturity" (1976, p. 32n). The "facts" that are analyzed in this fashion are man's symbolic, created products—myths and language. He described a genetic, self-analyzing activity and examination of his own spirit (mind) in its interaction with the external world.

All of this bears an uncanny resemblance to the activity of psychoanalysis. The analogy between the psychoanalytic and the historic methods was noted by many historians, especially Walter Langer (1963), as well as by philosophers such as Ricoeur (1965) and Habermas (1968), whose work was examined in the previous chapter. The English historian-philosopher Collingwood saw historical knowledge as "the re-enactment of the past in the historian's mind" (1956, p. 163)—a view that bears a close resemblance to the psychoanalyst's use of empathy as a means of genetic reconstruction. Multiple historical contexts are employed in psychoanalysis: first, the patient's own reconstructed life history, whose outlines are constantly revised by emerging material; secondly, the context of the analyst's own life history and continuing life experiences which affect the range of his sensitivities; the historic context of Erikson's life cycle—that is to say, the same patient material may be viewed differently by the same analyst at different stages of his own life.

The analogy between history and the methods of psychoanalysis has not escaped the notice of psychoanalysts themselves (Klauber, 1968). A partial list would of course include Erikson, whose theory of the life cycle is essentially historical. Erikson (1964) also described in detail how a psychoanalyst actually gathers his clinical evidence. Waelder (1962) saw psychoanalysis as a hermeneutic discipline. In deciphering a code or script, he wrote, certain designs frequently recur; forgotten language is a historical interpretation because what is reconstructed is the meaning of the sign to those who put it there. The only evidence to support the interpretation is the fact that the reconstruction fits an enormous mass of data from many sources.

Novey (1968), whose views are close to our own, also understood the function of the communication of affects and the use of historical method in psychoanalysis.

In his paper "Constructions in Analysis" (1937b), Freud recognized that the analyst's daily work is analogous to that of the historian archaeologist. He thought that the term "construction" or "reconstruction" more appropriately related to analytic activity than the term "interpretation." And, further, that correct historical reconstruction produced a change in that which was being observed: "The analyst finishes the piece of construction and communicates it to the subject of the analysis, so that it may work upon him; he then constructs a further piece out of the fresh material pouring in upon him, deals with it in the same way and proceeds in this alternating fashion until the end" (p. 261).

In this description of the psychoanalytic process Freud acknowledged that the historical awareness of the observer influenced what was being observed. In contrast to the ethologist, who observes the behavior of a species that has remained unchanged for hundreds of thousands of years, the analyst observes neuroses that are not so fixed and

178   PSYCHOANALYTIC KNOWLEDGE

relatively immutable. We have every reason to believe that since the beginning of psychoanalysis the nature of our patients has been continually changing.[2] The symptomatic neuroses were replaced by the character neuroses. Indeed, we are in the midst of a rapid change in the phenomenology of neurosis. It is not too much to say that Auden's "Age of Anxiety" has been replaced by "The Age of Narcissism," or the "Age of Anomie." Although we do not know the mechanism of change, the neuroses may be the reflectors of unknown social forces. The analyst observer is not outside of these forces but is himself subject to the same neuroses as are his patients. Our fundamental clinical concepts, such as the notions of the nature of defense and transference, are not absolutely fixed but are linked to a particular form of classical transference neurosis. As the neuroses themselves change, so do the terms that apply to them.

We are faced with two seemingly incompatible views of psychoanalysis, both well supported by observation. We believe that psychoanalysis cannot be separated from biology in that the communication of affects is the perceptual basis of psychoanalytic knowledge. We also believe, despite our emphasis on the influence of the analyst upon what he observes, that there is a core in the neuroses linked to psychic structure that may have a determining effect upon the form of the transference, that is, whether there is a manifest transference neurosis or a recapitulation of a developmental arrest. Hence, the unfolding of the analytic process is also relatively independent of the influence of the personality of the analyst. From this assumption, gen-

[2]Waelder (1962) made the same point: The psychoneuroses seem to have changed since the early days of psychoanalysis with simple and rather transparent cases of Grande Hysterie retreating from sophisticated urban quarters and being reported from backwaters only; and, in general, with repression, the simple form of defense is giving way to more complicated mechanisms.

eralizations can be made, and upon it all our clinical knowledge rests. The method of observation used here is analogous to that of the naturalist observer. But we must also recognize a counterclaim, namely, that psychoanalytic knowledge is in essence historical knowledge.[3] What, then is the truth? Is it possible that both views represent aspects of the truth? We need to be reminded here that physics was faced with a similar insoluble paradox. A considerable body of experimental evidence supported the inference that light possessed the properties of a wave. Opposed to this was a substantial amount of incontrovertible evidence which was consistent with the thesis that light possessed a discrete particularity. We know that the way out of this dilemma was found by Niels Bohr through an epistemological device which, I believe, has far-reaching relevance for psychoanalysis—that is, the notion of complementarity. (I shall apply the strategy of complementarity to the larger issue contained in this work—psychoanalysis as a two-person and as a one-person psychology in Chapter 15.) Instead of attempting to resolve this paradox by a new synthesis, Bohr proposed that both views were correct, that basic dualities could be accepted without straining for their mutual dissolution or reduction.

Bohr specifically acknowledged a close analogy between the analysis of atomic phenomena and the problem of observation in human psychology. He stated: ". . . such a comparison is in no way intended to suggest a closer relation between atomic physics and psychology but merely to stress an epistemological argument common to both fields" (p. 27).

I propose that we adopt for psychoanalysis the episte-

---

[3] It must be acknowledged that evolution can also be considered as a historical narrative (Mayr, 1982). This historicism does in effect separate biology from physics, but there is a fundamental difference between man-created cultural history and the strictly materialistic history of the evolutionary process.

mological device of complementarity; that is, that we accept two opposed and contradictory views of the epistemology of psychoanalysis, both of which are correct.[4] Each view carries with it its own assumptions, models, and metaphors. What has been described as "The Fusion of Science and Humanism" in Freud (Gedo and Pollock, 1976) is widely recognized. In an earlier attempt to grapple with this problem, I suggested that the model of the mental apparatus is applicable only when one can generalize about man as a species (Modell, 1971a). That is, one can frame generalizations about the mind if one sees man as a phenomenon in nature subject to the laws of other natural phenomena. This is a view of man from the outside. Such models based on such general laws are not applicable to man's self-created environment, that is, to culture, which does not have this degree of generalizability. At that time I thought it was possible to classify the subject matter of psychoanalysis: to apply the models of natural science to phenomena that are species-generalizable and to apply the methods of historical inquiry to the products of culture.

As I hope to demonstrate in the following sections, I realize now that such a view is not possible, as biology and culture are so inextricably fused that separation through classification cannot be achieved. We require a new advance of thought—the epistemological device of complementarity which permits us to accept without striving for synthesis the two opposing traditions of natural science and the science of the mind. In this way the divergent traditions of *Naturwissenschaft* and *Geisteswissenschaft* may be brought into some relation to each other.

The inextricability of culture and biology can be demonstrated by means of the classic example cited by Freud

---

[4]The complementarity principle was applied by Edelheit (1976) as a means of dealing with the mind/body problem in psychoanalysis, an area quite distinct from the application we are proposing here.

of the linking of a specific fantasy with a specific character formation; it is as well an illustration of the type of generalization that can be made by means of a psychoanalytic method. Freud discovered a specific fantasy in the fetishist—that the woman has a penis and that the fetish is a substitute for the penis. This observation has withstood the test of time and can be repeated as often as one wishes. The fact that a specific ideation can be correlated with a specific character formation implies a certain stability of character to which we apply the metaphor of structure.

This stability of character structure permits us to observe differences in the unfolding of a psychoanalytic process so that the psychoanalytic process itself can be used as an operational method for establishing a nosology. Kohut (1971) did just this to establish the syndrome of the narcissistic character disorder, which can be differentiated from the transference neuroses. I believe this to be a generalization that is repeatable and capable of confirmation by independent observers.[5]

Although this statement has by no means achieved the status of an uncontroverted clinical fact since some analysts do not agree that the narcissistic character disorders present a separate syndrome, it is, however, a matter that can be empirically verified. We can refer to no crucial experiments: Instead, the verification or rejection of this assertion will be accomplished over time by independent psychoanalytic observers who will sooner or later arrive at a consensus—a process not dissimilar from what goes on in other sciences.

Yet I also believe even though it cannot be proven that

[5]I have disagreed with Kohut concerning the central aspect of the phenomenology of the narcissistic character disorder (Chapter 8, Chapter 6), and regarding the use of confrontation, but these disagreements should not obscure the fact that I have been able to confirm the existence of this syndrome by means of the psychoanalytic method itself.

the narcissistic character, although not new, is increasing in frequency as a result of poorly understood social processes (Chapter 16). The structure of character represents an inseparable amalgam of the biological and the cultural.

The repeatable configurations of character that psychoanalysts observe have been metaphorically described as structures. This has proved to be a heuristic device of great value inasmuch as we are able by this means to provide a theoretical scaffolding for the differentiation of nosological entities (Gedo and Goldberg, 1973). But there is another sense in which psychic structure is not to be taken simply as a metaphor, for the unfolding of psychic development is not left to chance. We do not believe that the development of the organism is totally plastic; the development of the personality is also in a literal sense an epigenesis, one that is determined by genetic history. Thus the concept of structure is not only a metaphor but also a biologic actuality. Though we believe that the changing form of the neuroses reflects unknown psychosocial pressures, this cultural plasticity has biologic limitations. Cultural and biologic determinants are inextricably interwoven in character structure.

THE COMPLEMENTARITY OF AFFECTS

Affects are therefore endowed with a complementarity of biologic and historic meaning. When we ask a patient what something means, we ask simultaneously: What is its function and where does it come from? A historical and a teleological question.

This duality of historical and teleological meaning is implicit in Freud's (1893, 1894) first description of the mechanism of a conversion symptom. It is the history of a trauma in which the affective component has persisted though the ideational component has been removed by means of repression. The affect is in this sense a signifier of a meaningful historical event.

It has long been recognized that the affects experienced in the transference are the affects that are historically meaningful to the patient. It does not matter whether the affects refer to actual or subjectively created historical events. It is upon this that we base our familiar observation that transference affects provide us with the most direct opportunity for historical reconstruction. Simultaneously, Freud also considered the affects of the hysteric as capable of discharge, thus serving the function of reducing the level of excitation of the central nervous system. The fact that Freud based his teleologic reasoning on the now-obsolete concept of Fechner's constancy principle need not concern us here. We wish simply to demonstrate that meaning in psychoanalysis involves a historic and biologic duality. Freud would probably have denied that the constancy principle was teleologic; Jones stated that "Freud never abandoned determinism for teleology" (1953, p. 45). And today biologists do not readily admit to belief in teleology. Yet, as Polanyi observed, "You cannot enquire into the functions of living organisms without referring to the purpose served by these functions. . . .teleology is a woman of easy virtue that the biologist disowns in public but lives with in private" (1974b, p. 139).

Scientists outside of biology, such as Bohr (1958) frankly acknowledged as did Polanyi that biology cannot exclude the notion of teleology:

> Owing to this essential feature of complementarity, the concept of purpose, which is foreign to mechanical analysis, finds a certain field of application in biology. Indeed, in this sense, teleological argumentation may be regarded as a legitimate feature of physiological description which takes due regard to the characteristics of life in a way analogous

to the recognition of the quantum of action in the corresponding argument of atomic physics [1958, p. 10].

We believe that Freud's speculation regarding the evolution of affects was in this sense teleologic, despite his adherence to the principle of scientific determinism. Freud (1926a), following Darwin, believed, as do contemporary biologists, that affects serve the adaptive needs of the group which exists prior to the adaptive needs of the individual. (I have discussed this in Chapter 5.) If we leave aside Freud's Lamarckian beliefs that affects are the "precipitates of primeval traumatic experiences," the use of affects as signifiers of vital information in the prehistory of the race is analogous in a profound sense to the storing of vital information (precipitated by trauma) in the history of the individual. Lorenz (1965), who is in no sense a Lamarckian, proposed a similar analogy when he noted that despite the enormous differences in the respective time scales, the functional analogies between the phylogenetical and the individual processes of acquiring and storing information are such that it seems well justified to create a concept encompassing both.

Affects are thus simultaneously understood in a historic and a biologic context: *Affects are at the crossroads of biology and history.*

The speculation that the evolution of affects serves the adaptive needs of the group receives some support from psychoanalytic observation as described in Chapters 4 and 5. There I commented on a particular form of guilt that follows from the satisfaction of egoistic strivings, that is, the satisfaction of getting something for oneself. The alternative would be the survival of a few stronger individuals, weakening the group as a whole. That altruism preserves the group in preference to the individual is a teleological principle.

IMPLICATIONS FOR AN EPISTEMOLOGY OF PSYCHOANALYSIS

We have proposed that affects are the starting point for the development of an epistemology of psychoanalysis; affects signify simultaneously what is historically meaningful and what is or has been biologically purposeful. We have further proposed that affects are the primary data of psychoanalysis (Chapter 9), that ideation becomes meaningful only when that ideation is "invested" with affect. This is no more than to say that affects are at the center of empathic communication (see also Kohut [1959]). Empathy belongs to the method of historical knowledge, and it has long been recognized as a tradition divergent from that of "objective" science (where the observer is outside and does not participate in the intersubjective experience between the knower and the known).[6] If the means of observation are those of history, by what right does psychoanalysis claim that it is a science?

We have also described the psychoanalyst in the position of a naturalist observer. This claim for science rests on the fact that the data of psychoanalysis are repeatable; this repeatability is not reconcilable with the essence of historical knowledge, from which static, lawlike generalizations are not possible.

Psychoanalysis is essentially a hybrid enterprise. It receives its data by means of empathy, but this fact alone does not categorize it as a purely historical discipline. We have to make the claim that it is unlike any other science (see also Wallerstein [1976]). As we believe that psychoanalysis stands firmly in both a historical and a scientific tradition, and as these traditions are in a certain sense irreconcilable, we have proposed that Bohr's epistemolog-

---

[6]These divergent traditions have been admirably reviewed from the standpoint of psychoanalysis by Habermas (1968).

ical device of complementarity be used as a method for resolving this paradox.

This brief essay is not an outline for an epistemology of psychoanalysis but a proposal of a method for removing an impediment to the development of such an epistemology. We have made no attempt to consider the extensive current literature concerning the epistemology of psychoanalysis (for excellent reviews, see Thomä and Kächele [1975] and Rubinstein [1976]), nor have we considered the function of psychoanalytic theory, especially the relationship of clinical theory to metapsychology. Nor have we touched upon the more vexing problem of how the truthfulness or proof of psychoanalytic observations is established.

Our wish is simply to show how the intellectual device of complementarity can prevent the polarization of those who view psychoanalysis as a branch of the humanities from those who view psychoanalysis as a science.

Chapter 12

The Transitional Object and the Creative Act

This chapter, which was originally intended as part of a *Festschrift* for Winnicott, discusses his idea of the "potential" space between the individual and the environment as it applies to the problem of creativity. The paper can be considered a commentary on the limits of narcissism.

I believe that originality is not something that arises completely anew within an individual. It is based on an acceptance of separateness, that is, a limitation of narcissism and omnipotence. Although I have focused on artistic and scientific creativity, the principles here apply equally well to the psychoanalytic situation itself. Something new, when it is discovered, cannot be said to belong either to the analyst or the patient; it is a conjoined activity, experienced as a sudden, unexpected creative act.

Freud suggested in "Totem and Taboo" that the social institutions of primitive man functioned in a manner analogous to the inner reality of modern man; the dread of incest, the intensity of ambivalence, the belief in the omnipotence of thought, which form the rubric of primitive religions, have become the content of inner reality of modern man. Freud said, "We are thus prepared to find that primitive man transposed the structural conditions of his own mind into the external world . . ." (1913a, p. 91). If Freud was correct, we would expect that the tangible products—that is, the art work associated with man's oldest institution, paleolithic religion, might in some respect be interpreted as the externalization of a process that has become internalized and unconscious in modern man.[1] There are specific aspects of paleolithic art which, as we shall describe, may be interpreted as these tangible expressions of the psychology of the creative process itself—an externalization of something that remains internal and relatively hidden in modern man.

Paleolithic art, perhaps the oldest known cultural product of Western man, consists not only of cave drawings but also of statuary, sculpture, and engraved ornaments. According to recent authorities (Graziosi, 1960; Laming, 1959), this art existed, with only minor stylistic changes, over a span of time so long that we can apprehend it only with difficulty. The chronology of the art (supported in part by radioactive carbon dating) covers the period from approximately 30,000 B.C. to approximately 12,000 B.C.—nearly 20,000 years. Within this almost unimaginable period of time, there were minor stylistic changes suggesting an evolution from cruder to more sophisticated forms, although the assigning of periods to the stylistic changes remains controversial and a problem for the specialist.

For our purpose, it is enough to note that this art is the creation of *Homo sapiens*, that is, Cro-Magnon man, and

[1]Jones (1938) also recognized the importance of paleolithic art as a tangible expression of the primitive mind. Unfortunately, his comments were based upon questionable archeological data, namely, that the female genitals were portrayed more frequently in the earlier Aurignacian period, whereas phalluses were more frequently used in the later sculpture of the Magdalenian period.

not of Neanderthal man, who coexisted with him and whom he eventually replaced. The homogeneity of this art, found over a large area of southern Europe, and its great stability suggest that it was part of a nearly indestructible religious institution and not an expression of man's decorative urge, an example of *Homo ludens*, or "art for art's sake." The facts that the paintings are relatively inaccessible, found for the most part in deep, dark recesses of limestone caves, and that many of them, such as those at Lascaux, appear on the ceilings of the caves, which must have presented an extraordinarily difficult task of execution, suggest that the caves were not family dwellings but instead sacred shrines for the performance of magical rites. In another publication I have described these paintings in some detail (Modell, 1968) and speculate on the more general aspects of their symbolism, especially in relation to separation anxiety and the fear of death. In this essay I restrict my attention to the specific characteristics of paleolithic art that suggest a correspondence to Winnicott's concept of the transitional object.

Not infrequently, the paleolithic artists made use of the natural geologic formation of the walls, floor, and ceiling of the cave itself. In Altamira, rounded protuberances on the ceiling of the cave were covered with paint and transformed into bisons in various postures. On the clay floor of the cave at Niaux, there are ten round cavities caused by the dripping water. Lines were engraved around the holes to transform the area into the image of a bison. One hole became the pupil of the animal's eye:

and others were elaborated as wounds, when arrows were drawn extending from the hole:

The created and the actual environment interpenetrated.

In Castillo, a formation of stalagmites was transformed

into the figure of a bison rearing up on its hind quarters. There are many more instances of this process of the interpenetration of reality with the artistic vision. In Pech-Merle, a stalagmite formation was used as the head and trunk of a hairy mammoth and the rest of the animal was completed with a few schematic black strokes. Bulges of rock were transformed into animals, and where body parts were missing they were completed by the artist with colored paint. It is as if the cave itself and the artists were combined in harmonious collaboration; mother earth fused with the created symbol.

It could be argued that these natural formations merely suggested the animal to the artist, perhaps by means of a kind of eidetic imagery. This suggestion was made by Herbert Read (1965).[2] Although this is a possible interpretation, it is not to be supposed that the use of these natural accidents, or found objects, was caused by a lack of imagination or skill; the modeling of these objects was exquisitely sensitive.

I should like to suggest another interpretation, one in accord with Freud's earlier hypothesis that primitive institutions represent an externalization of inner mental processes: namely, that this interpretation of the symbol and the real world is a tangible expression of the mental process of creation itself. The psychological significance of the use of these "natural accidents" or "found objects" of paleolithic art, which are now a common element in pop painting and sculpture, was noted by Fairbairn (1938). He interpreted their use as representative of an intermediate point between the attitude of the artist and the beholder. He suggested that "insofar as the artist is not responsible for the existence of the object, but simply 'finds' it, he may

---

[2]After this paper was written, I learned that Lewin (1968) also interpreted paleolithic art as a type of eidetic image, as an "image in the head."

be said to play the role of a beholder as much as any
member of the general public who 'finds' such an object
in a surrealistic exhibition."
   The notion that there is something intermediate between the attitude of the creator and the beholder approaches Winnicott's concept of the transitional object.
This is also analogous to Polanyi's "personal" knowledge.
The interpenetration of the actual environment—that is,
the walls and ceilings of the cave itself—with the created
image may represent an externalization of a psychic process: the child's first creative relationship with the environment, which Winnicott described as the transitional object
and transitional phenomena (1971). The created image
invests an inanimate object with significance, but the image
is not entirely a psychic process: what is created is not a
hallucination. The cave itself has collaborated with the creator to give substance, hardness, and permanence to what
is created. By analogy, the transitional object is an object
that is part of the environment: it is something—it is not
a hallucination—it is an inanimate object that is invested
with the qualities of life by the child.[3] It is a thing created
by the infant and yet at the same time provided by the
environment. As with paleolithic paintings, the inner process interpenetrates the objects of the environment and
gives them life.[4]
   Winnicott (1971) also recognized that in the child's play
there are those psychological motives that may have contributed to the origin of culture itself. The mother is the
child's first environment, and in the child's later relationship to the inanimate environment are employed those
psychological forces that were first used in relation to his
human environment. That is, magical thought, which mit-

---

[3]Searles (1960) expressed a similar view in *The Nonhuman Environment*.
[4]I discussed this in detail in a monograph, *Object Love and Reality* (Modell,
1968).

igates separation anxiety, makes no distinction between human and inanimate objects. The illusory sense of connectedness between the child and his transitional object is analogous to the illusory connection between the created symbol of the paleolithic artist and the real object that the symbol denotes. We believe that for paleolithic man, symbols were not used in a denotative sense—the symbol *was* the object, and symbol and object were fused; action upon the symbol affected the "object in the environment."

I view the transitional object as a watershed concept, a great psychological divide: On one side, there is a sense of connectedness of the subject to the object, a sense of connectedness that supports a denial of separation, whereas on the other side, there is an acknowledgment of that which is outside the self; the transitional object is a thing in the environment and not entirely self-created. Therefore, I would interpret the paleolithic artist's use of the actual formation of the cave walls and ceilings themselves as a concretization of the interpenetration of the inner and the actual environment; that is, the art work itself is a tangible expression of the psychology of the creative process.

What is created is not an entirely new environment but a *transformation* of that which already exists. This suggests that an essential element of creativity is an *acceptance* of that which is outside the self. This acceptance implies some mastery of the attitude of primitive ambivalence toward the original (maternal) object, a testimony to the synthetic powers of Eros. In the creative process, whether of art or of science, it is convention and tradition that are equated with the nonself. This equation has been noted by Milner (1957), who stated that the artist "may contribute to this convention, enrich it and enlarge it, but he cannot start off without it, he cannot jump off from nothing." And Winnicott observed, "The interplay between originality and the acceptance of tradition as the basis for inventiveness seems to me to be just one more example, and a very exciting one, of the interplay between separateness and union" (1967b, p. 370). The creation of the transitional object is therefore seen as a derivative of the child's first object relationship. We have suggested that the environment itself may be equated with this, the child's first love object. The psychology of creativity, which is the psychology of a created environment, can therefore be modeled on the psychology of object relations. If we understand the transitional object concept as a great psychologic divide with a progressive and a regressive side, we can discern an analogy in creative processes between primitive and more mature modes of loving. Mature love requires an acceptance of the nonself. We believe that true creativity, whether in art or science, also requires the acceptance of a prior tradition which stands for the nonself, that is transformed by the creative act. What appears as a scientific revolution cannot be entirely self-created. Greenacre (1957) noted that there has been an undue emphasis on the narcissistic aspects of creativity. As she viewed it, "the artistic product has rather universally the character of a love gift." A "collective love affair with the world" may be an obligatory condition for the development of great talent.

A necessary precondition for scientific creativity, one that parallels the capacity for mature love relationships, is the quality of fidelity. Those who have created scientific revolutions, such as Darwin[5] and Freud, have first shown a fidelity to, one could say a love of, the tradition that they subsequently transformed. This fidelity was accompanied by an identification with a great man who exemplified that tradition. In Freud's life that man was Brucke (Bernfeld,

---

[5]See his relation to Lyell's geology (Himmelfarb, 1959).

1944; Jones, 1953), and the tradition was the school of Helmholtz. Although Freud transformed this tradition, to a significant extent he remained loyal to it and never completely abandoned it. This is shown in his continued interest in psychophysical models that would characterize the mental apparatus as a whole.

The failure of creativity, if we may continue to compare it to a love relationship, might correspond to more primitive forms of loving, that is, the regressive side of the transitional phenomena. The failure to accept that which exists outside of the self reflects a failure to resolve ambivalence. There may be an actual hatred of the recognition of the existence of objects outside of the self. On this regressive side of the psychological divide are those phenomena that we label psychotic. Kris (1952) observed that psychotic art fails to retain its communicative function as it does not accept the need for others to comprehend. Indeed, it does not even accept the existence of "others." In psychoanalysis we may observe similar psychotic-like defenses in people who are not fundamentally psychotic. For in the psychoanalysis of certain creative people we can observe the failure of creativity where there is an excessive reliance on fantasies of omnipotence, an attempt to be entirely self-creative, an inability to acknowledge the contribution of others, which is at bottom a failure to accept the existence of objects outside of the self. Creativity can also be considered as an experience of ordinary life among those who are not particularly endowed with talent: the capacity to learn something new from experience. It is this capacity that contributes to a sense of vitality. To put it in the obverse, those who do not have this capacity are psychically dead. Learning here is not a reference to something transitory, a quick imitation, but rather to that which becomes a permanent part of the self.

We are aware of this process when it is absent. For there

is a group of individuals, fortunately comparatively few in number, who in fact do not learn from experience and who, therefore, cannot profit from psychoanalysis. (McDougall (1980) described them as the antianalysands.) Although these people are not psychotic, they seem unable to master the primitive ambivalence that accompanies the separation from their first object. Accordingly, they are unable to mourn the loss of the object and they remain psychically frozen in a state of rejection or saying no to all the "good" that comes to them from the outside world. They believe in the omnipotence of their own thoughts to the extent that they are convinced there is nothing they can obtain from others. This is analogous to a state of psychic death. Learning remains at the stage of the "as-if"; they can imitate or temporarily identify, but nothing lasts or becomes part of themselves. Learning is ephemeral, and to offer such people interpretations is an exercise in futility, for everything is written in sand.

I have employed the analogy of the transitional object to describe the creative illusion of transference in certain borderline and schizophrenic people (Modell, 1968). In them, the element of illusory connectedness between self and object is retained to the point where the analyst's separateness, that is, his uniqueness, cannot be fully acknowledged. Yet an element of transitional object relations is retained alongside of or beneath more mature modes of loving—it is a necessary illusion of connectedness that deepens one's relation to reality. If we each experience the world uniquely, we require a sense of connectedness to others to provide the necessary illusion that we are sharing a common reality. Winnicott described this as "the place where cultural experience is located in the *potential space* between the subjective object and the object objectively perceived . . ." (1967a, p. 371).

The analogy between the transitional object, paleolithic

art, and creativity in modern man breaks down in one significant respect. In our society, where originality is idealized, the source of the creative image is attributed to the individual experience of the creator. The almost incomprehensible stability of paleolithic art, extending for nearly 20,000 years, demonstrates that this art could not have been the self-conscious creation of individuals; the individual artists themselves were simply the instruments of a rigidly enforced religious tradition. If this paleolithic society was at all analogous to contemporary primitive peoples it is likely that these artists were shamans (Muensterberger, 1951), a class of men endowed with special powers but whose reactive performance is ritualized, like that of a modern priest who celebrates mass. To preserve such a tradition there may have been a positive prohibition against the variations that are the consequence of individuality. The sense of individuality is a cultural and not a biological given. It is difficult for us to imagine the time when even the idea of distinguishing the characters of individual men was an incredible novelty.

Although the paleolithic artists possessed sufficient skill to render animals with such naturalistic fidelity that now-extinct species can be accurately identified (Laming, 1959), representations of human beings are few in number, and by comparison to the animal paintings, human portraits are stylistically crude and subject to peculiar distortions. The few human figures found are seen mostly as engravings on bone or stone. In contrast to the elegant naturalism of the animal portraits, the human figures lack three-dimensional modeling, and frequently the heads and faces are distorted. The human heads may be left empty or blank or may have been replaced with animal heads, such as the famous "sorcerer" of Les Trois Freres, who has the genitals of a man with the tail possibly that of a horse, and with head, ears, and antlers resembling those of an elk. In other hybrid figures, the human face has been replaced by that of an animal, but it is not possible to recognize the species. These hybrid figures have been interpreted as either portraits of shamans wearing animal masks, or perhaps representations of godlike or mythical ancestors. Other human figures associated with paleolithic art include so-called Venus statues, female figures, faceless, with exaggerated breasts, buttocks, and vulva. Although the function of these figures is not known, they are thought to be associated with worship of a mother goddess (Levy, 1963). A not unreasonable conclusion is that the paleolithic artist possessed the ability to portray himself with the same naturalistic fidelity with which he could portray animal species, but that he was prohibited from doing so by a taboo similar to the one the Jews observe regarding the production of graven images. Prohibition of the sense of individuality insured the preservation of an unchanging, historically frozen, paleolithic culture. The creative act of the paleolithic artist is not analogous to the spontaneous product of the child's play. In the baby, that which is created is spontaneous, whereas for the paleolithic artist, the art work is not attributable to the creative act of an individual but is part of a holy ritual. But the infant who creates a transitional object is also unaware of a sense of self that is responsible for the creation. As Winnicott reiterated (1951), "Of the transitional object it can be said that it is a matter of agreement between us and the baby that we will never ask the question, 'Did you conceive of this or was it presented to you from without?' The important point is that no decision on this point is expected. The question is not to be formulated (p. 240)."

But if we leave this objection aside, we can still discern a convergence between the child's first creative act and the origin of culture. The cultural transformation of the environment may be understood in part as a process modeled on the child's relation to his primary environment, that is, his mother. Separation anxiety provides the motive for the child's first creative play, and separation anxiety (to which the fear of death is added) may also be the motive for the institution of a magically created environment. Both symbolic processes serve to mitigate the experience of total helplessness.

These speculations are, I believe, consistent with the theory of the origin of culture suggested by Freud (1913a, 1930) and elaborated by Roheim (1942). The motive for the origin of culture is derived in part from man's prolonged and helpless infancy. Instead of the stereotypic relations to the environment that are dictated by instinct in other animals, man places his reliance on the protection afforded by external objects. This leads to prolongation of the period in which the mother is the environment of the developing child. Hence culture, which is the creative transformation of the environment, bears the imprint of the psychological equation, mother[6] = environment. In this larger sense, then, the creation of cultural forms is analogous to a love relationship. It requires sufficient mastery of ambivalence so that the acceptance of the existence of something outside of the self can be achieved. A cultural form cannot be completely self-creative; there must be a certain limitation upon narcissism that enables the expression of fidelity to, and a love of, the tradition that has been transformed.

[6]"Mother" here stands for all protective parental objects.

Chapter 13

The Ego and the Id: Fifty Years Later

PREFATORY NOTE

Although I have modified my views in the years that have followed the appearance of this paper, I have decided to include it in this volume because I believe, not that the paper is incorrect, but rather that it is one-sided and incomplete. It is essentially a transitional statement, standing between acceptance of the "classical" position and the views I present in Chapters 15 and 16. I attempt to preserve the paradigm implicit in Freud's "The Ego and the Id," while recognizing the discrepancy between clinical observation and Freud's metapsychology. Object relations are not discharge phenomena. Freud's concept of instinct as something arising from within the interior of the organism does not apply to the observation that the formation of object relations is a process of caring encompassing two people (a process that does not include climaxes or peaks of discharge). Further, the concept of instinct itself has not received its necessary backing from contemporary biology, which tends to view a transcendent organizing principle of this type as an antique notion. I believe, as does Bowlby

(1969), that object relations have their analog in the attachment behaviors of other species. Were one to retain the concept of instinct, it would not only be as a motivating system but as urges which require the facilitating process of socially learned behavior (Freedman, 1982). This is as true for man as it is for other species. For example, human beings or animals raised in social isolation cannot perform the sexual act.

What is still clinically valid, however, is Freud's broad description of internalization, resulting in complex identifications with both parents during the oedipal period. We know that this observation has been extended to the preoedipal period (Jacobson, 1964) and to the postoedipal period, the period of adolescence (Erikson, 1959). These identifications result in certain abiding structures which have been given a variety of names. As yet, their theoretical function remains unclear, but their clinical validity is unquestioned. I am referring to the observation that "good enough" object relations lead to a sense of self that persists over time; whether we call this a self-representation or an ego-identification is a problem for psychoanalytic lexicography. It is an undeniable clinical fact that in borderline states and certain narcissistic personalities, this process miscarries. To this extent I believe that structural concepts are still clinically verifiable and have value.

As I shall describe more fully in Chapter 15, this description is one-sided and must be supplemented by an entirely different system of concepts and terms to account for processes where internalization has not yet taken place. It is misleading to assert, as a general principle, as Hartmann has done, that maturation is equated with internalization. We remain social beings whose sense of self requires the continued affirmation of others. Therefore, the paradigm implicit in Freud's "The Ego and the Id," that is, the paradigm of individual psychology, is clinically relevant, but only in a restricted sense—a description of structure formation after internalization has taken place. We need another set of concepts to describe the continued interaction of the self and the human environment. The terms "self" and "self-representation," or "ego-identity," belong to different conceptual contexts; "self" belongs to the context of a two-person psychology, whereas "self-representation," or "ego-identity," as well as the term "ego" itself, belong to the context of a one-person psychology. This is discussed more fully in Chapter 15.

I.

In this assessment of "The Ego and the Id" after the passing of half a century, there is an implicit question that refers to the nature of scientific change itself. The history of science is essentially discontinuous (if we are to follow Kuhn's description [1962]); the impetus for scientific work may reside in the discrepancy between the facts of a science and its theory. "Once it has achieved the status of paradigm a scientific theory is declared invalid only if an alternate candidate is available to take its place" (Kuhn, 1962, p. 77). The fit between theory and observation is always imperfect. When there is a tacit agreement among the practitioners of a science that the fit is good enough, the fundamental theory, the central paradigm, remains unquestioned. This corresponds to what Kuhn described as the phase of "normal science," a period where there is a sense of well-being concerning the future of the science; it is a period of optimism and confidence. For example, Anna Freud's *The Ego and the Mechanisms of Defense* (1936) is a direct expansion of "The Ego and the Id" (Freud, 1923), an elaboration of her father's observation that defensive processes are themselves unconscious. This book, as is well known, led to a deepening of psychoanalytic technique to include careful analysis of the ego defenses. This in turn consolidated the phase of psychoanalytic history that is associated with the term "ego psychology," a time of comparative confidence and optimism in the future of our science.

The second phase of scientific evolution occurs when there is less certainty regarding the ability of the central paradigm to organize the facts of the science. In this phase, in contrast to the sense of optimism of "normal science," there is a sense of disquietude which may at times approach the intensity of an actual crisis regarding the future of the science itself. There are two possibilities: Either the central paradigm can be modified in accordance with new facts, or the paradigm itself has to be abandoned, in which case a scientific revolution has taken place (provided, of course, that a more successful theory can be found).

Psychoanalysis is at present in this second phase of scientific development. "The Ego and the Id" remains the central paradigm of psychoanalysis: Can it be modified in accordance with new facts of clinical experience or, as some critics have maintained, should it be abandoned? The historian of science provides us with some comfort, for he tells us that our own uncertainty and disquietude regarding the future of our science, which Anna Freud described as a sense of anarchy (1972), are reflections of nothing more than necessary processes of scientific change. We know that "The Ego and the Id" was itself the result of the discrepancy between clinical facts and theory—a previous phase of Freud's psychoanalytic thinking that might be termed "prestructural" (Gill, 1963; Arlow and Brenner, 1964). The new clinical fact was Freud's recognition of the ubiquity of unconscious guilt, so that the quality of consciousness could not be used to differentiate the repressed from the repressing forces.

The new clinical knowledge that now provides the most

direct challenge to "The Ego and the Id" can be subsumed under the broad term "the psychopathology of object relations." In contrast to the more classical character neuroses, such as the obsessive-compulsive or hysterical character neuroses, where internal versus environmental etiological factors are understood to be a complementary series, here the balance of the etiological agents are weighted in the direction of an actual failure of the human environment. The arrest and regression of instinctual and ego development are thought to be secondary to this environmental failure. The environmental failure may be massive and obvious, such as a failure of a constant and reliable maternal object in the first and second years of life, or the failure may take more subtle forms, such as a failure of the mother to accept the growing autonomy and individuality of the young child, thus interfering with its sense of identity and separateness.

Several nosological terms have been used to describe the patients from whom these fundamental observations are drawn. Although the syndromes to which the terms refer differ from each other and there is as yet no commonly accepted psychoanalytic nomenclature, such patients have been described as "schizoid," as having "narcissistic character disorders" or being "borderline" cases. In contrast to the more "classical" neurotic, they have great difficulty in forming a therapeutic alliance, and in contrast to the patients whom Freud described, one does not always have the sense that there are two separate people in the consulting room. In addition to overwhelming intrapsychic conflicts there are fundamental conflicts between the person and the environment—conflicts that Freud once believed to be characteristic of the psychoses (Freud, 1924a, b). It is this new dimension of object relations that has yet to be integrated within Freud's model of "The Ego and the Id."

If the need for object ties is instinctive, where shall these instincts be placed—are they to be in the ego or the id? Fairbairn's answer was that they were ego instincts—that the ego was primarily object seeking and not pleasure seeking:

> The basic conception which I advanced on that occasion and to which I still adhere, is to the effect that libido is primarily object-seeking (rather than pleasure-seeking, as in the classical theory), and that it is to disturbances in the object relationships of the developing ego that we must look for the ultimate origin of all psychopathological conditions [1944, p. 82].

Fairbairn concluded quite logically that if it is true that no impulses can be regarded as existing in the absence of an ego structure, it will no longer be possible to preserve any psychological distinction between the id and the ego.

Fairbairn's theory has not replaced "The Ego and the Id." His was an unsuccessful revolution. As he has few adherents among contemporary psychoanalysts, it may be thought that I have exaggerated his influence. Nevertheless, the questions he raised remain unanswered. Are the instincts that underlie object relations part of the id or the ego? What is the influence of object relations upon the impulses of the id? If these questions cannot be answered, i.e., if object relations theory cannot be integrated within "The Ego and the Id," the latter will not survive as the central paradigm of psychoanalysis. This chapter represents an attempt to show how such an integration is possible. To return to the earlier question, it is my belief that "The Ego and the Id" can be revised in accordance with these newer clinical facts, that "the paradigm can be preserved," and that we are not yet at the stage of scientific anarchy or scientific revolution.

II.

From the beginning Freud was led to his formulations of the structure of the mind through the description of antithetical forces. In a larger sense, antithetical relationships provide a certain classificatory schema. Thus "The Ego and the Id" serves to place phenomena in different classes. Starting from the age-old distinction between reason and passion, Freud differentiated two categories of energy: the bound energy of the rational ego from the free energy of the irrational id. Further, he contrasted the relative organization of the ego with the relative disorganization of the "steaming cauldron" of the id.[1] Perhaps the most fundamental antithesis that Freud described resulted from the fact that the ego alone has direct contact with the external world, whereas the id is confined to the interior of the mental apparatus.

. . . the ego is that part of the id which has been modified by the direct influence of the external world through the medium of the *Pcpt.-Cs.;* in a sense it is an extension of the surface-differentiation. Moreover, the ego seeks to bring the influence of the external world to bear upon the id and its tendencies, and endeavours to substitute the reality principle for the pleasure principle which reigns unrestrictedly in the id. For the ego, perception plays the part which in the id falls to instinct. The ego represents what may be called reason and common sense, in contrast to the id, which contains the passions [1923, p. 25].

Freud here is basing his differentiation of the ego from the id upon the fundamental biological distinction between the individual and the species. If the ego is formed as a result of the interaction of the id and the external world,

---

[1]Gill (1963) and Schur (1966) observed that the id, too, is organized.

it rests as it were as a follicle upon the id and reflects the individual's acquired experience, whereas the id, as the repository of instincts, contains the experience of the species acquired through the processes of evolution. (The fact that Freud believed in Lamarckian mechanisms of inheritance does not detract from this fundamental differentiation.)

> The experiences of the ego seem at first to be lost for inheritance; but, when they have been repeated often enough and with sufficient strength in many individuals in successive generations, they transform themselves, so to say, into experiences of the id, the impressions of which are preserved by heredity [Freud, 1923, p. 38].

Unfortunately, however, as is true of most sciences, the initial clarity of a theoretical vision may be blurred by the accretion of further knowledge. Freud's vision of the ego as a plastic organ moulded by individual experience has been blurred by our general acceptance of Hartmann's (1939) view that the ego is in part autonomous, as it contains certain prestructured, biologically given modes of adaptation to the environment. Our more sophisticated knowledge of the ego has unfortunately marred the beautiful simplicity of Freud's earlier tripartite model. There can no longer be sharp differentiation of biological categories: assigning to the id that which is inherited and assigning to the ego that which is formed principally "by accidental and contemporary events." This in turn has led, as we all are aware, to an expansion of the concept of the ego at the expense of the concept of the id, so that now for many psychoanalysts, the concept of the id has suffered from an erosion of meaning (Marcovitz, 1963; Hayman, 1969).

Whereas the earlier model implied distinctions between

structures of the mind shared by the species and those created by man himself through culture, Hartmann showed convincingly that the ego is not simply formed anew in each individual: "The individual does not acquire all the apparatuses which are put into the service of the ego in the course of development: perception, motility, intelligence, etc. rest on constitutional givens" (1939, p. 101).

Rapaport (1958) extended the description of the ego's autonomy to include "memory apparatus, the motive apparatus, the conceptual apparatus and the threshold apparatuses, including the drive and affect discharge thresholds." It should be noted, however, that these biologically determined ego functions are analogous, not to instincts but more to physiological regulatory mechanisms. They are not instincts for they are not powerful motivating forces. For this reason Hartmann's contribution, although a significant modification of "The Ego and the Id," did not threaten the paradigm itself but limited its usefulness as a classificatory schema, for the ego not less than the id is formed by the experience of the species transmitted by the evolutionary process. It no longer could be maintained that the id is phylogenetically or ontogenetically older than the ego. Hartmann's contribution led to the new conceptualization that the ego and the id develop out of an undifferentiated phase (Hartmann, Kris, and Loewenstein 1946).

Now it is also well known that Freud seemed to have modified his view of the ego in "Analysis Terminable and Interminable," where he also indicated an undifferentiated phase: "But we shall not overlook the fact that the id and the ego are originally one; nor does it imply any mystical overvaluation of heredity if we think it credible that, even before the ego has come into existence, the lines of development, trends and reactions which it will later exhibit, are already laid down for it" (1937a, p. 240). But there is some question whether Freud really modified his earlier view of the ego. For in the "Outline" (1940a) Freud appears to have returned to his original formulation:

> The other agency of the mind, which we believe we know best and in which we recognize ourselves most easily—what is known as the *ego*—has been developed out of the id's cortical layer, which, through being adapted to the reception and exclusion of stimuli, is in direct contact with the external world *(reality)*. Starting from conscious perception it has subjected to its influence ever larger regions and deeper strata of the id, and, in the persistence with which it maintains its dependence on the external world, it bears the indelible stamp of its origin (as it might be, 'Made in Germany') [1940a, p. 198].

And Freud says: "We have repeatedly had to insist on the fact that the ego owed its origin as well as the most important of its acquired characteristics to its relation to the real external world" (p. 302). In his final position it seemed that he acknowledged the ego's inherited characteristics but considered them to be of secondary importance in comparison to the ego's acquired characteristics.

III.

The relative strength of the ego in regulating the instinctual demands of the id was expressed by Freud in his famous metaphor of the man on horseback

> . . . who has to hold in check the superior strength of the horse; with this difference, that the rider tries to do so with his own strength while the ego uses borrowed forces. The analogy may be carried a little further. Often a rider, if he is not to be parted from his horse, is obliged to guide it where it wants to go; so in the same way the ego is in the

habit of transforming the id's will into action as if it were its own [1923, p. 25].

The clinical process that gives added content to this metaphor is that of identification. It is by means of identification that the ego is able to gain power over the id and mitigate its demands. The clearest example of this is given by Freud in his description of the formation of the super-ego as the heir to the Oedipus complex. The intense instinctual demands of the Oedipus complex are modulated, i.e., partly desexualized or sublimated, by a complex set of identifications with both parents. Freud summarized it as follows:

> The broad general outcome of the sexual phase dominated by the Oedipus complex may, therefore, be taken to be the forming of a precipitate in the ego, consisting of these two identifications in some way united with each other. This modification of the ego retains its special position; it confronts the other contents of the ego as an ego ideal or super-ego [1923, p. 34].

Freud suggested, "It may be that this identification is the sole condition under which the id can give up its objects" (1923, p. 29).[2]

It is now an accepted and undisputed fact that identifications of this sort take place not only during the oedipal period, but during the preoedipal period as well. Further, and most significantly, these earlier identifications, primarily with the mother, the first loved object of both sexes, are taken not only into the superego but into the ego or,

---

[2]Freud's discussion of instinctual defusion may belie this point, for he indicated that with the formation of the superego a quantum of aggression is freed. It is possible, as Jacobson (1964) proposed, that Freud was thinking in this instance of the superego of the severely depressed person—a pathological miscarriage of a normal process.

more accurately, as will be discussed, the self (Jacobson, 1964). Although Freud (1923) described primarily super-ego identifications, it would be perfectly consistent to consider ego identifications as well. He himself had made the same distinction in discussing identifications (Freud, 1921). Freud, however, did not always carefully distinguish ego identifications comprising the sense of self, or, as we call it now, the sense of identity, from the use of the term "ego" referring to a system.

Patients who have disturbances in object relations invariably have an abnormality in the sense of identity. This clinical fact has occupied analysts for at least the last 20 years, and the literature in this area is voluminous. This is not, as we have said, a subject that Freud considered in 1923 in "The Ego and the Id."

The study of borderline and narcissistic character disorders (schizoid disorders, in the older English literature: see Fairbairn [1940], Modell [1963], Kernberg [1967], and Kohut [1971]) has confirmed Freud's central thesis that an identification serves to mitigate the intensity of instinctual demands. For in the borderline patient we can observe a miscarriage of the process of identification, a failure of the process, a failure to take something in (Modell, 1968). We suspect that this failure occurs in the preoedipal period and results in the failure to identify with the "good" mother. But this failure of identification may also involve the father and result in a relatively defective formation of the superego with the persistence of an inordinate quantum of unconscious guilt (Modell, 1971b). While the failure of paternal identifications represents a more controversial observation, the failure of maternal identification has been widely observed and can today be taken as an uncontested clinical observation, despite the diversity of theoretical formulations. These observations confirm Freud's prediction that a failure of identification would lead to a failure in the capacity to sublimate instinctual demands. For the borderline patient demonstrates an intensity of ambivalence and an inability to distinguish between instinctual needs and instinctual wishes. Affects associated with anger and love are experienced with such intensity as to induce a sense of annihilation (see Zetzel, 1965). It would appear that the drive/affect discharge thresholds that Rapaport suggested as autonomous ego functions may be modified by this relative miscarriage of the process of identification.

These studies have further taught us that in order for a "good" identification to take place there must be something provided for by the environment, i.e., provided by the quality of the object relationship (Winnicott, 1960, 1962b). This is an area of clinical knowledge that Freud did not have available to him, but it may not be too much to suggest that these clinical observations demonstrating the need for an environmental fitting in, that is, the need for, in Winnicott's terms, a "good enough" object relationship, go to the heart of the problem of the relationship between object ties and instincts.

The objection will be raised that the failure to form an identification cannot be equated with a failure in object relationships, for we know that identifications are not absent in borderline patients; indeed, it would be difficult to imagine a human being whose ego and superego were devoid of identifications. However, if we examine the identifications of borderline patients more closely, we note that they are restricted to objects created by the subject or to the negative aspects of the object. The clearest example of identification with an object created by the subject is that with the fantasied omnipotence of the parents, in both its positve and negative forms. Identifications with the negative aspects of the object are not necessarily created by the subject; they serve fundamentally defensive purposes and are not used in the process of sublimation of instinct.

In this category is Anna Freud's (1936) observation of the child's identification with the aggressor, where the child becomes the frightening one rather than the one who was frightened. Such identifications with negative qualities are also characteristic of depressive illnesses; it is as if the person is saying, "I would preserve my belief in the goodness of my parents by taking their badness into me."

With these qualifications in mind, we can repeat: The ego is able to gain control over the instincts of the id by means of an identification with a "good" object. This identification, in turn, requires the fitting in of something provided by the human environment, i.e., the fitting in of "good enough" object relations.

IV.

If the need for an object reflects the workings of an instinct,[3] it will have to be acknowledged that the concept of instinct here is quite different from Freud's use of the term. As Freud (1915a) acknowledged, instinct is a biological and not primarily a psychoanalytic concept, and to this extent psychoanalysis remains dependent upon biology. This, in turn, has led to some confusion regarding the relationship of psychoanalysis to other sciences: On one extreme, there are those (Peterfreund, 1971) who see psychoanalysis simply as a branch of biology, and others (Loewald, 1971) who would wish to see psychoanalysis more completely self-sufficient, with reference to no other science but itself. There is a significant distinction between sciences that are complete unto themselves—i.e., that re-

---

[3]It would appear that the need for other human objects is a biological given, perhaps a reflection of man's prolonged infantile dependency. The biological significance of object relations was clearly demonstrated by Spitz (1945), who showed in his well-known study that hospitalized infants who are grossly deprived of adequate mothering may actually withdraw from their environment to the point of death.

main independent of other sciences by restricting the field of observation—and sciences that are unrestricted. The only restricted science is physics. Most sciences are unrestricted in the sense that an investigator must be prepared to follow problems into any other science whatsoever (Pantin, 1968). A science may utilize the findings of other branches of knowledge and yet remain unique. This is true, I believe, of psychoanalysis in that it rests upon both biology and the social sciences, but its fundamental data come from the psychoanalytic situation itself, a unique field of observation. Although we can assume that the evolution of instinct is continuous, that there are elements in man's instinctual life that he shares with lower animals, biology also demonstrates that instincts are species-specific—that the instinctual life of man in certain regards may be unique. This fact was acknowledged by Freud's English translators, who adopted the convention of using the term "instinctual" to refer to the instincts of man and reserving "instinctive" for the instincts of other animals.

This brief discussion of the relationship of biology to psychoanalysis was necessary, as the instinctual nature of object ties has received considerable confirmation from recent ethological studies. The principal psychoanalytic spokesman for this point of view has been Bowlby (1969). Unfortunately, Bowlby chose to take the stance of a behavioral scientist and ignore the distinction between instinctual and instinctive, as if man were simply another species observed from the outside. (For a similar criticism, see A. Freud, Schur, and Spitz [1960]; Engel [1971].) Because of this epistemological error, his work tends to remain unaccepted by most psychoanalysts, and this criticism has tended to deflect attention from Bowlby's most important contribution—his demonstration of the instinctual basis of object relationships.

V.

In "The Ego and the Id" Freud employed the concept of instinct that he had already elaborated earlier, principally in "Instincts and Their Vicissitudes" (Freud, 1915a). Instinct was viewed as a stimulus applied to the mind. It is something arising from *within* the organism, from a physiological source which exerts pressure, that is, a demand upon the mind for work. It has an aim, which is to "establish satisfaction by removing a state of excitation" (see also Schur [1966], p. 43). The essential qualities of what we shall now call the instincts of the id are that they arise from within the organism, that gratification involves some form of discharge. This is true of both sexual and aggressive instincts. In contrast to the instincts of the id, the instincts associated with object relations are quieter. Furthermore, it is difficult regarding the instinct of object relations to speak of a specific physiological source, as is true for those instincts arising within the organism. The stimulus for the gratification of the instincts arises, not from within the organism but from the environment; the gratification of the instinct requires a fitting in of specific responses from other persons. The model of an individual mental apparatus isolated from the environment is not applicable to those ego instincts underlying the formation of object relationships.[4] The model here is one of process and interaction, not of discharge (this is the point that has been most criticized by the movement described as general systems theory; see von Bertalanffy, [1968]); it is a view of an organism in its environment; it is a view based principally upon observations of the earliest object relationship, that of an infant and its mother. As Winnicott stated, "The

---

[4]The ethologist Hinde (1970), who prefers the term "motivational systems" to the term "instinct," described such systems as either stable or labile in the face of environmental influences.

infant and the maternal care together form a unit; there is no such thing as infant" (1960, p. 39). The existence of the ego instincts of object relations does not in any sense negate the existence of the instincts of the id, as Freud described. What I am proposing is that there are two transcendent classes of instinct, classes that correspond to the divisions between the ego and the id. I propose that we retain the concept of the id as the locus for Freud's dual instinct theory—those instincts arising from *within* the organism seeking tension reduction. As the ego, in contrast to the id, is the sole portion of the mind in contact with the environment, the locus for the instincts of object relations must be placed within the ego. This formulation preserves Freud's fundamental distinction between the ego and the id. In this regard, I believe that Fairbairn was essentially correct in stating that the ego is object-seeking and not pleasure-seeking, but he impeded acceptance of his major contribution by denying the existence of the instincts of the id. As the instincts of object relations require a fitting in of something from the environment, they must be assigned to that portion of the mind that is orientated to the external world, i.e., the ego. Although we have of necessity used the term "ego instincts," this must not be confused with Freud's earlier usage that was intended to denote the instincts of self-preservation, as contrasted with the sexual instincts (see Bibring [1969]). Although the instincts of object relations are indeed, as Spitz showed, essential to the preservation of the self, they should not for this reason be confused with the older notion of a uniform instinct of self-preservation.

VI.

Having established that there are two transcendent classes of instinct, we must examine their relationship.

Observations derived from child development and the psychoanalyst's knowledge obtained directly from psychoanalytic situations suggest that object relationships provide the setting for the normal unfolding of the instincts of the id. As we have said, the instincts of object relations, unlike those of the id, operate quietly. In normal development they are taken for granted and their presence is known only through psychopathology. We have come to believe that, in addition to the transference, there is an actual object tie between the analyst and his patient (see Gitelson, 1962; Stone, 1961; Greenson and Wexler, 1969, 1970; Zetzel, 1958). The importance of the "actual" object relationship is in direct proportion to the degree of privation the patient has suffered in his object relationships during his development. When the privation has been minimal, this actual relationship can be taken for granted, and accordingly, the therapeutic alliance can be established without undue difficulty. This corresponds to the situation of the "well chosen" or "ideal" analytic patient. Most people depart from this ideal to some degree.

We have learned from recent experience that the analytic relationship itself, at its deepest unconscious level, is, in Winnicott's words, a "maternal holding environment" (see also Gitelson [1962]). We have learned the necessity of abstaining from any gratification of the instincts of the id during the process of psychoanalysis. However, this rule of abstinence does not apply to the instincts of object relations. Here, in contrast to instincts seeking discharge, the gratification itself remains silent. Where there has been marked privation, the gratification derived from the analytic situation in this fashion seems to take precedence over everything else. We are familiar with the period at the beginning of the analysis where nothing seems to be happening, where the therapeutic alliance is minimal and where it seems as if the work of analysis has not yet begun.

We learn in retrospect that the analytic relationship itself is a holding environment, providing a reaffirmation of the constancy and reliability of the person of the analyst. A silent process of instinctual gratification occurs. For some patients, such as those designated as borderline cases, this process may extend for a period of years; in other patients it is present only at the start of the analysis; for the "ideal case" it may be absent. If successful, we believe that this silent process results in an identification with a "good" object. As emphasized above, this identification requires that something is provided by the human environment: There must be a fitting in of something given by the other person.

The development of object relations is a necessary precondition of the taming or sublimation of the instincts of the id. Although Loewald (1971) did not propose these two separate classes of instinct, he did state something that comes very close to our own position: "Instincts understood as psychic, motivational forces become organized as such through interactions within a psychic field consisting originally of the mother-child (psychic) unit" (p. 118). I would not, however, limit the consideration of object relations to the earliest object relation, that is, the child and his mother. We must include later stages as well, encompassing the paternal as well as the maternal object. For, as I have described earlier (Modell, 1968, 1971b), object relationships with the father may, as Freud also suggested, play a special role in the formation of the superego.

VII.

We spoke in general terms of a fitting in of something from the environment and the processes of instinctual gratification of object relations that proceed silently. We must now examine these processes more specifically and precisely. As mentioned above, these are processes that are taken for granted in normal development but appear with greater clarity when there is psychopathology. There seems to be general agreement that in addition to the reliability and constancy of the first object, the maternal object must be able at an appropriate time to introduce some measure of privation. Winnicott expressed this as follows:

> There comes into existence an ego-relatedness between mother and baby, from which the mother recovers, and out of which the infant may eventually build the idea of a person in the mother. From this angle the recognition of the mother as a person comes in a positive way, normally, and not out of the experience of the mother as the symbol of frustration. The mother's failure to adapt to the earliest phase does not produce anything but annihilation of the infant's self [1956, p. 304].

Mahler described this process as an emergence from a symbiotic stage to one of individuation (Mahler [1967]; see also Pollock [1964]). The term "symbiosis" does underline the instinctual nature of the infant-mother tie but is, I believe, misleading as it implies an equivalence of need.

Good-enough object relations not only lead to the ego's control of the id but are essential for the formation of a special structure of the ego itself—the sense of self or the sense of identity. The developing child is dependent upon the mother for this sense of his own uniqueness. The earliest sense of identity may be induced by the experience of the child perceiving its mother's face responding to it (Spitz, 1945).

This recognition and support of individuation embody a process that is distinct from the reliability and consistency of the object. When all is well, this process occurs silently and goes unnoticed. However, mothers who are unable to accept the child's separateness and individuality may pro-

mote the development of a primary rather than a secondary identification with herself. This is seen in certain
narcissistic character disturbances, where the sense of individuality is obliterated as a result of a total rather than
a partial identification with the maternal object. This total
identification with the maternal object may also lead to a
certain "falseness" of affective expression, a condition similar to that of the "as if" personality described by Deutsch
(1942) and to the formation of the "false self" of Winnicott
(see also Mahler [1967]; Khan [1971]). The mother's inability to accept the separateness and uniqueness of her
child may be repeated in the transference with the roles
reversed. Here the patient is unable to accept the analyst's
separateness and uniqueness and is unable to believe that
the analyst is different in any way from the patient. This
has been described as the "mirror transference" by Kohut
(1971).

   The promotion of individuation by means of an object
tie may be repeated silently in the analytic process itself.
For the analyst's perception of the patient (in Buber's term)
as "thou" may provide a gratification that has been absent
in earlier development. Erikson's observations regarding
the restructuring of the sense of identity that occurs in
adolescence are well known. They refer to an analogous
process where, instead of the instinctual tie between
mother and child, a peer group assumes the role of the
mother in the bestowal of identity.

   As noted above, the concept of identity and self-representation was absent in "The Ego and the Id." Hartmann
showed that this concept can be fitted into the fundamental
paradigm without challenging the paradigm itself (Hartmann, 1950, p. 85): "It would therefore be clarifying if we
define narcissism as the libidinal cathexis not of the ego
but of the self. (It might also be useful to apply the term
self-representation as opposed to object representation.)"

Hartmann wished to make it clear that the self that Freud described as beloved in narcissistic states is not theoretically equivalent to the concept of the ego. He suggested that the self that is loved can be conceptualized as an ego structure—a part of the ego, but not equivalent to the ego itself. Because the concept of self-representation was seen by Hartmann as analogous to object representation, there has been a tendency on the part of some authors (especially Jacobson) to reify the latter concept; they treat it as if it were equivalent to and symmetrical with self-representation. Although there are undoubtedly memories of fantasies and objects that can be called object representations, they are not organized into a psychic structure as is the self-representation. It would not be an exaggeration to speak of the sense of self as a psychic organ; for the content of this sense influences one's perception of others. Without the development of a sense of self that is unique and separate from others, one is unable to perceive and acknowledge the existence of the separateness and individuality of other persons. Such functions cannot be attributed to the "object representations."[5]

VIII.

Our suggestion regarding the instincts that motivate object relations do not negate Freud's concept of instinct, as Fairbairn has proposed—instead they are to be understood as two different classes of instinct that have direct application to the psychoanalytic theory of affects. The usefulness of a theory resides in its ability to unify seemingly disparate phenomena, to effect a synthesis that had pre-

---

[5] I discussed elsewhere the fact that the concept of object representations is derived originally from the eighteenth-century philosophy of John Locke, which may have been uncritically incorporated into the fabric of psychoanalytic theory (Modell, 1968).

viously been lacking. It has long been known that the psychoanalytic theory of affects has remained outside the paradigm of the ego and the id. Rapaport's statement of 1953 has remained unchallenged: "We do not possess a systematic statement of the psychoanalytic theory of affects." This has largely been due to the fact that although the ego has been viewed as the locus of affects, the sources of affects were understood as drive representations, instinctual derivatives serving as safety valves for drive cathexis (Rapaport, 1954). This so-called discharge theory would view affects as arising within the interior of the mind as if the mental apparatus were isolated from its environment. This conception is belied by the obvious communicative function of affects, the contagiousness of affects that Freud observed in groups and which forms the basis of empathy (Burlingham, 1967), i.e., the basis of psychoanalytic knowledge itself.

We may still retain the Freudian view that affects are instinctual representations, but representations of both the instincts of the id seeking discharge and the instincts that motivate object relations—instincts oriented toward the human environment. Affects, as is the ego, are Janus-faced—they face both the interior of the organism and the external objects of the environment.

A clinical example may demonstrate this duality more clearly. The isolation of affects in an obsessive-compulsive person may superficially appear similar to the withdrawal of a narcissistic individual. However, the affect blocks may relate to different psychic systems. In the obsessive-compulsive, we understand his isolating affects from ideation because of his fear of being overwhelmed by the intensity of feeling. Here the affects can be correctly linked to the instincts of the id—the danger comes from within the psychic apparatus itself. This corresponds quite accurately to the classical description given by Anna Freud in *The Ego and the Mechanisms of Defense.* However, in the narcissistic person the affect block is a reflection of his state of non-relatedness (Chapter 2). He acts as if he is self-sufficient and does not seek gratification from the person of the analyst. The absence of affects reflects the fundamental disturbance of the object relationship between the patient and the analyst, for the existence of an object tie is signified by the sharing and communication of affects. (Of course, disturbances in both affect systems may occur simultaneously.)

The instinctual origin of the communicative aspects of affects has been observed by ethologists who noted that for a primate group affects are the medium through which intergroup communication is achieved, the medium through which vital motivational information is conveyed. Knowledge of these moods is necessary to ensure the survival of the group as a whole (quoted by Modell, 1971b). It can be seen that psychoanalytic knowledge itself also rests upon a similar instinctual base.

IX.

We have noted above that Freud's model of the mind formed in a certain sense a classificatory schema, a schema that would bring antithetical processes into some relationship with one another. We have seen also how certain antithetical relationships had to be discarded as a result of further knowledge. Hartmann's contribution has destroyed the antithesis of the ego as the repository of the accidental and experiential as contrasted to the evolutionary structure of the id.

What then are the antitheses that are preserved? Freud's fundamental antithesis concerning the ego and the id is as true now as it was 50 years ago: that the ego alone is in contact with the external world and the id corresponds to that which is the interior of the organism cut off from the external world. This antithesis has far-reaching implications, for it encompasses the fact that the psychic agency that mediates the development of object relations is the ego; hence we have posited the necessity for placing the instincts of object relations within the ego. We can also adhere to Freud's description that the ego obtains control of the id by means of the process of identification. However, we must add to Freud's description the observation derived from the psychopathology of object relations: that for identification to serve the process of "taming" the id, identification must be supported by a "good enough" object relationship.

Although the antithesis between the ego and the id in terms of what is experiential and what is biological can no longer be maintained, it can still be claimed that although both the ego and the id have an evolutionary history, the ego alone contains a record of created history, that is, of culture. The ever-changing nosology of the neuroses is the most direct indication of the impact of historical processes upon the ego. There is little doubt, for example, that the increased number of narcissistic character disorders reflects in part the changing pattern of child-rearing. This psychohistorical point of view has been associated with the contribution of Erikson (1959), who demonstrated in his theory of the life cycle that the ego itself is modified by historical forces. This has important and far-reaching epistemological implications for psychoanalysis. It means that the search for general laws of the mind, analogous to the laws of physiology or biology, is applicable only to the id, and those portions of the ego that are ahistorical. Further, the notion of a species-generalizable psychic apparatus is something that would also be applicable only to the id and ahistorical portions of the ego. For those portions of the ego that are culturally and historically determined, we must employ a different epistemology—one that would share certain assumptions with the epistemology of social science (see Abrams [1971]).

Acknowledgement of two transcendent classes of instincts, as we have suggested, preserves the distinction between the ego and the id. As we have noted, the early studies of the psychopathology of object relationships, such as the work of Fairbairn, tended to obliterate the distinction between the ego and the id by denying the existence of the instincts of the id. Object relation studies have emphasized the importance of the contribution of the human environment, the fact that the instincts subserving object relations do not arise only from the interior of the organism but require a fitting in from the external human environment for their normal development. This has led to certain modifications of Freud's earlier view of the relationship between the ego and the environment. We no longer think of the ego and its human environment as sharply demarcated. We know both from Winnicott's studies of the transitional object and from certain primitive transference phenomena that the external object, that is, the human environment, is in part subjectively created by the subject. This is a phenomenon that is not limited to psychopathology as it may be the base upon which all esthetic experience rests (Winnicott, 1971; Modell, 1970).

Winnicott suggested that in addition to subjective psychic reality and objective external reality, there is a transitional intermediate area of shared subjectivity. This is an area which we are only beginning to understand and which will undoubtedly lead to further modifications of Freud's model of "The Ego and the Id."

Chapter 14

Does Metapsychology Still Exist?

Metapsychology has been attacked recently from many directions. In this broadly based attack one should distinguish those who wish to discard or modify Freud's metapsychology because it is no longer congruent with observation and those who see metapsychology as irrelevant as they no longer share Freud's belief that psychoanalysis is a form of natural science. For critics in the latter category the problem is not only empirical, for they question the very nature of psychoanalysis itself.

An early example of one who discarded Freud's metapsychology on empirical grounds was Fairbairn (1952), who, through observation of what was then called the schizoid personality, questioned the validity of Freud's libido theory and the significance of erogenous zones for ego development. He believed that libido is essentially object-seeking in that the erotogenic zones are not the primary determinants of libidinal aims but channels mediating the primary object-seeking aims of the libido. He replaced Freud's description of the mental apparatus in terms of ego, id, and superego with structures that represent the relationship of objects that have been internalized. He substituted for Freud's metapsychology the concept of the central ego, the libidinal ego, and the internal saboteur.

More recently Kohut (1977), as the result of observations of what he termed "narcissistic personality" (a designation that I suspect may cover the same nosological territory as Fairbairn's schizoid personality) also proposed a sweeping revision of Freud's metapsychology. It was based not so much on internalized structural representations of object relations but on the psychology of the self. Kohut, as did Fairbairn before him, also cast doubts on Freud's libidinal theory but, unlike Fairbairn, he minimized the importance of the superego. In Kohut's view, the superego is associated with the Oedipus complex (thus minimizing its preoedipal history); as the Oedipus complex is no longer viewed as the center of the neurosis, the superego also disappears from view. Tragic Man has replaced Guilty Man. What is called for here is a revision of metapsychology and not necessarily a decision as to the continued existence of metapsychology itself.

For those who believe that psychoanalysis is a hermeneutic discipline more allied to historical or textual interpretations and not a branch of natural science, metapsychology is viewed as irrelevant. For these critics the study of linguistics and the philosophy of language, not biology, provides the elements of coherence. Such critics include Lacan (1977), who claimed that the unconscious is structured as a language, believing that linguistic theory and not metapsychology is the instrument that brings some measure of order and coherence to the psychoanalytic experience. Here we would also include Schafer (1976), who also asserted that structured language will bring some measure of coherence to psychoanalysis. Unlike Lacan, he relied not on the contributions of the continental school but on the English studies of the philosophy of language, with special emphasis on the work of Wittgenstein and his notion of "language games." He believes that psychoanalytic observations and psychoanalytic propositions can be restated in everyday "action" language and that is what frees psychoanalysis from the misleading biological and mechanistic metaphors of Freud's metapsychology.

There are others who are not necessarily identified with this hermeneutic point of view but nevertheless question the continued existence of metapsychology. George Klein (1976) thought that there are two psychoanalytic theories: a clinical theory which he wished to preserve and a metapsychological theory which he claimed is a theory employed "to explain" the clinical theory.

It can be demonstrated that metapsychology does not explain clinical theory but that clinical theory is derived from metapsychology. For example, Anna Freud's (1936) book, *The Ego and the Mechanisms of Defense*, preeminently clinical theory, could not have been written if Freud had not revised his metapsychology to provide a new mental model in which the unconscious forces were viewed not as a system separate from the ego but as part of the ego itself.

Klein believed that metapsychology contains biological assumptions that are irrelevant to clinical understanding and that "Freud's metapsychology is not distinctly psychoanalytic . . . it reduced human behavior to a conceptual domain which requires a different kind of observational data from that available in the analytic situation" (p. 48). Klein (1976) raised questions that are not only empirical but also epistemological. He saw metapsychology simply as an expression of Freud's philosophy of science. Gill (1976) carried Klein's argument one step further to state that metapsychology contains biological or physiological assumptions couched in the language of psychology, that metapsychology is not psychology at all.

From all this it can be inferred that the definition of metapsychology is in the eye of the beholder. Yet despite

Freud's own ambiguities concerning this definition, there are certain texts which by general agreement can be labelled metapsychological. Freud's five papers on metapsychology were originally part of a collection of twelve papers that Freud had intended to publish as a book under the title "Preliminaries to Metapsychology" which, according to Strachey (Freud, 1915a, p. 105), was to provide a stable theoretical foundation for psychoanalysis. Freud stated explicitly (1917a, p. 222): "The intention of this series is to clarify and carry deeper the theoretical assumptions on which a psycho-analytic system could be founded." Of the original twelve papers only five have survived, and the fate of the other seven remains unknown; it is presumed that Freud destroyed them. One also applies the term "metapsychological" to all of Freud's major theoretical works, which would include the five papers just mentioned, "Group Psychology," "The Ego and the Id," and "Beyond the Pleasure Principle." Although Freud did not use the term "metapsychology" in "The Interpretation of Dreams," it could be applied retrospectively to the seventh chapter.

If we view these works as a totality, it appears to me that there are at least three different functions that can be attributed to metapsychology.

One: A selection of psychological phenomena that could be termed universal in the sense that they are characteristic of the human species. A partial list would include: the primary and secondary processes; the repetition compulsion; identification and internalization; the origin and development of the Oedipus complex; the development of the superego and the ego ideal. It is evident that this attempt to select and describe the psychological processes of the highest generalizability is also an attempt to reach a biological bedrock. Processes that are common to the species as a whole are by definition biological.

Two: Metapsychology is not only generalization of the highest order but also contains, as Freud observed, theoretical assumptions upon which a psychological system can be founded.

Although Freud was undoubtedly burdened by the intellectual baggage of his particular historical and cultural stratum (as has been so frequently asserted in recent years), his account of the use of theory would not be rejected by contemporary epistemologists (1915a):

> We have often heard it maintained that sciences should be built up on clear and sharply defined basic concepts. In actual fact no science, not even the most exact, begins with such definitions. The true beginning of scientific activity consists rather in describing phenomena and then in proceeding to group, classify and correlate them. Even at the stage of description, it is not possible to avoid applying certain abstract ideas to the material in hand, ideas derived from somewhere or other but certainly not from the new observations alone. Such ideas—which will later become the basic concepts of the science—are still more indispensable as the material is further worked over [p. 117].

Freud understood that the assumptions underlying psychoanalytic theory were themselves historically determined and therefore in a state of constant evolution. In addition to the historically bound nature of these assumptions underlying our theory, Freud further recognized its dependent nature: that some of its fundamental assumptions are derived from other neighboring sciences such as biology.[1]

[1]Gill (1976) was correct that metapsychology refers to biological phenomena, but to conclude as he did that metapsychology is not psychology would label as nonpsychological most of what we know as psychoanalysts.

The clearest example is the theory of instincts. We know that metapsychology has been most vulnerable to criticism because Freud accepted as true an assumption from the psychobiology of the nineteenth century—an assumption that unfortunately has proved to be wrong. This is Fechner's constancy principle: "[that] the nervous system is an apparatus which has the function of getting rid of the stimuli that reach it, or of reducing them to the lowest possible level; or which, if it were feasible, would maintain itself in an altogether unstimulated condition" (Freud, 1915a, p. 120).

The problem is not, as some critics would have it, that Freud confused psychology with biology, but that he employed a fallacious biological principle. The mischief that followed from this was considerable: reification of the concept of energy, which in turn lent support to a discharge theory of affects that was not congruent with clinical observation, and so on. Freud based his definition of metapsychology on its second function, that is, consideration of the underlying theoretical assumption: "I propose that when we have succeeded in describing a psychical process in its dynamic, topographical and economic aspects, we should speak of it as a metapsychological presentation" (Freud, 1915b, p. 181). These terms, "dynamic," "topographic," and "economic" carry with them a network of connected notions which may or may not be compatible with each other. This collection of assumptions brought into some systematic relation with each other leads us to the third and final definition of the functions of metapsychology.

Three: Metapsychology as a modeling device; a model is in this sense an imaginary entity, an experiment in thinking that will bring some measure of order to the raw data of psychoanalysis derived from the psychoanalytic situation itself.

In the ideal model there is a "frictionless correspondence" (Berlin, 1979, p. 115) between the perceived entities and the model. As this ideal is never achieved, the usefulness of the model corresponds to the degree to which this ideal is fulfilled. It is important to note that Freud's strategy here is analogous to Galileo's, who dared to describe the world as we do *not* experience it. The world Galileo described cannot be confirmed by direct observation, for our vision tells us that a feather and a cannon ball do not fall at the same rate. Von Weizsacker (1964) contrasted Galileo to Aristotle; Aristotle was too empirical in that he made too much use of common-sense observation in his attempt to preserve the phenomena.

It is, I believe, in recognition of this purely imaginary nature of metapsychology that Freud referred to the "witch" metapsychology (1937a, p. 225). "Without metapsychological speculation and theorizing—I had almost said 'phantasying'—we shall not get another step forward."

When we refer to metapsychology we are describing, therefore, not a single entity but a broad heading that covers at least three distinct functions: one, a generalization of those psychological processes that are species specific; two, an explicit enunciation of those assumptions that underly psychoanalytic theory, including assumptions borrowed from neighboring disciplines, such as biology; and three, a modeling device which is in the nature of a thought experiment, an imaginary entity that brings a measure of order to the primary data of psychoanalysis but does not correspond directly to those data. It is a heuristic device whose usefulness is measured by its correspondence to the perceived entities.

The assumptions that are borrowed from neighboring

sciences are themselves in the process of constant transformation. It is otiose to claim that metapsychology should be discarded as it reflects Freud's now outmoded philosophy of science (Klein, 1976). That Freud's philosophy of science is no longer current we take for granted. One does not for this reason discard metapsychology, but one must revise the epistemological assumptions of metapsychology so that it is in accord with our current outlook.

As metapsychology is also a set of generalizations of the highest order, we assume that such generalizations must rest upon biological assumptions. But this does not mean that such observations are isomorphic with neurophysiological events, as Gill (1976) claimed. What psychoanalysts observe are the psychological representations of the outcome of evolutionary processes which to date are not simply isomorphic with neuropsychology. (A possible exception to this is the distinction between primary and secondary process, which appears to have its analogue in neurophysiology. However, the evidence is still inconclusive [Pribram and Gill, 1976].) The Oedipus complex and its attendant incest taboo are perhaps the clearest example of a psychological generality which rests on the bedrock of biology. It is not isomorphic with any known neurophysiological events and its evolutionary significance is unquestioned. For example, Darlington, a leading geneticist, acknowledged that the incest taboo is the source of a genetic advantage that "has been the decisive agent in holding together not only each human tribe, but also the whole human species" (1969, p. 61).

METAPSYCHOLOGY AND THE FACTS OF PSYCHOANALYSIS

Those who claim that psychoanalysis is a hermeneutic or historical discipline and not a natural science receive

their strongest support from the observation that the relation between the observer and the observed in psychoanalysis is unlike that in any other natural science. Men
have recognized at least since Vico (d. 1744) that there are
two broad categories of knowledge: there is a sense in
which we can know more about other men's experience,
in which we act as participants, than we can ever know
about nonhuman nature, which we can observe only from
the outside. Vico, as we have seen in preceding chapters,
described empathy as a source of knowledge. As a mode
of knowing, empathy has an evident connection to the
esthetic experience—the use of creative imagination. In
psychoanalysis the Cartesian split between the observed
and the observer cannot be maintained. Subject and object
in some fashion enter into each other, so that an intersubjective I-Thou relationship replaces the I-It relationship,
the observational mode of natural science.[2] This was recognized in the early nineteenth century by the poet-psy-
chologist Samuel Taylor Coleridge, whose theory of
knowledge rests on the "coalescence of subject and object"
(Richards, 1969, p. 57): "Into the simplest seeming 'datum'
a constructing, forming activity from the mind has entered.
And the perceiving and the forming are the same. The
subject (the self) has gone into what it perceives and what
it perceives is, in a sense, itself. So the object becomes the
subject and the subject the object." Coleridge was claiming
that the activity of the subject gives meaning to the object.
This view is nearly identical to Winnicott's description of
the subjectively created object. This undoing of the split
between subject and object may be experienced not as an
oceanic merging but as an oscillatory state where sepa-

[2]There is a corrective trend in the contemporary philosophy of science which
acknowledges the psychology of the human observer. See, for example, the work
of Polanyi and Chapter 9.

rateness and fusion are continuously undone (Milner, 1957).

But the analogy of the psychoanalytic situation to an aesthetic experience cannot be carri d too far. Literature and works of art may communicate to us, but they do not respond to our communications. And words by themselves, as we have argued, do not constitute the primary data of psychoanalysis. What endow words with meaning and what constitute the primary data of psychoanalysis are affects. The capacity to know the mind of another rests on the most primitive perceptions of all—the capacity of a child to know the affective state of its mother and conversely the capacity of the mother to "know" the affective state of the child. In this sense the capacity to know the affective state of another antedates the acquisition of language and persists after the acquisition of language. So affects and symbolization are inseparable. This obvious fact has been obscured by the persistent belief that there are separate faculties of feeling and cognition. Freud unfortunately perpetuated this distinction between affects and ideation perhaps, as Pribram and Gill (1976) suggested, because of his proto-neurological theories. Freud believed that the topographic transformations between the preconscious and the unconscious, and ideation and affects, have separate fates. Ideas, unlike affects, have a special relation to verbal residues and therefore a special relationship to the preconscious. This wrong turning of Freud's was especially noted by Green (1977), who emphasized that affects are the carriers of semantic content. In this we fully concur.

If we assume that the affect charges, or their absence, are what give meaning to the communicated words, a great deal falls into place. We are able to describe empathic knowledge on a developmental gradient. There is a state of primitive communication analogous to that between mother and child where affects arising from the object are "placed" in the subject without evidence of conscious intent or the wish to communicate. I refer here to the phenomenon of induced or countertransference affects, which I have discussed in Chapter 2, and which I believe is coincident with the concept of projective identification. In this more primitive form of empathic knowledge, the analyst may observe in himself affects as specific fantasies that may be alien to his own character and infer that certain imagos created within him correspond to imagos within the patient. In the more mature form of empathic knowledge the analyst is said to gain insight by making active use of what he first experiences unconsciously or preconsciously. Here there may be partial or trial identifications with the subject, and the self-object differentiation is maintained. A creative use of empathy may involve, as Milner (1957) indicated, an oscillation between states of fusion and separateness. There are, however, states of noncommunication or of communication of inauthentic affects where the analyst's empathic instrument may have been rendered temporarily inoperative (Modell, 1980). These are states of intense defensiveness or resistance where the patient converts the I-Thou relationship to an I-It relationship. We are now in the position of an outside observer characterizing methods of defense.[3] Observation of such defensive processes places us in the position of a naturalist observer rather than that of a participant observer. We know that shifts from empathic knowledge to the observation of defenses as viewed from the outside may occur rapidly. It requires little effort to shift one's observational set from the I-Thou to the I-It, and indeed such shifts

---

[3]Ricoeur seems to have modified his former view that psychoanalysis is an exclusively hermeneutic discipline. For he also noted that the process of resistance has the nature of a force which may require a natural science model for its interpretation (1977, p. 849).

occur without eliciting any particular notice on the part of the analyst.

The "facts" of psychoanalysis can be described in two broad categories depending on the relation of the observer to the observed. When the analyst and the patient are conjoined in the I-Thou relationship, the facts of psychoanalysis are closer to that of the interpretive, that is, hermeneutic disciplines. It is in this context that psychoanalytic "truth" is established (Loch, 1977). However, the analyst is also in the position of an outside observer searching for diagnostic categories, categorizing forms of resistance, identifying recurrent configurations, and so on. The analyst has stepped back from participant to onlooker, from the I-Thou position to the I-It position. Facts in this sense are prestructured, as it were, out of our theoretical preconceptions, out of our metapsychology. Without metapsychology we cannot begin to think.

In the I-It position metapsychology provides elements of structure and coherence that enable us to organize the buzzing confusion of immediate clinical experience. Those who wish to discard metapsychology must give us an alternative method that will provide intellectual order and coherence.

Lacan (1977) argued that the theory of linguistics provides such elements of coherence. Lacan's ideas are notoriously opaque and nearly incomprehensible. But his well-known aphorism is clear enough: "If psychoanalysis is to become instituted as the science of the unconscious, one must set out with the notion that the unconscious is structured like a language" (Lacan, 1978, p. 203). He believes that psychoanalysis will either establish its foundations in an adequate linguistics or have no serious foundations at all. The patient's words are the sole medium of psychoanalytic action and it is the task of the analyst, as it is that of the logician, linguist, and anthropologist, to discover the deep-lying structures of the patient's discourse, for only then can psychoanalysis make claim to scientific generality. "It follows that the unconscious is structured, that it has a syntax, precisely in the sense made familiar to us by the deep-structured postulate of transformational generative grammars and by the Levi-Straussian model of binary symbolic arrangements underlying all social and aesthetic forms of human understanding and activity" (Steiner, 1978, p. 53).

In a penetrating review of Lacan's intellectual edifice, Wollheim (1979) observed that Lacan's attempt to reinterpret all of psychoanalysis as language reaches a point of absurdity when Lacan apparently interpreted the erotogenic zones as psycholinguistic phenomena.

Schafer (1976) also believes that the structure of language provides the elements of coherence which are an alternative to metapsychology. He differed from Lacan in that his work is influenced not so much by the discipline of psycholinguistics as by English philosophers such as Wittgenstein, Austin, and Ryle. Schafer clearly stated his objection to metapsychology:

> The terms of Freudian metapsychology are those of natural science. Freud, Hartmann, and others deliberately used the language of forces, energies, functions, structures, apparatus, and principles to establish and develop psychoanalysis along the lines of a physicalistic psychobiology. It is inconsistent with this type of scientific language to speak of intentions, meanings, reasons, or subjective experience [1976, p. 103].

He concluded that in principle all mechanistic models of this kind must turn into an anthropomorphic model, that the model of the biological sciences, which includes concepts such as cause, effect, impulse, charge, or force, are inherently unsuitable for rendering the concerns of a person who intends, decides, or acts for reasons (Anscombe, 1981). It is interesting to note that Wittgenstein (1958), who influenced Schafer, is distinctly apsychological in that he believes that the meaning of language is determined not so much by private mental states but by "the role which these signs are playing in a system of language." Wittgenstein described "systems of communication which we shall call 'language games' . . . they are more or less akin to what in ordinary language we call 'games.' We are not, however, regarding the language games which we described as incomplete parts of a language, but as languages complete in themselves, and as complete systems of human communication" (p. 81). Individual psychology lies outside of Wittgenstein's language games.

By offering proposals that have elicited a growing literature of rebuttal, Schafer served the very useful function of forcing us to question our fundamental assumptions. This literature has now become so extensive that I shall only attempt to summarize some of its major arguments.

1. Schafer's proposals are intentionally abiological. He wishes to remove every reference to evolutionary biology as an agent in human psychology. With the removal of biological processes as agents or forces, Schafer must find a substitute and here he posits the self as a single monolithic agent. In doing this, as Barratt (1978) and Anscombe (1981) observed, Schafer may have destroyed the unique contribution of psychoanalysis—the recognition that there are multiple determinants.

2. Moreover, it is difficult to find a place for the unconscious in Schafer's action language. Barratt stated:

> It could be said that Schafer's new "action language" stands Freudianism on its head and thus demolishes it.

Freud's psychology is constructed upon the discovery of the fundamental alienation of human discourse, the rupture of conscious and unconscious meaning. Schafer's psychology is arsy-versy, being founded upon the abstract, unspoken ideal of psychoanalysis: the whole integrated person. Under Schafer's ministrations, the repressed unconscious is ablated [1976, p. 302].

3. Schafer's "self" is an Aristotelian unmoved mover which, as Anscombe observes, lies outside of developmental and maturational considerations—how does one account for the agency of the self in the young child who has not yet developed a cohesive self?

4. Schafer's abiological stance forces him into a linguistic definition of affects—an affect is an abstract noun (p. 166).

5. Finally, Schafer's attempt to avoid the contaminating effect of metaphor may deprive thinking itself of its necessary elements (Meissner, 1979).[1]

Lacan's proposal that psychoanalysis be interpreted through a Saussurian psycholinguistics and Schafer's reinterpretation of psychoanalysis by means of action language are announcements of programs yet to be realized. There are, I believe, reasons to doubt whether such programs are realizable.

Another alternative to metapsychology is Habermas' proposal of "general interpretations." Habermas (1968) observed correctly that the language of theory is narrower than the language in which technique is described. To remedy this, Habermas wishes to supplant metapsychology

---

[1]There is nothing new in the wish to "purify" thinking by eliminating metaphor—in the seventeenth century, Berlin (1980, p. 84) informed us, the Royal Society in England formally set itself against the use of metaphor and other forms of rhetorical speech and demanded language that was plain, literal, and precise.

with interpretations restricted to the ordinary language in which the psychoanalyst and his patient converse (see also Modell, 1978b). There is no need to go outside of psychoanalysis for a theoretical structure. This is a method that is consistent with the I-Thou relationship. But as we noted above, the analyst is not always in intrasubjective agreement with his patient—there are times when he steps back and makes use of categories. The analyst observes a particular mechanism of defense, a particular pattern in the unfolding of the analytic process, and decides that he is observing a narcissistic transference rather than a transference neurosis. He has substituted an I-It relationship for the I-Thou relationship.

In Habermas' proposal there is, as was also true of Schafer, an Aristotelian wish to preserve the phenomena at the expense of denying to ourselves the theoretical tools that we require to think about what we have just observed. Here we are in agreement with Feyerabend (1978), who recognized that learning does not go from observation to theory, but always involves both elements. Experience arises together with theoretical assumptions. To eliminate theoretical knowledge is disorienting.

It is not too much to claim that psychoanalysis is a unique discipline. It shares with the hermeneutic disciplines the use of empathy as a mode of observation, viewing man from the inside. It subjects these observations to metapsychology, which views man from the outside. This form of double vision is not without precedent. I have suggested (1978a) a close analogy of this principle in Bohr's concept of complementarity: that the same phenomenon may be viewed from two opposing and seemingly disjunctive points of view without striving for a synthesis. Vico's separation of human knowledge into what was later called *Geisteswissenschaft* and *Naturwissenschaft*, the I-Thou and the I-It, are disjunctive categories. It is possible to shift in our thinking from one category to the other without blurring the distinctions or attempting a synthesis.

We have remarked elsewhere (Modell, 1978a) how psychoanalysis describes phenomena that are unique and nonrepeatable so that the psychoanalyst is in a position analogous to the historian. (Of course evolutionary biology is also historical but that is of a different order from creating history, that is, culture.) However, as we are also observing an organism, this analogy to history is inaccurate—there are repeatable configurations that reflect biological structures. Although psychoanalysis is in a certain sense a linguistic enterprise, words cannot be separated from affects, and affects have unquestionably evolutionary, that is, biological, significance. Although analogies between psychoanalysis and history and esthetics and linguistics can be found, these analogies are all imperfect, for at bottom the psychoanalyst is unlike the historian in that he observes the psychological representations of biological phenomena. We are forced to make the claim that psychoanalysis is a unique discipline that cannot be fitted into any ready-made epistemology but requires, as Ricoeur has observed, a new advance of thought (see also Wallerstein, 1976).

SOME EMPIRICAL DISCREPANCIES

Those who do not necessarily question psychoanalysis' status as a natural science have objections to metapsychology. Their objections are made on empirical grounds, namely, that the model provided by metapsychology is not congruent with clinical experience. However, these objections refer not only to clinical observations but also to the assumptions borrowed from the neighboring science of biology, which contribute to the body of metapsychology.

In this regard Freud readily acknowledged his dependency on biology:

> I am altogether doubtful whether any decisive pointers for the differentiation and classification of the instincts can be arrived at on the basis of working over the psychological material. This working-over seems rather itself to call for the application to the material of definite assumptions concerning instinctual life, and it would be a desirable thing if those assumptions could be taken from some other branch of knowledge and carried over to psychology [1915a, p. 124].

The biology of Freud's intellectually formative period did not appreciate the dynamism that exists between the organism and its environment. It was a field dominated by the laboratory experiment in which the environmental conditions were assumed to be constant. From this arose the notion of an instinct of an organism—an organism relatively cut off from its environment. Correspondingly, the environment was seen principally as a source of adventitious or learned responses. This is not the position of contemporary biology, which no longer sees any correlation between the innate and the interior and the learned and the environment. As Lorenz wrote, "In regard to behavior the innate is not only what is not learned, but what must be in existence before all individual learning in order to make learning possible" (1965, p. 44). Similarly, Lorenz quoted Hebb: "I strongly urge that there are not two kinds of factors determining animal behavior and that the term 'instinct' is completely misleading, as it implies a nervous process or mechanism which is independent of environmental factors and different from those nervous processes into which learning enters" (Hebb, 1953, p. 4).

Contemporary biology is now dominated by concepts of information theory which views the dynamic interplay of

all biological units with the environment from the level of
the cell to that of the organism. The false equation of the
innate with the interior of the organism and the environment with the adventitious contributed to Freud's model
of the ego and the id when he stated that "It is easy to see
that the ego is that part of the id which has been modified
by the direct influence of the external world through the
medium of the Pcpt.-Cs. In a sense it is an extension of
the surface differentiation" (1923, p. 25). This differentiation Freud also saw as corresponding to the distinction
between the individual and the species. If the ego was
formed as a result of the interaction of the id and the
external world, it contains the individual's acquired experience, whereas the id is the repository of the instincts
contained in the collective experience of the species acquired through the process of evolution. The term "instinct" now hardly exists in the index of contemporary
ethologists, but if it exists at all it refers to a fitting in for
the organism to an environment of which it has no experience but about which it has instead genetically acquired
information.

Hartmann's work (1939), *Ego Psychology and the Problem
of Adaptation*, did take cognizance of the new biology. In
a sense it was a corrective applied to Freud's "Ego and the
Id": The ego has, Hartmann claimed, prefigured innate
modes of adaptation to the average expectable environment. The ego did not, as Freud (1940a) assumed, owe
"its origin as well as most important of its acquired characteristics to its relation to the real external world" (p. 201).
"Man does not come to terms with his environment anew
in every generation; his relation to the environment is
guaranteed by—besides the factors of heredity—an evolution peculiar to man, namely, the influence of tradition
and the survival of the works of man" (Hartmann, 1939,
p. 30).

However, in my opinion Hartmann, took a wrong turning when he stated that "In phylogenesis, evolution leads to an increased independence of the organism from its environment" (p. 40). Although this may be true in the broadest sense if one compares warm-blooded creatures, which are able to control their bodily temperatures independently of the environmental temperature, to reptiles, which are totally dependent on the environment, as a broad psychological principle, I submit that it is misleading. This equates maturation with internalization, which is partially true in regard to certain functions such as that of the superego but remains grossly misleading in the area of object relations. For we never outgrow in a certain sense the need for the "fitting in" of the other. There is a need to acknowledge what everybody knows, that there is a form of mature dependency upon objects in that one does not outgrow one's need for the validation of the self. This was understood many years ago by Fairbairn (1952), who contrasted mature and infantile dependency, and Balint (1950), who believed that psychoanalytic theorizing was unduly weighted in the direction of the clinical model of the obsessive-compulsive because in this neurosis all the conflicts and mental processes are internalized. We achieve autonomy from the environment with regard to other processes. The fact that our need for a certain "fitting in" from the other has been labeled as narcissistic may be misleading, for this carries with it a pejorative implication that it is childlike.[5]

What I am referring to has been described as the process of mirroring. It must be acknowledged that Lacan was perhaps the first to recognize the importance of the func-

[5]Perhaps Kohut (1977) had the persistence of narcissistic structures in mind when he claimed a separate developmental line for narcissism and object relations. But this too is misleading for the continued need for validation *is* a function of object relatedness.

tion of the mirror. Lacan's contribution was intended more as a metaphor, or an "as if" story, than a clinical observation. For Lacan (1949) the child's seeing himself in the mirror as a unified whole helps to heal the sense of fragmentation that exists before the child has acquired the capacity to use symbols, that is, to use language. The mirror concept was later elaborated by Winnicott in the context of the mother-child relationship. Winnicott (1967b) acknowledged his indebtedness to Lacan; Winnicott, however, focused, not on the inanimate mirror, but instead on the mother's face, which served a mirroring function. That is, the child's inner affective state was communicated to the mother, who in turn reflected it back to the child, providing an early validation of the sense of self. We have understood the mirroring function as a manifestation of a continuing affective bond between the self and the object. What we shall describe further forces us to reformulate our concept of certain defenses—defenses directed against the vulnerability of the self that is inherent in this mirroring process. We see this need for a "fitting in" as something which may be exaggerated because of earlier privations, as in the character disturbance that Kohut described as mirror-hungry but which is nevertheless universal. As Loewald (1960) also understood, the mirror function is central to the therapeutic action of psychoanalysis in the sense that the analyst communicates to the patient an image of the person that the patient can become.

This alteration in our fundamental metapsychological assumptions has been described in various ways. Balint (1950), many years ago (quoting Rickman), spoke of a two-body psychology as opposed to a one-body psychology which he saw, as we do, as stemming from a model of physiology of an organism cut off from its environment. This has also been described as an open system as compared to a closed system.

We know that Freud modified his metapsychology because of his deepening clinical experience; his observation that defense mechanisms were themselves unconscious led to his development of structural psychology as we know it in "The Ego and the Id." We are proposing that the newer knowledge resulting from our increased technical facility in the treatment of narcissistic disorders necessitates a similar modification of metapsychology.

If the ego and its relation to the human environment are not seen as a closed system, it is then possible to conceive of defenses against object relationships without abandoning a psychoanalytic stance. If our metapsychological model is not closed off, it is then possible to describe events between the self and the object without basing the description on a simplistic theory of interpersonal relationships or a reified system of "internalized" objects. Balint (1950) observed: "All the events which lead ultimately to therapeutic changes in the patient's mind are initiated by events happening in a two-person relationship, i.e. happening especially between two people and not inside only one of them." The concept of the self or self-psychology still remains to be integrated with Freudian metapsychology. This is not a reason, as some would have it, for the abandonment of metapsychology, but a reason for its modification.

Chapter 15

Contexts and Complementarity

In the previous chapter I observed that the newer clinical knowledge gained from the psychoanalysis of the narcissistic personality has created a problem for metapsychology. I framed the question as follows: How is it possible to describe events between the self and the object without reverting to a simplistic theory of interpersonal relationships or a reified system of "internalized objects"? I suspect that we are currently in a position analogous to that of Freud when he faced the fact that the topographic theory could not account for the clinical observation of unconscious resistance, especially that of unconscious guilt. We may now again be on the threshold of a major theoretical revision. But lacking Freud's genius, we must attempt to do collectively what Freud accomplished by himself. We know that Freud solved the problem of unconscious resistance by means of structural ego psychology, the roots of which can be traced back to the beginning of psychoanalysis, but which had remained dormant until Freud was faced with the necessity for a systematic revision. It is also probable that every advance of this sort solves certain problems but creates new ones in its wake. The English term

247

PSYCHOANALYTIC KNOWLEDGE

"ego" obscures, as many have observed, the ambiguity of the German *"das Ich."* As Strachey noted in his introduction to the "Ego and the Id" (Freud, 1923): "The German term 'das Ich' has two usages, one in which the term refers to the person's self as a whole (including perhaps his body), the other being a denotation of a particular part of the mind characterized by its attributes and its functions" (1923, p. 7).

Further, as Strachey noted, it is not always easy to draw a line between these two different senses of the word. We know that for many ego psychologists it is only this structural attribute of the self that is thought to be of relevance for psychoanalysis.[1] The self concept was grafted onto ego psychology in only one of its denotations; it has, until recently, been convenient to ignore the ambiguity of the ego concept and focus on Freud's statements concerning identification and internalization, which can be easily assimilated to a one-person structural psychology. For example, he declared, "At any rate, the process, especially in the early phases of development, is a very frequent one, and makes it possible to suppose that the character of the ego is a precipitant of abandoned object cathexis and that it contains the history of these object choices" (Freud, 1923, p. 29).

Instead of the term "self"[2] with its ambiguities, American psychoanalysts focused on the concept of ego identity, a concept quite compatible with structural ego psychology. This trend was supported by Strachey's substitution of the impersonal Latin term "ego" for Freud's "ich" (Ornston, 1982). With this strategy it was possible, for the time being

---

[1]Gedo (1979) suggested that the term "ego" be restricted to define a hierarchy of defensive functions, and that the term "self" apply (following George Klein) to superordinate functions.

[2]Grossman (1982) and Spruiell (1981) would restrict the term "self" to endopsychic perceptions or what Grossman calls "phantasy," and use the term "ego" to refer to objective structure.

at least, to ignore the paradox that the self is also an endopsychic perception: not an internalized structure but a something that is exquisitely dependent on affirming or negating objects.

Hartmann (1950, p. 85) also gave a further theoretical respectability to the notion of the self as an internalized representational entity: "It therefore would be clarifying if we define narcissism as the libidinal cathexis not of the ego but of the self. (It might also be useful to apply the term self-representation as opposed to object representation.)"

This structural approach to the problems of the self appeared to have considerable clinical validation in its application to the so-called borderline personality. In my own work with the borderline personality in the 1960's I emphasized the relative failure of internalization, the failure to take something in (Modell, 1963, 1968). This in turn was understood as the consequence of an actual failure of the parental holding environment. Instead of a cohesive sense of self, one observed a self based on omnipotent fantasies (both in their negative and positive valences) or a sense of self based on an identification with the feared qualities of the parents.

The endopsychic perception of the self, so exquisitely dependent on the affirming or negating object, was described in structural terms as a "self-representation" and in place of the actual object, there was the term "object representation." These concepts are, in my opinion, not at all symmetrical and are all too easily subject to reification (Modell, 1968). Can the image of the object and the image of the subject be considered separate structures in the mind with equal potentials for organized functions? The organizing functions of the self are not to be compared with the image of the object. Kernberg (1975), following Fairbairn, went so far as to speak of "internalized object relations," as if everything takes place in the mind of the subject. The concept of internal objects and their representations "in the mind" is, I believe, conceptually much too frail to bear the weight of clinical observations of processes which occur between two people.

The self as an internalized structure is one context. Another is implicit in the work of Winnicott (1965b). Although Winnicott took pains not to accentuate his theoretical differences with classical Freudian theory, he understood the self as something provided for by the object. It takes form from the immediacy of experience. The very existence of the self is dependent upon the caretaking functions of the other. Whereas the self conceived as an internalized structure can be fitted without any problem into the one-person theoretical system of classical psychoanalysis, the other self cannot. The paradox of the self-concept, present from the beginning, temporarily evaded by ego psychology, is now in full view.

There is something here that appears to be irreconcilable: How can the self which is defined by the immediacy of experience in relation to the other also be considered as an ego structure, defined by its functions? If, as we have indicated in the previous chapter, one of the functions of metapsychology is the framing of theories of the highest generalizability, how can this function be reconciled with a dual context of the self, that of a one-person and two-person psychology? One might answer that it is simply a matter of selecting the appropriate example; it is a problem of classification. An analogy could be found in contemporary physics: classical mechanics was not proved false by quantum mechanics; rather, it was that its range of application was restricted to large bodies.

To develop this analogy further, it could be proposed that classical metapsychology be restricted to those universal phenomena of mental functioning: the process of dreaming, the primary and secondary processes, the universal regulatory principles, such as the pleasure principle and the reality principle. These phenomena would be analogous to the large bodies to which the older metapsychology would still apply. We could then turn to a new metapsychology that would encompass two-body phenomena such as the process of mirroring.

Unfortunately, the analogy breaks down at this point, for upon further reflection it is evident that the fields of observation of psychoanalysis cannot be so easily classified into a one- or two-person psychology. Countertransference provides a clear example. We have said that affects are object-seeking and that the process of mirroring is based on this two-way communication of affects. As we have stated in Chapter 10, an affective interchange between the patient and the analyst can be classified either as an empathic or a complementary response (H. Deutsch, 1926; Racker, 1968). In the first instance, there is an act of resonance, an act of pleasurable recognition, a partial identification by the analyst with a portion of the patient's self. This is contrasted with the complementary identification, where the patient treats the analyst as an internal object, and the analyst accordingly is acted upon by the patient's projected affects, as if the patient were a stage director, but in this instance a director whose actions are unconscious. For the analyst this is not a pleasurable act of recognition for it is more likely to be accompanied by a sense of being manipulated or having affects thrust upon one. A theoretical understanding of this process assumes the activation, in both personalities, of internalized structures. Internalized structures belong to a one-person psychology; and yet the projection and communication of affects that accompany the activation of these internalized objects produce a mirroring response in both the patient and the analyst. The self experience of both patient and analyst is affected in the transference/countertransference processes.

In the latter example we have shifted our theoretical context from that of a one-person to a two-person psychology. The phenomena of countertransference cannot be classified as either within a one-person or a two-person psychology. This is also true for most of what we observe as psychoanalysts. (In preceding chapters I have described the one-person *and* two-person aspects of defense, certain forms of guilt, and their implications for affect theory.) From these considerations it follows that nosological categories cannot be used to separate one-person from two-person phenomena. Kohut's (1977) dichotomy of Guilty Man and Tragic Man does not support any separation between the older, structural, guilt oriented, one-person psychology and a "new" psychology of the self (see Chapter 8). It would appear that the attempt to resolve the dilemma of maintaining theories of the highest generalizability in the face of disparate clinical phenomena has come to nought.

A different strategy would be to abandon the aim of seeking a broad, encompassing theory and to accept a theoretical pluralism. Gedo and Goldberg (1973) offered a hierarchical series of models of the mind corresponding to hierarchical levels of psychic development. Their proposal addressed the complexity of the human personality, the fact that in all of us there are multiple levels of organization, from the more primitive to the more mature. Although the concept of hierarchies is attractive because of its order and logic, I question whether our personalities are in fact organized along such logical lines. I find their proposal congenial in that it recognizes the impossibility of using a simple nosology as a line of cleavage, but in abandoning the search for theory of the highest generalizability they open the door to a potentially confusing multitude of ad hoc theoretical constructions. As I hope to demonstrate, there are other alternatives.

THE TWO CONTEXTS OF THE SELF

Kohut (1977) made essentially two incompatible suggestions: that self-psychology and classical psychoanalysis are complementary, and that self-psychology is essentially a superordinate psychology that would eventually contain classical psychoanalysis: "We might indeed speak of a psychological principle of complementarity and say that the depth psychological explanation of psychological phenomena in health and disease requires two complementary approaches: that of a conflict psychology and that of a psychology of the self" (p. 78). However, elsewhere in the same work he repeatedly considered drive-related conflicts not as complementary to self-psychology but as subordinate to it. For he stated that drives appear as a disintegration product of an unsupported self: "I trust I have succeeded in demonstrating the relevance and explanatory power of the hypothesis that the primary [sic] psychological configurations in the child's experiential world are not drives, that drive experiences occur as disintegration products when the self is unsupported" (p. 171). Later, Kohut would drop all references to complementarity as he had come to view self-psychology as having replaced classical psychoanalysis (Kohut, 1982).

It will be recalled that I have used the strategy of complementarity to apply to the epistemological dilemma that psychoanalysis is both a heuristic discipline and a natural science (Chapter 11). It is evident that I am following a suggestion of Kohut's in applying complementarity to the problem of the self. It is a suggestion once proposed and later retracted. However, the lines of cleavage pointing to an intrinsic paradox are different from that to which Kohut had applied the idea of complementarity. The distinction is not that between classical psychoanalysis and self-psychology; the paradox is not the irreconcilability of the concepts of drive, conflict, and structure with the concept of the self; the paradox is that psychoanalysis encompasses both a one-person and a two- (or multiperson) psychology. The self has been described within the rubric of these two separate contexts, but the distinction between these two usages—that is, between that of a one-person and a two-person psychology—was not recognized. Further, the failure to make explicit these two different networks of theoretical assumptions leads, as many have recognized, to a state of confusion, for our terms and concepts are context bound.

When I described the developmental disturbance in the narcissistic personality in Chapter 2, I suggested that failures in the parental holding environment lead to a precocious maturation, that is, a precocious internalization of the self. This is a description using the terms and concepts of classical one-person psychology. However, when we describe the defense of nonrelatedness and noncommunication that protects the self against the unempathic or intrusive response of the other, we are describing a very different self. Here, the self is not a structure but an endopsychic perception, the configuration of which is bestowed or negated by the other. The paradigm for this self is not Freud's structural metapsychology, but Winnicott's proposal that the continued existence through time of the child's sense of self is provided for by the holding environment; disruption of this holding leaves the child with a sense of fragmentation, going to pieces, a fear of annihilation. It is presumed that derivatives of this early annihilation anxiety persist in the adult who needs to employ a massive defense against the possibility of negative mirroring. Structural concepts referring to developmental arrests and the concept of mirroring are both necessary to account for what is observed clinically. We do not of course have two selves: a developmental, structural self belonging to ego psychology and a self, in Winnicott's sense, belonging to a two-person psychology. There is only one self; but there are two ways of thinking about this self, and these two ways require different terminologies and are supported by different networks of theoretical assumptions. What then is the value of the notion of complementarity? This is intended as a crude verbal analogy compared to the formal mathematical complementarity of physics, by means of which seemingly irreconcilable bodies of observation may be accepted without straining for their mutual dissolution or reduction. Using the notion of complementarity will also enable us to maintain clarity as to the system of thought to which disparate concepts belong. We recognize that in the clinical situation, as in nature, elements of a one-person and a two-person psychology are hopelessly intermixed. I have used the illustration of countertransference, where it is necessary to think in terms of internalized objects as well as the process of affect communication that occurs between both participants. To choose one explanatory system alone, to focus exclusively upon internalized objects or alternatively upon the communication of affects is misleading and does not do justice to what is actually observed. As Habermas stated (1968, p. 245), "For Freud the language of the theory is narrower than the language in which the technique is described."

There are those who would state that this claim for a complementarity between a one-person and a two-person psychology is not really required. Freud's structural metapsychology was by no means solipsistic; he did not ignore the external environment. He described the ego as a portion of the id, modified by the influence of the perceptual system—the representation in the mind of the external world. Why cannot some means be found to incorporate the interplay of the self and the object within traditional ego psychology?

The elaborate representational psychology of Kernberg (1975) moved in this direction, but in its attempt to maintain what is thought to be a classical intrapsychic position, representational psychology was pushed beyond its capacity to account for what we observe clinically (see Chapter 1). Structural metapsychology cannot provide in itself an adequate framework that corresponds and reflects the interplay that occurs between the self and the object. Structural concepts describe the outcome of that process, that is, what exists after internalization has occurred. Therefore, in a sense, structural psychology presents us with an essential record of developmental history but is not adequate to provide us with theories for the "here and now." As Bion (1970) noted, a science of relationships has yet to be established: that is, a discipline that would relate one element in the structure of the subject to one element in the personality structure of the object. What is needed is a structural psychology that moves beyond internalization, one that can be applied to the psychology of the psychoanalytic group of two.

There is another helpful analogy, this time from biology. When investigating the cause of a biological phenomenon such as bird migration the biologist needs to consider both the *ultimate* evolutionary cause, which traces the history of the species through thousands and millions of years, as well as the *proximate* cause of migration, which is in the realm of physiology, such as the bird's hormonal response to the shortening hours of daylight. Evolutionary and physiological thought occupy disparate conceptual realms; it took nearly a century for biologists to recognize this disparity and then reconcile both modes of thinking into what is now called the modern synthesis (Mayr, 1982). The strategy of complementarity as applied to the paradox of the ego/self is a similar first step—the recognition of a conceptual disparity.

If we consider the self as a structure formed in the course of individual development, with its history of lost objects retained as identifications, this is a mode of thinking that is analogous to the *ultimate* cause in biology. The analogy is only with regard to the way of thinking and not to the facts, for the time span of individual development is, of course, infinitely shorter. However, when we consider the self as an endopsychic perception provided for by the affirmation of the other person, this is analogous to the *proximate* cause in biology—it is immediate and adaptive. If our structural concepts are, to follow this analogy, *ultimate* causes, an example would be precocious maturation, that is, the precocious internalization of the self in the narcissistic case. This description is perfectly congruent with a one-person psychology. The defensive process, however, observed in psychoanalysis, the states of noncommunication and states of nonrelatedness, require a two-person context. The anxiety that is defended against by nonrelatedness is the dissolution of the self; the self, with its extreme sensitivity to the response of the other, is protected by creating an illusion of the absence of desire or interest in the other.

Affects are in this sense object-seeking and their noncommunication creates the illusion of self sufficiency. Here we are describing something that is analogous to a *proximate* cause. It is something that is immediate and adaptive and in a broad sense analogous to a physiological response. But not a physiological mechanism; it is not a freestanding machine that we are describing but a process between two people. Although internalized ego structures and the affective processes between two people belong to two different conceptual realms, there is a possibility that these two apparently irreconcilable contexts may eventually be brought into some relation to each other.

In Chapter 11, "Affects and the Complementarity of Biological and Historical Meaning," I noted that there is historical evidence that Neils Bohr may have been led to the idea of complementarity through William James' *Psychology*, where James struggled with the paradox, "How does the observing mind observe itself?" (Holton, 1973). The mind is both subject and object.

Complementarity may be for psychoanalysis only a temporary expedient: It is possible that what appears now to be irreconcilable will at some later date be brought into a new synthesis. On the other hand, it is also possible that the existence of insoluble paradoxes may reflect an intrinsic quality of the human mind, so that complementarity may remain a permanent feature of the psychoanalytic landscape. Bohr (1958) suggested that the existence of paradox is central to human psychology, in so doing making the analogy between complementarity and human psychology quite explicit:

> However unexpected this development may appear in the domain of physics, I am sure that many of you will have recognized the close analogy between the situation as regards the analysis of atomic phenomena, which I have described, and the characteristic features of the problem of observation in human psychology. Indeed, we may say that the trend of modern psychology can be characterized as a reaction against the attempt to analyze psychical experience into elements which can be associated in the same way as are the results and measurements in classical physics. In introspection, it is clearly impossible to distinguish sharply between the phenomena themselves and their conscious perception, and although we may often speak of lending our attention to some particular aspect of psychical experience, it will appear on closer examination that we really

have to do, in such cases, with *mutually exclusive* situations [emphasis added]. We all know the old saying that, if we try to analyze our emotions, we hardly possess them any longer, and in that sense we recognize between psychical experiences, the description of which words such as "thoughts" and "feelings" are adequately used, a complementary relationship similar to that between the experiences regarding the behavior of atoms obtained under different experimental arrangements and described by means of different analogies taken from our usual ideas. By such a comparison it is, of course, in no way intended to suggest any closer relation between atomic physics and psychology, but merely to stress an epistemological argument common to both fields, and thus to encourage us to see how far the solution of the relatively simple physical problems may be helpful in clarifying the more intricate psychological questions with which human life confronts us, and which anthropologists and ethnologists so often meet in their investigations . . .[p. 27].

We affirm Niels Bohr's observation that the idea of complementarity may be intrinsic to human psychology. We have suggested that there is not necessarily a single paradox—there may be several. I have used the strategy of complementarity in two different senses. In Chapter 11 I showed that complementarity can be applied to the question of the "placement" of psychoanalysis, that it can be simultaneously viewed as a hermeneutic discipline and a natural science. Here complementarity is used in a different context from that which separates a one-person from a two-person psychology. It is therefore necessary at this point to examine in greater detail the term "context."

The idea of context is intrinsic to the human mind, but unlike the term "complementarity" it is part of everyday speech and is not an analogy borrowed from another discipline. It is difficult to think of our cognitive and percep-

tual processes without introducing some notion of context.
Written as well as spoken words are only comprehensible
when placed in a certain context. Context in this sense is
everything. Erikson (1981) believes that our sense of reality
is marked by "Factuality"—the world of cognitively given
facts, "Actuality"—the mutual activation of individuals
sharing such facts, and "Contextuality"—a principle by
which the selection of facts suddenly appears to be "really
existing" because they appear to be comprehensible within
a compelling context. Context determines meaning, whether
in science or in art. Gregory Bateson (1979) observed that

> Without context, words and actions have no meaning at
> all. This is true not only of human communication in words,
> but also of all communication whatsoever, of all mental
> process, of all mind, including that which tells the sea ane-
> mone how to grow and the amoeba what he should do next.
> I am drawing an analogy between context in the superficial
> and partly conscious business of personal relations and con-
> text in the much deeper, more archaic processes of em-
> bryology and homology. I am asserting that whatever the
> word *context* means, it is an appropriate word, the *necessary*
> word, in the description of all these distantly related proc-
> esses [p. 15].

When I describe the complementarity of a one-person
and a two-person psychology, I am simply demarcating
one context from another. It is the introduction of a formal
ordering principle into what we do, whether consciously
or unconsciously as a part of our everyday life. We do it
no less in our work as psychoanalysts. The psychoanalytic
process itself unfolds within the organizing effect of a certain context. The same material presented earlier in an
analysis can be understood quite differently as a result of
the different context present later in the analysis. This is
all taken for granted as part of the nature of our work. I

am suggesting that the selection of a specified context is but a natural outgrowth of what we do as clinicians. The notion of complementarity introduces a formalized recognition of the use of a given context along with all of the concepts and theoretical assumptions that can be understood only within a given context. In this sense the self can be understood both as an evanescent endopsychic experience as well as a structure defined by its functions (in which case we refer to it as an ego).

Although it is tempting to do so, the principle of complementarity and the specification of context cannot be used as a simple method of classification. If it were true that the theories of self psychology could be applied to certain narcissistic disorders and Freud's metapsychology could be reserved for the classical case, we would have in our hands a powerful classificatory tool. Unfortunately, human psychology does not permit this easy classification. One might ask, are there not certain conditions where it is appropriate to view phenomena entirely from the context of a one-person psychology? These conditions can be met in the state of dreaming, which is truly a solipsistic state, as the individual is effectively cut off from his human environment. The dream process itself can be understood as a quasi-neurological regulatory process, and the process of the regulation of affects during dreaming can be considered in the context of Freud's so-called discharge theory of affects. For when affects occur in the mind of the dreamer, they are in a certain sense "discharged into the interior" in order to maintain a steady state and to prolong the condition of sleep. These are processes that can be classified under the heading of nonexperiential regulatory principles (Sandler, 1974) and appropriately placed within the context of a mental apparatus. If we restrict our attention to these phenomena alone, it would appear that a two-person psychology is not needed. If, however, we

consider the dream of someone who is in psychoanalysis
or psychotherapy, we know that that which prompts the
dream may have its origin in an ongoing relationship, that
the remembering and forgetting of dreams, as well as their
content, may be determined by the transference.

There is hardly anything that comes under the purview
of psychoanalytic observation that exists as a completely
solipsistic phenomenon. Although almost everything can
be viewed either from the context of a one-person or a
two-person psychology, let us not forget that there is an
underlying unity to the thing observed; and it is only the
need of the observer to place it within an appropriate context. It is like those drawings or paintings which seem to
change in appearance as the observer stands to the right
or to the left; this is, of course, only an illusion, being only
a matter of the placement of the observer.

Part IV

A Sociological
Postscript

Chapter 16

Comments on the Rise of Narcissism

I have taken this final chapter as an invitation to lift the usual restraints that inhibit us in presenting our views unless we can accompany them with a modicum of proof. For this is a conjecture—a conjecture based on clinical experience, but not one that can be tested by clinical experience alone, inasmuch as I am in the domain of the psychohistorian and sociologist.

What I shall propose is that the ever-changing nosology of the neuroses is the most direct indication of the impact of historical processes upon the ego: that the neuroses are, in effect, a social barometer. There is agreement that the manifest forms of the neuroses are continually evolving; that the symptomatic neuroses have been replaced by character neuroses and, in turn, that the character neuroses have come to be replaced by what has been labeled the narcissistic neurosis, or the narcissistic personality. Character neuroses are still very much with us, but there has been a relative increase in narcissistic disorders (I am excluding from this consideration borderline and psychotic cases). What I am suggesting is that a shift in the ecology of neuroses is the response to historical change.

The relationship between culture and character formation is a very large subject indeed, and in this brief chapter I will not even attempt to summarize the existing literature. Waelder (1962) wrote in 1962 that "the psychoneuroses seem to have changed since the early days of psychoanalysis, with simple and rather transparent cases of *grande hystérie* retreating from sophisticated urban quarters and being reported from backwaters only; and, in general with repression, the simple form of defense, giving way to more complicated mechanisms" (p. 625). Gitelson (1954) also had no question that the neuroses were continually evolving. He noted an increase of narcissism in his 1954 paper but he understood this to occur within the context of the character neuroses, suggesting that with the changes in moral and ethical outlooks the boundaries between license and deprivation had become blurred and the personality itself has become the carrier of the symptom. He stressed the adaptive aspects of narcissism in that narcissistic character defenses hide behind a façade of normality. This same observation was developed by Tartakoff (1966) in her paper, "The Normal Personality in Our Culture and the Nobel Prize Complex," where she described an infantile grandiosity that is supported and given the cachet of normalcy as it is congruent with certain values of American culture. And we know that Kohut (1977) expressed the similar view that the increase in the numbers of narcissistic personalities is the result of what he termed "psychotropic social factors" (see also Samitca [1981]).

The assertion that narcissistic personality types are on the increase usually elicits the skeptical question, are we proposing that the narcissistic neurosis is something new? Contemporary life has not produced a new form of neurosis, but there is reason to believe that something—and this something we shall examine further—has increased their numbers. The skeptic may grant that there has been an increase in the numbers of narcissistic personalities but would claim that this is merely an epiphenomenon: Human nature remains essentially unchanged and the influence of society produces a stylistic change, merely what appears on the surface. A comparison of the unfolding of the analytic process in the so-called classical case with that in the narcissistic personality will easily demonstrate that the differences are no epiphenomenon. The uniform transferences of the narcissistic personality, based as they are on a relative failure of self/object differentiation, point to a developmental disorder and can be contrasted to the infinitely more variegated transference neuroses which reflect the internal elaboration of the individual's early history.

Many aspects of the narcissistic personality can be understood as the defensive response to developmental trauma. I have focused especially in this work upon the defensive responses of nonrelatedness and noncommunication.

From our analyses we are able to reconstruct characteristic disturbances in the interactions between our patients and their parents. Different authors may emphasize different aspects of this process, use different terminology or are influenced by different theoretical preconceptions, but I think the fundamental clinical observations are essentially non-controversial. The parental failures[1] are usually those of emotional unresponsiveness or an excessive degree of psychological or physical intrusion.

The reader will have noted an apparent paradox: I asserted above that the changing nosology of the neuroses is perhaps the most direct indication of the impact of his-

[1]This is not to "blame" the parents for the child's neurosis. The etiology of the neurosis is still elusive and still consists of Freud's complementary series of internal and environmental determinants. Environmental trauma may need to be conjoined with certain internal events to produce neurosis—but it goes in the face of clinical evidence to ignore the effect of failures in the parental holding environment.

torical processes on the ego. Yet I, along with Kohut and others, have been able to confirm that narcissistic defenses result in part from inauthentic mirroring. If it is true, as we have asserted, that the increase of narcissism is, in part, secondary to cultural change, then how does culture influence development? There are two general hypotheses: one, that cultural change is transmitted through the personality of the parents. This could be described as indirect cultural transmission. Another hypothesis, and one to which we subscribe, is the belief that the individual experiences directly the impact of culture during adolescence and that this impact may accentuate the already existent character traits. This second hypothesis can be termed a theory of direct cultural transmission. These two hypotheses are not, of course, incompatible.

If parents are increasingly emotionally unavailable to their children or are unempathic and intrusive, what we are essentially indicating is that the parents are themselves more narcissistic; so that we would then have the further question of accounting for the increase in parental narcissism. Let us suppose, which I think likely, that the increase of narcissistic personalities has occurred during the last ten to fifteen years. (I have the impression from participating in selection committees that there has been a change in the ecology of candidates, a change different from that previously reported by Knight [1953]. We are, I believe, selecting an increasing number of candidates who describe many difficulties in the area of relating and commitment, which are characteristic of narcissistic personalities.) If we are correct in observing an increase in narcissistic personalities in the last ten or fifteen years, we are describing young adults who were adolescents in the late 1950's and 1960's and had their infancy and childhood in the years following World War II. Their parents, therefore, would for the most part have been children in the middle 1920's.

We would have to explain why this group of parents would have become increasingly narcissistic. The end of the 1920's, of course, marked the beginning of the Great Depression, but the previous years were ones of relative stability compared to our own era.

As an alternative hypothesis, we need not posit that there has been an increase in parental narcissism, but only that the effect of the parents' neurosis has been magnified because of the loss of the extended family. The latter change may be due to an increased mobility as a result of which the nuclear family leaves behind the support of its maiden aunts and grandparents, who may mitigate the pathogenic effect of the parents' narcissism. To this would be added also that the middle class, with changing lifestyles, gave up the nanny and the resident maid. This is a plausible, but essentially unproved, hypothesis. I do not find it fully convincing, for I suspect that there is a more profound relationship between society and character formation.

Kohut (1977) proposed that the loss of the extended family plus a changing pattern of work activity may contribute to a state of affairs where children are understimulated. This is reinforced by the fact that in modern life children do not have the same opportunities to observe their parents at work (as opposed to leisure activities) and that this failure to observe their parents' competence directly contributes to a certain diminution of the nuclear self.

The critic Lionel Trilling (1971), in his celebrated essay, "Sincerity and Authenticity," grappled with the same problem. As he was a literary critic and not a clinician, he examined literature and not patients. He believed that in the late sixteenth or early seventeenth century something like a mutation of human nature took place, with the formation of a new type of personality, a personality centered on the virtue of sincerity. Trilling defined sincerity as the degree of congruence between feeling and avowal. Sincerity is judged to be a virtue as it supports the working of society. Social institutions require a measure of trust in order to function so that sincerity is a measure of truthfulness. Trilling further believed that this mutation of personality coincided with the emergence of the idea of society much as we now conceive it. The breakdown of sincerity as Trilling defined it corresponds to what we have described as states of nonrelatedness and noncommunication.

We believe that the shaping of character is biphasic. The first phase is the familiar one of early development. The second phase may consist of a certain selective reinforcing or reorganization of the personality which can occur during adolescence when the individual begins to interact with, and perceive directly, the social environment in which he/she will become a full member. Our contemporary world confronts the adolescent with failures in the protective environment analogous to those experienced earlier in relationship to the parental environment. This second disillusionment will involve similar coping strategies.

There is little doubt that during the last twenty years we have experienced an accelerating disillusionment with our social institutions (Morganthau and Person, 1978), a disillusionment which is based in part on the fact that there is, in public life, no longer any congruence between what people believe and what they say. It was not very long ago, some time in the fifties, when this nation was shocked to learn that President Eisenhower had lied to us concerning the U2 spy mission. It was during President Johnson's administration that the press coined the euphemism "credibility gap" instead of saying outright that the President is lying. Today we are no longer shocked—we take the credibility gap for granted and expect to be lied to. As Lionel Trilling observed, sincerity was rightly considered to be a moral virtue as it supported the notion of society. Spurious or counterfeit communication from the leaders of our society may reinforce the same response that the individual learned earlier in relationship to his/her parents and their affective falseness. There is a reflexive reinforcement of the privacy and secrecy of the self which is hidden behind a façade of compliance, that is, a façade of playing the game. The authenticity of the self remains private. For good social adaptation the authentic self must remain inaccessible to others. In psychopathology the authentic self may be split-off and remain inaccessible to the rest of the personality. It is the tragedy of the people who present themselves to us as patients that they are cut off from this private authenticity of the self.

In 1950 David Riesman and his collaborators (Riesman, Glazer and Denney, 1950), in a remarkably prescient book, *The Lonely Crowd,* described a change in American character—a shift from "inner directed" to "other directed"—a character change in the direction of compliance, turning off, and playing the game. This would suggest that a certain degree of counterfeiting affects is socially adaptive. Pathology ensues when the counterfeiting of affects extends from the outer public sphere to the inner private sphere; the preservation of the private authenticity of the self is perhaps the paradigm of the normal narcissistic personality of our time. It is the failure to maintain this private authenticity that defines narcissistic illness.

There are additional analogies to be seen between our contemporary institutions and the early parental environment. Defensive narcissism in the child is frequently a reaction to an actual helplessness. The child correctly perceives that the parent cannot, in fact, protect him/her from the dangers of the real world. This is, of course, our present condition. The individual has always experienced a certain helplessness regarding his own fate. Human beings have always been at the mercy of uncontrolled social eruptions which can inalterably change their lives. Pasternak's *Dr. Zhivago* is perhaps the clearest example of this. But even after revolutions there is hope for the future. We all know that with the spread of atomic weapons there is a real possibility that civilization may be entirely destroyed—that is, we face a possibility that there will be absolutely no hope. Today we are made aware daily, through television and other media, that events anywhere in the world may threaten the permanence of our culture and there is really nothing we can do about it. The response of the individual has been a search for hopefulness not in relationship to the world, but in relationship to the self (Morgenthau and Person, 1978). One cannot master one's fate, but at least one can master the self. Of course this, too, is an illusion. Today the options for self-determination appear to be limitless—one even has the option of changing one's sex. The adolescent's search for consciousness-altering drugs and the adult's quest for some quick psychological technique that will alter the self is, I believe, in part a reflexive turning back to the self with the recognition that our institutions are hopeless as sources of protection.

There is another analogy between the situation of the child and that of our contemporary world. We all have a need for privacy and secrecy. We need to keep a part of ourselves isolated from others, a part that cannot be found. It is ironic that the social revolution that has resulted from Freud's discoveries may have inadvertently contributed to an intrusion upon this privacy. This is true for the unfortunate child whose psychoanalytically oriented parents interpret the unconscious meaning of his/her behavior. With the spread of psychological sophistication throughout our society, almost anyone can be an amateur psychoanalyst, which in turn has increased the need for us to remain hidden and unfound. Public inauthenticity has combined with a certain psychological intrusiveness which results in noncommunication.

If our conjectures are true, we expect that art as well as the nosology of the neuroses will reflect the impact of this inauthenticity in our contemporary world. I believe a case can be made for the existence of noncommunication in certain forms of contemporary art. The art historian Meyer Schapiro (1978) in his essay on recent abstract painting, expressed a similar view: "This art is deeply rooted in the self in its relation to the surrounding world. The pathos of the reduction or fragility of the self within a culture that becomes increasingly organized through industry, economy and the State . . . intensifies the desire of the artist to create forms that will manifest his liberty . . ." (p. 222). Schapiro suggested that the rigid, controlled, and impersonal messages of the mass media lead the artist to create works that are not obviously communicating to the audience but need to be found:

> What makes painting and sculpture so interesting in our time is their high degree of non-communication. You cannot extract a message from painting by ordinary means; the usual rules of communication do not hold, there is no clear code or fixed vocabulary. Painting, by becoming abstract and giving up its representational function, has achieved a state in which communication seems to be deliberately prevented [p. 223].

From this I conclude that the rise of narcissism is a response to our present difficult, troubled times, or, as the Chinese prefer to describe it, "our too interesting" times. It is a mistake to believe, as some popular commentators (Lasch, 1979) on the subject of narcissism have asserted, that the rise of narcissism is a sign of our national moral decay. It is not a moral issue at all—it is an issue of adaptation and survival.

References

Abrams, S. (1971), Panel report: Models of the psychic apparatus. *J. Amer. Psychoanal. Assn.*, 19:131-142.

Anscombe, R. (1981), Referring to the unconscious: A philosophical critique of Schafer's action language. *Internat. J. Psycho-Anal.*, 62:225-241.

Anthony, J. (1981), Psychoanalysis and environment. In: *The Course of Life*, ed. S. Greenspan & G. Pollock. Vol. 4. Washington: Dept. of Health and Human Services.

Arlow, J., & Brenner, C. (1964), *Psychoanalytic Concepts and the Structural Theory*. New York: International Universities Press.

Bak, R. (1953), Fetishism. *J. Amer. Psychoanal. Assn.*, 1:285-298.

Balint, M. (1950), Changing therapeutic aims and techniques in psychoanalysis. *Internat. J. Psycho-Anal.*, 31:117-124.

——— (1968), *The Basic Fault*. London: Tavistock Publications.

Barratt, B. (1978), Critical notes on Schafer's 'action language.' *Ann. Psychoanal.*, 6:287-303. New York: International Universities Press.

Basch, M. (1976), The concept of affect: A reexamination. *J. Amer. Psychoanal. Assn.*, 24:759-777.

Bateson, G. (1979), *Mind and Nature*. New York: E. P. Dutton.

Beres, D. (1958), Vicissitudes of superego functions and superego precursors in childhood. *The Psychoanalytic Study of the Child*, 13:251-324. New York: International Universities Press.

Berlin, I. (1969), A note on Vico's concept of knowledge. In: *Giambattista Vico*, ed. G. Tagliarozzo. Baltimore: Johns Hopkins University Press, pp. 371-377.

——— (1976), *Vico and Herder*. New York: Viking.

——— (1979), *Concepts and Categories*. New York: Viking.

——— (1980), *Against the Current*. New York: Viking.

Bernfeld, S. (1944), Freud's earliest theories and the school of Helmholtz. *Psychoanal. Quart.*, 13:341-362.

Bibring, E. (1937), (Contribution to the) Symposium on the theory of the therapeutic results of psychoanalysis. *Internat. J. Psycho-Anal.*, 18:170-189.

———— (1969), The development and problems of the theory of the instincts. *Internat. J. Psycho-Anal.*, 50:293-308.
Bion, W. (1959), Attacks on linking. *Internat. J. Psycho-Anal.*, 40:308-315.
———— (1970), *Attention and Interpretation.* New York: Basic Books.
Blum, H. (1971), On the conception and development of the transference neurosis. *J. Amer. Psychoanal. Assn.*, 19:41-53.
Bohr, N. (1958), Light and Life. In: *Atomic Physics and Human Knowledge.* New York: John Wiley & Sons, pp. 3-12.
Bonaparte, M., Freud, A., & Kris, E., Eds. (1954), *The Origins of Psychoanalysis.* New York: Basic Books.
Bowlby, J. (1969), *Attachment.* New York: Basic Books.
Brenman, M. (1952), On teasing and being teased. *The Psychoanalytic Study of the Child*, 7:264-285. New York: International University Press.
Brenner, C. (1979), The components of psychic conflict and its consequences in mental life. *Psychoanal. Quart.*, 48:547-567.
Brierley, M. (1937), Affects in theory and practice. In: *Trends in Psychoanalysis.* London: Hogarth Press, 1951, pp. 43-56.
Burlingham, D. (1967), Empathy between infant and mother. *J. Amer. Psychoanal. Assn.*, 15:764-788.
Chomsky, N. (1971), *Problems of Knowledge and Freedom.* New York: Pantheon.
Collingwood, R. (1956), *The Idea of History.* New York: Oxford University Press.
Darlington, C. D. (1969), *The Evolution of Man and Society.* New York: Simon and Schuster.
Deutsch, H. (1926), Occult processes occurring during psychoanalysis. In: *Psychoanalysis and The Occult*, ed. G. Devereux. New York: International Universities Press, 1970, pp. 133-146.
———— (1942), Some forms of emotional disturbance and their relationship to schizophrenia. In: *Neuroses and Character Types.* New York: International Universities Press, 1965.
Devereux, G. (1960), Retaliatory triumph over the father: A clinical note on the counteroedipal source of the Oedipus complex. In: *Basic Problems of Ethnopsychiatry.* Chicago: University of Chicago Press, 1980, pp. 138-147.
DeVore, I. (1965), *Primate Behavior.* New York: Holt, Rinehart and Winston.
Edelheit, H. (1976), Complementarity as a role in psychological research: Jackson, Freud and the mind/body problem. *Internat. J. Psycho-Anal.*, 57:23-29.
Engel, G. (1971), Attachment behaviour, object relations and the dynamic-economic points of view: Critical review of Bowlby's 'Attachment and Loss.' *Internat. J. Psycho-Anal.*, 52:183-196.
Erikson, E. H. (1959), Identity and the Life Cycle. *Psychological Issues*, Monogr. 1. New York: International Universities Press.
———— (1964), The nature of clinical evidence. In: *Insight and Responsibility.* New York: Norton, pp. 49-80.
———— (1981), On the generational cycle, an address. *Internat. J. Psycho-Anal.*, 61:213-223.
Fairbairn, W. R. (1938), The ultimate basis of aesthetic experience. *Brit. J. Psychol.*, 29:168-181.
———— (1940), Schizoid factors in the personality. In: *Psychoanalytic Studies of the Personality.* London: Tavistock, 1952, pp. 3-27.
———— (1944), Endopsychic structure considered in terms of object relations. In: *Psychoanalytic Studies of the Personality.* London: Tavistock, 1952.

——— (1952), *Psychoanalytic Studies of the Personality*. London: Tavistock Publications, p. 42.

Fenichel, O. (1938), Ego disturbances and their treatment. In: *Collected Papers*, 2nd. series. New York: Norton, 1954, pp. 109-128.

——— (1941), Problems of psychoanalytic technique. Albany: *Psychoanal. Quart.*

Feyerabend, P. (1978), *Against Method*. London: Verso.

Freedman, D. (1982), Of instincts and instinctual drives: Some developmental considerations. *Psychoanal. Inquiry*, 2:153-167.

——— (Unpublished), The Origin of Motivation.

Freud, A. (1936), *The Ego and the Mechanisms of Defense*. New York: International Universities Press, 1954.

——— (1969), *Difficulties in the Path of Psychoanalysis*. New York: International Universities Press.

——— (1972), Child-analysis as a subspecialty of psychoanalysis. *Internat. J. Psycho-Anal.*, 53:151-156.

——— Burlingham, D. (1944), *War and Children*. New York: International Universities Press.

——— Schur, M., & Spitz, R. A. (1960), Discussion of 'Grief and mourning in infancy' by J. Bowlby. *The Psychoanalytic Study of the Child*, 15:53-94. New York: International Universities Press.

Freud, S. (1893), On the psychical mechanism of hysterical phenomena. *Standard Edition*, 3:27-39. London: Hogarth Press, 1962.

——— (1894), The neuro-psychoses of defence. *Standard Edition*, 3:43-70. London: Hogarth Press, 1962.

——— (1900), The interpretation of dreams. *Standard Edition*, 5:339-627. London: Hogarth Press, 1958.

——— (1905), Three essays on the theory of sexuality. *Standard Edition*, 7:135-245. London: Hogarth Press, 1953.

——— (1911), Formulations on the two principles of mental functioning. *Standard Edition*, 12:218-226. London: Hogarth Press, 1957.

——— (1912), Recommendations to physicians practicing psychoanalysis. *Standard Edition*, 12:111-120. London: Hogarth Press, 1958.

——— (1913a), Totem and Taboo. *Standard Edition*, 13:1-162. London: Hogarth Press, 1955.

——— (1913b), The claims of psychoanalysis to the interest of the non-psychological sciences. *Standard Edition*, 13:176-190. London: Hogarth Press, 1955.

——— (1914), On narcissism: An introduction. *Standard Edition*, 14:67-102. London: Hogarth Press, 1957

——— (1915a), Instincts and their vicissitudes. *Standard Edition*, 14:111-140. London: Hogarth Press, 1957.

——— (1915b), The unconscious. *Standard Edition*, 14:159-215. London: Hogarth Press, 1957.

——— (1916), Some character types met with in psychoanalytic work. *Standard Edition*, 14:311-333. London: Hogarth Press, 1957.

——— (1917a), A metapsychological supplement to the theory of dreams. *Standard Edition*, 14. London: Hogarth Press, 1957.

——— (1917b), Mourning and melancholia. *Standard Edition*, 14:237-258. London: Hogarth Press, 1957.

——— (1917c), Introductory lectures on psychoanalysis. *Standard Edition*, 16:243-463. London: Hogarth Press, 1963.

———— (1918), From the history of an infantile neurosis. *Standard Edition*, 17:3-122. London: Hogarth Press, 1955.

———— (1920), Beyond the pleasure principle. *Standard Edition*, 18:3-64. London: Hogarth Press, 1957.

———— (1921), Group psychology and the analysis of the ego. *Standard Edition*, 18:67-143. London: Hogarth Press, 1957.

———— (1923), The ego and the id. *Standard Edition*, 19:3-66. London: Hogarth Press, 1961.

———— (1924a), The loss of reality in neurosis and psychosis. *Standard Edition*, 19:183-187. London: Hogarth Press, 1961.

———— (1924b), Neurosis and psychosis. *Standard Edition*, 19:149-153. London: Hogarth Press, 1961.

———— (1925), Negation. *Standard Edition*, 19:235-239. London: Hogarth Press, 1957.

———— (1926a), Inhibitions, symptoms and anxiety. *Standard Edition*, 20:77-174. London: Hogarth Press, 1959.

———— (1926b), The question of lay analysis. *Standard Edition*, 20:179-258. London: Hogarth Press, 1959.

———— (1927), Fetishism. *Standard Edition*, 21:149-157. London: Hogarth Press, 1961.

———— (1930), Civilization and its discontents. *Standard Edition*, 21:59-145. London: Hogarth Press, 1961.

———— (1932), New introductory lectures. *Standard Edition*, 22:3-182. London: Hogarth Press, 1964.

———— (1937a), Analysis terminable and interminable. *Standard Edition*, 23:216-253. London: Hogarth Press, 1964.

———— (1937b), Constructions in analysis. *Standard Edition*, 23:257-269. London: Hogarth Press, 1964.

———— (1939), Moses and monotheism. *Standard Edition*, 23:3-137. London: Hogarth Press, 1964.

———— (1940a), An outline of psychoanalysis. *Standard Edition*, 23:141-207. London: Hogarth Press, 1964.

———— (1940b), Splitting of the ego in the process of defence. *Standard Edition*, 23:271-278. London: Hogarth Press, 1964.

Gedo, J. (1979), *Beyond Interpretation*. New York: International Universities Press.

———— Goldberg, A. (1973), *Models of the Mind*. Chicago: University of Chicago Press.

———— Pollock, G., (1976), The Fusion of Science and Humanism. *Psychological Issues*, Monogr. 34 & 35. New York: International Universities Press.

Gill, M. M. (1963), Topography and Systems in Psychoanalytic Theory. *Psychological Issues*, Monogr. 10. New York: International Universities Press.

———— (1976), Metapsychology is not psychology. In: Psychology versus Metapsychology. *Psychological Issues*, Monogr. 36. New York: International Universities Press, pp. 71-105.

———— (1982), Analysis of Transference, Vol. I. *Psychological Issues*, Monogr. 53. New York: International Universities Press.

Gillespie, W. (1940), A contribution to the study of fetishism. *Internat. J. Psycho-Anal.*, 21:401-415.

———— (1952), Notes on the analysis of sexual perversions. *Internat. J. Psycho-Anal.*, 33:397-402.

Gitelson, M. (1954), Therapeutic problems in the analysis of the 'normal' candidate. In: *Psychoanalysis: Science and Profession.* New York: International Universities Press, 1973.
—— (1958), On ego distortion. *Internat. J. Psycho-Anal.*, 39:245-257.
—— (1962), The curative factors in psychoanalysis. *Internat. J. Psycho-Anal.*, 43:194-205.
Glover, E. (1932), The relation of perversion formation to the development of reality sense. In: *On the Early Development of Mind.* New York: International Universities Press, 1956, pp. 216-234.
—— (1937), Symposium on the theory of the therapeutic results of psychoanalysis. *Internat. J. Psycho-Anal.*, 18:125-132.
Gombrich, E. (1960), *Art and Illusion.* New York: Pantheon.
Graziosi, P. (1960), *Palaeolithic Art.* London: Faber and Faber.
Green, A. (1975), The analyst, symbolization and absence in the analytic setting. *Internat. J. Psycho-Anal.*, 56:1-22.
—— (1977), Conceptions of affect. *Internat. J. Psycho-Anal.*, 58:129-156.
Greenacre, P. (1953), Certain relationships between fetishism and faulty development of the body image. *The Psychoanalytic Study of the Child*, 8:79-98. New York: International Universities Press.
—— (1957), The childhood of the artist. *The Psychoanalytic Study of the Child*, 12:47-72. New York: International Universities Press.
Greenson, R. R. (1960), Empathy and its vicissitudes. *Internat. J. Psycho-Anal.*, 41:418-424.
—— (1974), Transference: Freud or Klein. *Internat. J. Psycho-Anal.*, 55:37-48.
—— Wexler, M. (1969), The non-transference relationship in the psychoanalytic situation. *Internat. J. Psycho-Anal.*, 50:27-39.
—— —— (1970), Discussion of 'the non-transference relationship in the psychoanalytic situation.' *Internat. J. Psycho-Anal.*, 51:143-150.
Grossman, W. (1982), The self as fantasy: fantasy as theory. *J. Amer. Psychanal. Assn.*, 30:919-937.
Guntrip, H. (1968), *Schizoid Phenomena, Object Relations, and the Self.* New York: International Universities Press.
Habermas, J. (1968), *Knowledge and Human Interests.* Trans. by J. Shapiro. Boston: Beacon Press, 1971.
Hamburg, D. (1963), Emotions in the perspective of human evolution. In: *Expression of the Emotions of Man.*, ed. P. H. Knapp. New York: International Universities Press, pp. 300-317.
Hartmann, H. (1939), *Ego Psychology and the Problem of Adaptation.* New York: International Universities Press, 1958.
—— (1950), Comments on the psychoanalytic theory of the ego. *The Psychoanalytic Study of the Child*, 5:74-96. New York: International Universities Press.
—— (1959), Psychoanalysis as a scientific theory. In: *Psychoanalysis, Scientific Method and Philosophy.*, ed. S. Hook. New York: New York University Press.
—— Kris, E., & Loewenstein, R. (1946), Comments on the formation of psychic structure. *The Psychoanalytic Study of the Child*, 2: 11-38. New York: International Universities Press.
Havens, L. (1976), *Participant Observation.* New York: Jason Aronson.
Hayman, A. (1969), What do we mean by 'id'? *J. Amer. Psychoanal. Assn.*, 17:353-380.
Heimann, P. (1950), On counter-transference. *Internat. J. Psycho-Anal.*, 31:81-84.

Hendrick, I. (1936), Ego development and certain character problems. *Psychoanal. Quart.*, 5:320-346.

Himmelfarb, G. (1959), *Darwin and the Darwinian Revolution*. New York: W. W. Norton & Co., Inc., 1968.

Hinde, R. A. (1970), *Animal Behaviour*. New York: McGraw-Hill.

Holt, R. R. (1975), The past and future of ego psychology. *Psychoanal. Quart.*, 44:550-576.

Holton, G. (1973), The roots of complementarity. In: *Thematic Origins of Scientific Thought*. Cambridge, Mass.: Harvard University Press, pp. 115-161.

Home, H. J. (1966), The concept of mind. *Internat. J. Psycho-Anal.*, 47:42-49.

Hook, S., Ed. (1969), *Psychoanalysis, Scientific Method and Philosophy*. New York: New York University Press.

Horton, P. R. (1981), *Solace*. Chicago: University of Chicago Press.

Jacobson, E. (1957), Denial and repression. *J. Amer. Psychoanal. Assn.*, 5:61-92.

—— (1964), *The Self and the Object World*. New York: International Universities Press.

Jones, E. (1916), The theory of symbolism. In: *Papers on Psychoanalysis*. Baltimore: Williams and Wilkins, 1948, pp. 87-114.

—— (1929), Fear, guilt and hate. In: *Papers on Psychoanalysis*. London: Baillere, Tindall and Cox, 1948, pp. 383-397.

—— (1938), A psycho-analytic note on palaeolithic art. In: *Essays in Applied Psychoanalysis*, Vol. II. London: Hogarth Press, 1951.

—— (1948), Papers on Psychoanalysis. London: Baillere, Tindall and Cox.

—— (1953), *The Life and Work of Sigmund Freud.*, Vol. I. New York: Basic Books, pp. 40-41.

Kernberg, O. (1967), Borderline personality organization. *J. Amer. Psychoanal. Assn.*, 15:641-685.

—— (1974), Further contributions to the treatment of narcissistic personalities. *Internat. J. Psycho-Anal.*, 55:215-240.

—— (1975), *Borderline Conditions and Pathological Narcissism*. New York: Aronson.

Khan, M. M. R. (1963), The concept of cumulative trauma. In: *The Privacy of the Self*. New York: International Universities Press, 1974, pp. 42-58.

—— (1971), Infantile neuroses as a false-self organization. *Psychoanal. Quart.*, 40:245-263.

—— (1973), The Role of illusion in the analytic space and process. In: *Annual of Psychoanalysis*, 1:231-246. New York: Quadrangle.

Klauber, J. (1968), On the dual use of historical and scientific method in psychoanalysis. *Internat. J. Psycho-Anal.*, 49:80-88.

—— (1972), On the relationship of transference and interpretation in psychoanalytic therapy. *Internat. J. Psycho-Anal.*, 53:385-391.

Klein, G. (1976), *Psychoanalytic Theory*. New York: International Universities Press.

Klein, M. (1948), *Contributions to Psychoanalysis*. London: Hogarth Press.

—— (1957), *Envy and Gratitude*. New York: Basic Books.

Knight, R. (1953), The present state of organized psychoanalysis in the United States. *J. Amer. Psychoanal. Assn.*, 1:197-221.

Kohut, H. (1959), Introspection, empathy and psychoanalysis. *J. Amer. Psychoanal. Assn.*, 7:459-483.

—— (1971), *The Analysis of the Self*. New York: International Universities Press.

——— (1977), *The Restoration of the Self.* New York: International Universities Press.

——— (1980), Reflections on advances in self-psychology. In: *Advances in Self-Psychology.*, ed. A. Goldberg. New York: International Universities Press, pp. 473-554.

——— (1982), Introspection, empathy and the semi-circle of mental health. *Internat. J. Psycho-Anal.*, 63:395-407.

Kris, E. (1952), Approaches to art. In: *Psychoanalytic Explorations in Art.* New York: International Universities Press, 13-63.

Krystal, H., Ed. (1968), *Massive Psychic Trauma.* New York: International Universities Press.

Kuhn, T. (1962), *The Structure of Scientific Revolutions.* Chicago: University of Chicago Press.

Lacan, J. (1949), The mirror stage. In: *Écrits.* New York: Norton, 1977.

——— (1968), *The Language of the Self.* Trans. by A. Wilden. Baltimore: Johns Hopkins Press.

——— (1977), *Écrits.* New York: Norton.

——— (1978), *The Four Fundamental Concepts of Psychoanalysis.* New York: Norton.

Laming, A. (1959), *Lascaux.* Baltimore: Penguin Books, Inc.

Langer, S. K. (1967), *Mind: An Essay on Human Feeling*, Vol. 1. Baltimore: Johns Hopkins University Press.

Langer, W. (1963), The next assignment. In: *Psychoanalysis and History.*, ed. B. Mazlish. Englewood Cliffs, N.J.: Prentice Hall, pp. 87-107.

Langs, R., Ed. (1981), Truth therapy/lie therapy. In: *Classics in Psychoanalytic Technique.* New York: Aronson, pp. 495-515.

Laplanche, J. (1976), *Life and Death in Psychoanalysis.* Baltimore: Johns Hopkins University Press.

——— Pontalis, J. B. (1973), *The Language of Psychoanalysis.* New York: W. W. Norton.

Lasch, C. (1979), *The Culture of Narcissism.* New York: W. W. Norton.

Leroi-Gourham, A. (1967), *Treasures of Prehistoric Art.* New York: Harry N. Abrams.

Levy, G. R. (1963), *Religious Conceptions of the Stone Age.* New York: Harper & Row Torch Books.

Lewin, B. (1950), *The Psychoanalysis of Elation.* New York: Norton.

——— (1968), *The Image and the Past.* New York: International Universities Press.

Lifton, R. (1967), *Death in Life.* New York: Random House.

Loch, W. (1977), Some comments on the subject of psychoanalysis and truth. In: *Psychiatry and the Humanities*, Vol. 2, ed. J. Smith. New Haven: Yale University Press, pp. 217-255.

Loewald, H. (1960), On the therapeutic action of psychoanalysis. *Internat. J. Psycho-Anal.*, 41:16-33.

——— (1971), On motivation and instinct theory. *The Psychoanalytic Study of the Child*, 26: 91-128. New York: Quadrangle.

——— (1973), Review of Kohut's 'The Analysis of the Self.' *Psychoanal. Quart.*, 42:441-451.

——— (1980a), *Papers on Psychoanalysis.* New Haven: Yale University Press.

——— (1980b), Some considerations on repetition and repetition compulsion. In: *Papers on Psychoanalysis.* New Haven: Yale University Press, pp. 87-101.

——— (1981), Regression: Some general considerations. *Psychoanal. Quart.*, 50:22-43.

Lorenz, K. (1965), *Evolution and Modification of Behavior.* Chicago: University of Chicago Press.

Mahler, M. (1967), On human symbiosis and the vicissitudes of individuation. *J. Amer. Psychoanal. Assn.*, 15:740-763.

Marcovitz, E. (1963), Panel report: The concept of the id. *J. Amer. Psychoanal. Assn.*, 11:151-160.

Mayr, E. (1982), *The Growth of Biological Thought.* Cambridge: Harvard University Press.

McDougall, J. (1978), Primitive communication and the use of countertransference. *Contemp. Psychoanal.*, 14:173-209.

——— (1980), *Plea for a Measure of Abnormality.* New York: International Universities Press.

Meissner, W. (1979), Methodological critique of the action language in psychoanalysis. *J. Amer. Psychoanal. Assn.*, 27:79-105.

——— (1981), Internalization in Psychoanalysis. *Psychological Issues*, Monogr. 50. New York: International Universities Press.

Milner, M. (1957), *On Not Being Able to Paint.* New York: International Universities Press.

Mirsky, I. A., Miller, R. E., & Murphy, J. V. (1958), The communication of affect in rhesus monkeys. *J. Amer. Psychoanal. Assn.*, 6:433-441.

Modell, A. H. (1958), Theoretical implications of hallucinatory experiences in schizophrenia. *J. Amer. Psychoanal. Assn.*, 6:442-480.

——— (1961), Denial and the sense of separateness. *J. Amer. Psychoanal. Assn.*, 9:533-547.

——— (1963), Primitive object relationships and the predisposition to schizophrenia. *Internat. J. Psycho-Anal.*, 44:282-292.

——— (1965), On having the right to a life: An aspect of the superego's development. *Internat. J. Psycho-Anal.*, 46:323-331.

——— (1968), *Object Love and Reality.* New York: International Universities Press.

——— (1970), The transitional object and the creative act. *Psychoanal. Quart.*, 39:240-250.

——— (1971a), The psychic apparatus and psychoanalytic knowledge. *J. Amer. Psychoanal. Assn.*, 19:131-142.

——— (1971b), The origin of certain forms of preoedipal guilt and the implications for a psychoanalytic theory of affects. *Internat. J. Psycho-Anal.*, 52:337-346.

——— (1973), Affects and psychoanalytic knowledge. *Annual Psychoanal.*, 1:117-124. New York: Quadrangle Books.

——— (1975a), The ego and the id: Fifty years later. *Internat. J. Psycho-Anal.*, 56:57-68.

——— (1975b), A narcissistic defense against affects and the illusion of self-sufficiency. *Internat. J. Psycho-Anal.*, 56:275-282.

——— (1976), 'The holding environment' and the therapeutic action of psychoanalysis. *J. Amer. Psychoanal. Assn.*, 24:285-307.

——— (1978a), The conceptualization of the therapeutic action of psychoanalysis. *Bull. Menn. Clin.*, 42:493-504.

——— (1978b), The nature of psychoanalytic knowledge. *J. Amer. Psychoanal. Assn.*, 26:641-658.

——— (1978c), Affects and the complementarity of biologic and historical meaning. In: *Annual Psychoanal.*, 6:167-180. New York: International Universities Press.

——— (1980), Affects and their non-communication. *Internat. J. Psycho-Anal.*, 61:259-267.

——— (1981), The narcissistic character and disturbances in the 'holding environment.' In: *The Course of Life*, Vol. III, ed. S. Greenspan & G. Pollock. Washington: Publication of Dept. Health and Human Services, pp. 367-379.

——— (1983), Self psychology as a psychology of conflict: Comments on the psychoanalysis of the narcissistic personality. In: *Psychoanalysis: The Vital Issues*. Vol. II., ed. J. Gedo & G. Pollock. New York: International Universities Press, pp. 131-148.

Morgenthau, H., & Person, E. (1978), The roots of narcissism. *Partisan Review*, 45:337-347.

Muensterberger, W. (1951), Roots of primitive art. In: *Psychoanalysis and Culture*, ed. G. B. Wilbur & W. Muensterberger. New York: International Universities Press, 1965. pp. 371-389.

Nacht, S. (1958), Causes and mechanisms of ego distortion. *Internat. J. Psycho-Anal.*, 39:271-273.

Nichols, C. (1972), Science or reflection: Habermas on Freud. *Phil. Soc. Sci.*, 2:261-270.

Novey, S. (1959), A clinical view of affect theory in psychoanalysis. *Internat. J. Psycho-Anal.*, 40:94-104.

——— (1968), *The Second Look*. Baltimore: Johns Hopkins University Press.

Ornston, D. (1982), Strachey's influence: A preliminary report. *Internat. J. Psycho-Anal.*, 63:409-426.

Panel (1971), Models of the psychic apparatus, S. Abrams, reporter. *J. Amer. Psychoanal. Assn.*, 19:131-142.

Pantin, S. F. A. (1968), *The Relations Between the Sciences*. Cambridge: Cambridge University Press.

Peterfreund, E. (1971), Information, systems and psychoanalysis. *Psychological Issues*, Monogr. 25/26. New York: International Universities Press.

Polanyi, M. (1967), *The Tacit Dimension*. New York: Doubleday.

——— (1974a), *Personal Knowledge: Towards a Post-Critical Philosophy*. Chicago: University of Chicago Press.

——— (1974b), On the modern mind. In: Scientific Thought and Social Reality. *Psychological Issues*, Monogr. 32, ed. F. Schwartz. New York: International Universities Press, pp. 131-149.

Pollock, G. H. (1964), On symbiosis and symbiotic neurosis. *Internat. J. Psycho-Anal.*, 45:1-30.

Popper, K. (1959), *The Logic of Scientific Discovery*. New York: Basic Books.

Pribram, K., & Gill, M. (1976), *Freud's 'Project' Reassessed*. New York: Basic Books.

Racker, H. (1968), The meanings and uses of countertransference. In: *Transference and Countertransference*. New York: International Universities Press. pp. 127-173.

Rapaport, D. (1954), On the psychoanalytic theory of affects. In: *Psychoanalytic Psychiatry and Psychology*, ed. R. P. Knight & C. R. Friedman. New York: International Universities Press, pp. 274-310.

——— (1958), The theory of ego autonomy: A generalization. In: *Collected Papers*. New York: Basic Books, 1967.

——— (1960), The structure of psychoanalytic theory. *Psychological Issues*, Monogr. 6. New York: International Universities Press.

284   REFERENCES

Read, H. (1965), *Icon and Idea*. New York: Schocken Books, Inc.
Richards, I. A. (1969), *Coleridge on Imagination*. Bloomington: Indiana University Press.
Rickman, J. (1957), *Selected Contributions to Psychoanalysis*. New York: Basic Books.
Ricoeur, P. (1970), *Freud and Philosophy*. Trans. by D. Savage. New Haven: Yale University Press.
———— (1977), The question of proof in Freud's psychoanalytic writings. *J. Amer. Psychoanal. Assn.*, 25:835-871.
Riesman, D., Glazer, N., & Denney, R. (1950), *The Lonely Crowd*. New York: Doubleday Anchor Books.
Roheim, G. (1942), Origin and function of culture. *Psychoanal. Rev.*, 29:131-164.
Rosen, V. (1967), Disorders of communication in psychoanalysis. *J. Amer. Psychoanal. Assn.*, 15:467-490.
Rosenfeld, H. (1972), A critical appreciation of James Strachey's paper on the nature of the therapeutic action of psychoanalysis. *Internat. J. Psycho-Anal.*, 53:454-461.
———— (1974), Discussion of R. R. Greenson's 'Transference: Freud or Klein.' *Internat. J. Psycho-Anal.*, 55:49-51.
Rubenstein, B. (1976), On the possibility of a strictly psychoanalytic theory: An essay in the philosophy of psychoanalysis. In: Psychology Versus Metapsychology. *Psychological Issues*, Monogr. 36, ed. M. M. Gill & P. Holzman. New York: International Universities Press, pp. 229-264.
Rycroft, C. (1956), The nature and function of the analyst's communication to the patient. *Internat. J. Psycho-Anal.*, 37:469-472.
———— (1966), *Psychoanalysis Observed*. New York: Coward-McCann.
Sacks, M. (in press), Panel Report: The Oedipus complex—A reevaluation. *J. Amer. Psychoanal. Assn.*
Samitca, D. (1981), *L'influence des facteurs socio-culturels sur la demande en soins psychiatriques. Arch. Swisses de Neurologie, Neurochirurgie et de Psychiatre.*, 130:159-177.
Sandler, J. (1960a), The background of safety. *Internat. J. Psycho-Anal.*, 41:352-356.
———— (1960b), On the concept of the superego. *The Psychoanalytic Study of the Child*, 15:128-162. New York: International Universities Press.
———— (1974), Psychological conflict and the structural model: Some critical and theoretical implications. *Internat. J. Psycho-Anal.*, 55:53-62.
Sawyier, F. (1973), Commentary on Freud and philosophy. *Annual Psychoanal.*, 1:216-228. New York: Quadrangle.
Schachtel, E. (1959), *Metamorphosis*. New York: Basic Books.
Schafer, R. (1976), *A New Language for Psychoanalysis*. New Haven: Yale University Press.
———— (1982), The relevance of the 'here and now' transference interpretation to the reconstruction of early development. *Internat. J. Psycho-Anal.*, 63:77-82.
Schapiro, M. (1978), *Modern Art 19th and 20th Centuries*. New York: Braziller.
Schur, M. (1966), *The Id and the Regulatory Principles of Mental Functioning*. New York: International Universities Press.
Searles, H. (1960), *The Nonhuman Environment*. New York: International Universities Press.
———— (1965), *Collected Papers on Schizophrenia and Related Subjects*. New York: International Universities Press.

Sechehaye, M. A. (1951), *Symbolic Realization*. New York: International Universities Press.

Settlage, C. (1979), Conceptualizing the nature of the therapeutic action of psychoanalysis. Panel Report, M. Scharfman, reporter. *J. Amer. Psychoanal. Assn.*, 27:627-642.

Shane, M. (1979), The developmental approach to "working through" in the analytic process. *Internat. J. Psycho-Anal.*, 60:375-382.

Sharpe, E. (1931), Variations of technique in different neuroses. In: *Collected Papers on Psychoanalysis*. London: Hogarth Press, 1950, pp. 81-97.

Spence, D. (1982), *Narrative Truth and Historical Truth*. New York: W. W. Norton.

Spitz, R. A. (1945), Hospitalism. *The Psychoanalytic Study of the Child*, 1:53-74. New York: International Universities Press.

——— (1956), Countertransference. *J. Amer. Psychoanal. Assn.*, 4:256-265.

Spruiell, V. (1981), The self and the ego. *Psychoanal. Quart.*, 50:319-344.

Steiner, G. (1978), *On Difficulty and Other Essays*. New York: Oxford University Press.

Stone, L. (1961), *The Psychoanalytic Situation*. New York: International Universities Press.

Strachey, J. (1934), The nature of the therapeutic action of psychoanalysis. *Internat. J. Psycho-Anal.*, 50:277-292, 1969.

Sullivan, H. (1953), *The Interpersonal Theory of Psychiatry*. New York: W. W. Norton.

Tartakoff, H. (1966), The normal personality in our culture and the Nobel Prize complex. In: *Psychoanalysis: A General Psychology*. ed. R. Loewenstein, L. Newman, M. Schur, & A. Solnit. New York: International Universities Press, pp. 222-252.

Thomä, H., & Kächele, H. (1975), Problems of metascience and methodology in clinical psychoanalytic research. In: *Annual Psychoanal.*, 3:49-119. New York: International Universities Press.

Treurniet, N. (1980), On the relation between concepts of the self and ego in Kohut's psychology of the self. *Internat. J. Psycho-Anal.*, 61:325-333.

Trilling, L. (1971), *Sincerity and Authenticity*. Cambridge: Harvard University Press.

Valenstein, A. (1962), Affects, emotional reliving and insight in the psychoanalytic process. *Internat. J. Psycho-Anal.*, 43:315-324.

——— (1973), On attachment to painful feelings and the negative therapeutic reaction. *The Psychoanalytic Study of the Child*, 28:365-392. New Haven: Yale University Press.

Volkan, V. D. (1973), Transitional fantasies in the analysis of a narcissistic personality. *J. Amer. Psychoanal. Assn.*, 21:351-376.

Von Bertalanffy, L. (1968), *General Systems Theory*. New York: Braziller.

Von Weizsäcker, C. F. (1964), *The Relevance of Science*. New York: Harper and Row.

Waelder, R. (1962), Psychoanalysis, scientific method and philosophy. *J. Amer. Psychoanal. Assn.*, 10:617-637.

Wallerstein, R. (1976), Psychoanalysis as a science. In: Psychology Versus Metapsychology. *Psychological Issues*, Monogr. 36, ed. M. M. Gill & P. Holzman. New York: International Universities Press, pp. 198-228.

——— (1983), Self psychology and "classical" psychoanalytic psychology: The nature of their relationship. In: *The Future of Psychoanalysis*, ed. A. Goldberg. New York: International Universities Press, pp. 19-63.

Weisman, A. (1958), Reality sense and reality testing. *Behav. Sci.* 3:228-261.

———— (1972), *On Dying and Denying*. New York: Behavioral Publications.

Wilson, E. (1975), *Sociobiology*. Cambridge: Harvard UniversityPress.

Winnicott, D. (1951), Transitional objects and transitional phenomena. In: *Collected Papers*. New York: Basic Books, 1958.

———— (1954), Metapsychological and clinical aspects of regression within the psycho-analytical set-up. In: *Collected Papers*. New York: Basic Books, 1958.

———— (1956), Primary maternal preoccupation. In: *Collected Papers*. New York: Basic Books, 1958.

———— (1960), The theory of the parent-infant relationship. In: *The Maturational Processes and the Facilitating Environment*. New York: International Universities Press, 1965, pp. 37-55.

———— (1962a), A personal view of the Kleinian contribution. In: *The Maturational Processes and the Facilitating Environment*. New York: International Universities Press, 1965. pp. 171-178.

———— (1962b), Ego integration in child development. In: *The Maturational Processes and the Facilitating Environment*. New York: International Universities Press, 1965. pp. 56-63.

———— (1963a), Communicating and not communicating leading to a study of certain opposites. In: *The Maturational Processes and the Facilitating Environment*. New York: International Universities Press, 1965, pp. 179-192.

———— (1963b), Psychiatric disorders in terms of infantile maturational processes. In: *The Maturational Processes and the Facilitating Environment*. New York: International Universities Press, 1965, pp. 230-241.

———— (1965a), Ego distortion in terms of true and false self. In: *The Maturational Processes and the Facilitating Environment*. New York: International Universities Press, 1965. pp. 140-152.

———— (1965b), *The Maturational Processes and the Facilitating Environment*. New York: International Universities Press.

———— (1967a), The location of cultural experience. *Internat. J. Psycho-Anal.*, 48:368-372.

———— (1967b), Mirror role of mother and family in child development. In: *Playing and Reality*. New York: Basic Books, 1971, pp. 111-118.

———— (1969), The use of an object and relating through identifications. In: *Playing and Reality*. New York: Basic Books, 1971, pp. 86-94.

———— (1971), *Playing and Reality*. New York: Basic Books.

Wittgenstein, L. (1958), *The Blue and Brown Books*. New York: Harper Torchback.

Wollheim, R. (1979), Psycholinguistic guru. In: *The New York Review of Books*, 25 January, 1979.

Workshop, (1974), The fate of the transference neurosis after analysis, A. Balkoura, reporter. *J. Amer. Psychoanal. Assn.*, 22:895-903.

Yankelovich, D., & Barrett, W. (1970), *Ego and Instinct*. New York: Random House.

Zetzel, E. (1956a), An approach to the relation between concept and content in psychoanalytic theory. *The Psychoanalytic Study of the Child*, 11. New York: International Universities Press.

———— (1956b), The concept of transference. In: *The Capacity for Emotional Growth*. New York: International Universities Press, 1970, pp. 168-181.

———— (1958), Therapeutic alliance in the analysis of hysteria. In: *The Capacity for Emotional Growth*. New York: International Universities Press, 1970.

———— (1965), Depression and the incapacity to bear it. In: *Drives, Affects, Behavior*. Vol. 2., ed. M. Schur. New York: International Universities Press.

———— (1970), *The Capacity for Emotional Growth*. New York: International Universities Press.

INDEX

Abrams, S., 224, 275n.
Affects
 as communication, 23-25, 130, 221, 257
 complementarity of historical and biological meaning, 182-186
 countertransference, and, 162-167
 defenses against objects, and, 23-42, 130, 221-222
 discharge theory of, 2, 21,, 221
 feigned and manipulated, 27-29
 mirroring, and, 30-31; *see also* Mirroring; Self, vulnerability of, mother's affective state, and, 23-25
 negative, 33-36
 non communication, and, 23-42, 130
 psychoanalytic knowledge, and, 138, 159-169, 172-174, 185, 222, 230, 234-236
 repetition compulsion, and, 33-36
Anscombe, R., 238, 275n.
Anthony, E., 13, 275n.
Arlow. J., 202, 275n.
Auden, W., 178

Bak, R., 53, 275n.
Balint. M., 1, 16, 17, 40, 89, 118, 244, 245, 275n.
Barratt, B., 238-239, 275n.
Barrett, W., 161, 286n.
Basch, M., 172, 275n.
Bateson, G., 260, 275n.
Beres, D., 128, 275n.
Berlin, I., 138, 147, 176, 231, 239n., 275n.
Bernfeld, S., 194, 275n.
Bibring, E., 87, 215, 275n., 276n.
Bion, W., 26, 256, 276n.

Blum, H., 276n.
Bohr. N., 156, 162, 179, 185-186, 240, 258-259, 276n.
Bonaparte, M., 13, 276n.
Borderline disorders, 47, 203, 210, 249, 265
Bowlby, J., 199-200, 213, 276n.
Brenman, M., 276n.
Brenner, C., 41, 42, 202, 276n.
Brierley, M., 23, 276n.
Brucke, E., 12, 193
Burlingham, D., 24, 39, 221, 276n.

Chomsky, N., 169, 276n.
Cocoon transference, 29-33, 93-95, 103, 104, 168; *see also* Transference, developmental arrests; Illusion of self sufficiency
Coleridge, S., 233
Collingwood, R., 151, 176, 276n.
Complementarity, 8, 171-186, 247-262; *see also* paradox, acceptance of
 Bohr on, 156, 179-180, 185-186, 240, 258
 of hermeneutic and scientific knowledge, 139, 157, 179-186, 240-241, 259
 Kohut on, 253-254
 of a one and two-person psychology, 8, 21, 247-262
 Polanyi on, 156
Context as organizing frame, 11, 259-262
Contexts and Complementarity, 247-262
Counter Oedipus Complex, 14
Countertransference, 25-26, 35-36, 38, 162-167, 234, 252; *see also* Trans-

289

294   INDEX

Thoma, H., 150n., 186, 285n.
Transference, 93-99, 107-116
  actual object tie, and, 216
  countertransference, and, 25-26, 35-
    36, 111, 167-168
  developmental arrests, and, 93-99,
    109-116, 216-217; see also Co-
    coon transference
  two-person context, and, 3
Transference neurosis, 100-101, 113,
  133
Transitional object, 187-198
  as a watershed concept, 190, 192-
    193
Transitional Relatedness, 121-123
Treurniet, N., 127, 285n.
Trilling, L., 269-270, 285n.

Ultimate and proximate causes, analogy with, 256-257

Valenstein, A., 27, 35n., 285n.
Vico, G., 138, 147-148, 151, 233, 240
Volkan, V., 94, 285n.
Von Bertalanffy, L., 285n.
Von Weizsacker, C., 285n.

Waelder, R., 143, 177, 178n., 266,
  285n.

Wallerstein, R., 127, 85, 241, 285n.
Weisman, A., 46n., 52, 54, 285n.
Wexler, M., 92, 216
Wilson, E., 79, 286n.
Wilson, E., 79n.
Winnicott, D., 17, 33, 39, 285n., 286n.
  on communication, 28-29, 31-32
  on ego relatedness, 218
  on false self, 2, 27, 219; see also False
    self
  on mirroring, 245; see also Mirroring
  on potential space between subject
    and object, 139, 187, 195, 224,
    233
  on self, 250, 254
  on theory of technique, 3, 89-90, 95-
    96, 105, 115-116, 118, 134, 216
  on transitional object, 53, 189, 191-
    193, 197
  two person psychology, and, 1, 214-
    215
Wittgenstein, L., 237, 238, 286n.
Wolheim, R., 237, 286n.

Yankelovich, D., 161, 286n.

Zetzel, E., 87, 95, 167, 211, 216, 286n.,
  287n.